Hellenic Studies 31

ZEUS IN THE *ODYSSEY*

Other Titles in the Hellenic Studies Series

http://chs.harvard.edu

ZEUS IN THE *ODYSSEY*

J. Marks

CENTER FOR HELLENIC STUDIES
Trustees for Harvard University
Washington, D.C.
Distributed by Harvard University Press
Cambridge, Massachusetts, and London, England
2008

Zeus in the Odyssey
  by J. Marks
Copyright © 2008 Center for Hellenic Studies, Trustees for Harvard University
All Rights Reserved.
Published by Center for Hellenic Studies, Trustees for Harvard University, Washington, D.C.
Distributed by Harvard University Press, Cambridge, Massachusetts and London, England
Production: Kristin Murphy Romano
Cover design and illustration: Joni Godlove
Printed in Ann Arbor, MI by Edwards Brothers, Inc.

EDITORIAL TEAM
Senior Advisers: W. Robert Connor, Gloria Ferrari Pinney, Albert Henrichs, James O'Donnell,
  Bernd Seidensticker
Editorial Board: Gregory Nagy (Editor-in-Chief), Christopher Blackwell, Casey DuÈ
  (Executive Editor), Mary Ebbott (Executive Editor), Olga Levaniouk, Anne Mahoney,
  Leonard Muellner
Editorial Assistant and Project Manager: Emily Collinson
Web Producer: Mark Tomasko

LIBRARY OF CONGRESS CATALOGING-IN-PUBLICATION DATA:

Marks, J. (Jim)
  Zeus in the Odyssey / by J. Marks.
      p. cm. -- (Hellenic studies series ; 31)
  ISBN 978-0-674-02812-8
  1. Homer. Odyssey. 2. Zeus (Greek deity) in literature. I. Title. II. Series.
  PA4037.M324 2008
  883'.01--dc22

2008015347

PREFACE

Western literature begins with the *Iliad* and *Odyssey*, the monumental epics that already in antiquity had given rise to an extensive body of analysis and interpretation, from word studies and line-by-line commentaries to textual and literary criticism. Byzantine scholars preserved the texts and a portion of the ancient critical tradition through the Middle Ages, and reintroduced them to Renaissance Europe; Enlightenment- and Romantic-era scholars transformed the study of Homeric poetry into a profession. This profession today employs dozens, perhaps hundreds of scholars worldwide, who every year teach the epics to thousands of students, and publish hundreds of articles and dozens of books on matters Homeric in numerous modern languages.

This being the case, a new reading of the Homeric *Odyssey* requires some justification. To begin with, it is worth observing that, while the tradition of Homeric scholarship stretches back for millennia, less than a century has elapsed since Milman Parry and Albert Lord demonstrated that early Greek epic poetry is a phenomenon inseparable from oral performance, and in the process obviated much of previous scholarship. The Parry-Lord paradigm both remains a fertile field of inquiry and holds out the hope of further qualitative advances in our understanding of the epics.

Work within the Parry-Lord paradigm has convinced most scholars that orally-derived epics are conceived in performance as unified and carefully structured narratives. Attempts to understand how ancient Greek oral poets maintained this underlying unity, and how their audiences perceived it, however, have become entangled in complex and contested issues regarding the identity of the poet Homer and the origins of the Homeric manuscript tradition. As a consequence, analysis of the overall structure of the *Iliad* and *Odyssey* tends to proceed from the impulse either to deny or to defend the authenticity of specific sections of the poems, or to demonstrate that an individual composer could or could not have created the epics within a given historical context.

Yet the simple fact is that the precise circumstances under which the Homeric epics took shape are, and are likely to remain, irrecoverable. The aim of this book is to account for the unity of the overall narrative of the *Odyssey* in a way that is consistent with the Parry-Lord paradigm, and that remains agnostic as to the identity of Homer – or "Homer." To be sure, the argumentation is informed by current theories about the genesis of the epic, and is indeed more sympathetic to some than others. Nevertheless, the power of my model to explain the unity of the Homeric *Odyssey* does not depend on the answers to such questions as whether the text represents the effort of one person or many, or whether it took shape in Attica, Ionia, or some other locale.

Specifically, I argue that the plot of the *Odyssey* is represented within the narrative as a plan of Zeus, a *Dios boulê*, that serves as a guide for the performing poet and as a hermeneutic for the audience. Zeus' plan unfolds as the *Odyssey* negotiates its relationship with other accounts of Odysseus' story that would have been familiar to those for whom the poem was performed. Put another way, the character of Zeus maintains thematic unity as the narrative moves through a mass of potential narrative paths for Odysseus that was already dense and conflicting when the *Odyssey* was taking shape.

This book, then, offers a new perspective on the overall unity of the *Odyssey*, the tenor of interactions among the main characters, and the relationships among Homeric and other contemporary accounts of Odysseus' return. The commanding role that I hope to demonstrate for the Odyssean Zeus is functionally equivalent to that of his Iliadic counterpart, so that the two Homeric epics can be seen as more closely akin on a structural level than is generally appreciated. At the same time, I hope to show that a Zeus-centered reading of the *Odyssey* can help to explicate long-standing problems of interpretation, and to explain the literary success of the Homeric Odysseus.

TABLE OF CONTENTS

INTRODUCTION

The plan of Zeus

I N SOME ANCIENT GREEK EPICS, a *Dios boulē* 'plan of Zeus' helps to motivate and explain the plot. This theme is best known from its appearance at the beginning of the *Iliad*:

> μῆνιν ἄειδε θεά, Πηληιάδεω Ἀχιλῆος,
> οὐλομένην ἣ μυρί᾽ Ἀχαιοῖς ἄλγε᾽ ἔθηκεν,
> πολλὰς δ᾽ ἰφθίμους ψυχὰς Ἄιδι προίαψεν
> ἡρώων, αὐτοὺς δὲ ἑλώρια τεῦχε κύνεσσιν
> οἰωνοῖσί τε πᾶσι, Διὸς δ᾽ ἐτελείετο βουλή,
> ἐξ οὗ δὴ τὰ πρῶτα διαστήτην ἐρίσαντε,
> Ἀτρείδης τε ἄναξ ἀνδρῶν καὶ δῖος Ἀχιλλεύς.

Wrath: sing it, goddess, wrath of Peleus' son Achilleus,
destructive, which myriad woes on Achaians placed,
and many strong souls to Hades did send,
heroes' souls, and the men themselves made plunder
    for dogs
and for birds a banquet, and a plan of Zeus was reaching
    fulfillment
from when first they stood apart caught up in strife,
the son of Atreus ruler of men and godly Achilleus.

Iliad 1.1-7

The association of Zeus' plan with the main plot line here in the proem is, unsurprisingly, predictive: as the *Iliad* proceeds, the god engineers and maintains the momentum of the Trojan offensive that gives force to Achilleus' wrath, decides the fates of the major characters, and resolves conflicts that impede dramatic closure.

1

The Odyssean Zeus, on the other hand, seems reactive rather than proactive, unwilling or unable to control subordinate deities, and generally more remote from the action when measured against his Iliadic counterpart. At the same time, the two seem to differ in what might be termed leadership style. For the Odyssean Zeus acts and speaks in a manner that appears to be, if not more humane, at least less malevolent than that of the Zeus who repeatedly threatens violence against his fellow gods and gleefully pits them against each other in the *Iliad*. Some rough statistics can help to quantify these impressions. In the main narrative of the *Iliad*, Zeus has a speaking role in more than a dozen scenes, in which he maintains overall control of events by inducing divine characters to act or to refrain from action, and by sending some dozen omens to mortal characters; at one point, he even lends a hand in battle (*Iliad* 15.694-695). In all, Zeus' actions and words make up around 1000 of the *Iliad*'s approximately 15,000 lines (>6%). In the *Odyssey*, by contrast, Zeus appears four times in the main narrative; he neither incites nor impedes divine characters, at least overtly; and his direct involvement with mortal affairs is limited to four omens. All told, Zeus' actions and words make up around 250 of the *Odyssey*'s approximately 12,000 lines (<2%).[1]

In terms of sheer presence, then, Zeus is less prominent in the *Odyssey* than in the *Iliad*. It seems but a small and uncomplicated step to conclude that this quantitative difference reflects a qualitative one, that Zeus is relatively unimportant to the plot of the *Odyssey*. This has in fact long been and remains the dominant interpretation of the role of the gods in Homeric epic: the Odyssean Olympos is less hierarchical than the Iliadic one, and the Odyssean plot in general depends less on divine guidance.[2]

According to the arguments offered in this book, the significance of the differences between the Iliadic and Odyssean "divine apparatus" have been over-emphasized and misunderstood. The specific locution *Dios boulē* may not appear in the proem of the *Odyssey*, but I hope to demonstrate that Zeus' appearances at crucial points help to define the overall structure of the narrative, while the actions of subordinate deities, whether or not they so intend, reaffirm Zeus' own stated goals. Further, regarding leadership style, the harsher side of Zeus is not unknown to the *Odyssey*; thus for instance Hermes at one point warns Kalypso to beware the supreme god's wrath (Διὸς μῆνις, *Odyssey* 5.146). Conversely, the Iliadic Zeus resembles his Odyssean counter-

---

[1] See Appendix 1 for a tabulation of the passages on which these figures are based.

[2] Thus for instance N. Richardson *IC* 6:330 ad 24.525-6; P. Rose 1992:94; Burkert 1985:122; Kullmann 1985:5-7; Lloyd-Jones 1971:28-32; Fränkel 1962:1-6; Kirk 1962:159-178; Dodds 1951:32-33.

part in that he never, for all his bluster, has recourse to brute force within the bounds of the narrative.

Viewed from this perspective, the difference between the Iliadic and Odyssean visions of Zeus is not qualitative after all, but a difference of emphasis. Rather than offering mutually exclusive versions of Olympos, the epics each focalize the gods through the lens of the main hero. The Odyssean Zeus is assimilated to the heroics of Odysseus, which favor stratagems and covert action, while the Iliadic Zeus is assimilated to the heroics of Achilleus, which favor direct and forceful action. In other words, the epics offer mutually reinforcing visions of the same Olympos, one that motivates the plot in accordance with Zeus' wishes. In like manner, Achilleus and Odysseus are not so much opposed as complementary heroes. In neither epic is the former stupid, or the latter cowardly; and in the end Achilleus uses nonviolent means to settle his conflict with Agamemnon, while Odysseus kills roughly as many suitors in the *Odyssey* as Achilleus does Trojans in the *Iliad*.

Text and subtext in an oral medium

In the wake of Parry and Lord, any study of Homeric poetry must take into account the fact that the texts derive from an oral tradition. I will therefore defend at the outset the assertion that the significance of the gods in the *Odyssey* is revealed in large part through what might be called subtext. By my interpretation, Zeus is depicted in a manner that disguises the "true" extent of his involvement in the story, so that the poem communicates meaning in a way that belies the statistics cited above. Thus the Odyssean Zeus maintains through subtle manipulation a level of narrative control equivalent to that which the Iliadic Zeus exercises through more overt participation in the action.

During a performance of the *Odyssey*, where neither the composer-singer nor the audience had the opportunity to pause at will or to review, there are obvious limits to the amount of subtext the narrative could be expected to carry. Moreover, the significance of verbal repetition, which provides key evidence in this as in most work within the Parry-Lord paradigm, needs to be viewed within the context of mnemonic and other devices associated with oral composition.

On the other hand, interpretations that demand more of an orally-derived text than the sum of its words and syntax can be uncontroversial even from an oralist perspective. The *Odyssey* itself opens with a well-known example: the failure to identify "the man" (ἄνδρα) in the opening line as Odysseus until twenty verses later foreshadows the hero's penchant for deception. This effect is amplified in the four-book "delay" before Odysseus' own story commences, and is revisited in his delayed self-introductions to the Phaiakes and to his fellow Ithakans.[3] The suppression of the hero's name would be especially palpable for those familiar with epics like the *Iliad*, the opening line of which identifies the ingenuous Achilleus by both name and patronymic.

The audiences for whom the Homeric epics were composed and performed, I propose, would have found equally significant the absence of Zeus from the *Odyssey* proem. Non-Homeric epic in addition to the *Iliad* offers support for the conclusion that the *Dios boulē* was an established theme in ancient Greek poetry. Thus Hesiodic epic associates Zeus closely with the plot, not only in the Zeus-centered *Theogony* (e.g. 465, 572, 653, 730), but also in motivating the heroic deeds of Herakles (*Aspis* 27-29), as well as those associated with the Trojan War (*Works and Days* 173a-e; *Catalog of Women* fr. 204). Zeus likewise incites the Trojan War in an early non-Homeric epic known as the *Kypria* (38-39 Bernabé, 102-103 Allen). Similarly, in the *Homeric Hymn to Demeter*, Zeus engineers the kidnapping of Persephone (9), then negotiates a resolution to the crisis precipitated thereby (313-339).

Further examples will be cited in the course of this book, but these passages offer at least preliminary support for the proposition that the *Dios boulē* can be considered a traditional, and prominent, theme in early Greek epic. As such, Zeus' role has at least the potential to serve as the overall unifying principle of the Odyssean narrative.

Homeric vs. non-Homeric and the "facts" of ancient Greek myth

If the plan of Zeus is a traditional theme, however, it is not, by my interpretation, a universal one. Rather, the *Dios boulē* is specific to a particular class of traditional ancient Greek epics, namely those with a relatively heterogeneous constituency. It is well established that the *Iliad* and *Odyssey* were crafted to appeal to "Panhellenic" audiences, that is, ones drawn from

---

[3] Odysseus' delaying tactics are also singled out by Athene as key to his successful return (13.333-337). For the suppression of Odysseus' name in the proem, see de Jong 2001:7 ad 1.1; Cook 1995 18-21; Race 1993:91-92; Pedrick 1992:45-46; Clay 1983:26-29; Rüter 1969:34-35, 47. For Scodel 1999b:93, Odysseus' "evasiveness" in the *Odyssey* generally implies that "[audience] members must be expected to tolerate narrative that is not immediately transparent;" cf. Fenik 1974:41-43.

across ancient Greece, rather than from a single city or region. Iconographic and other external evidence makes it clear that many individuals among these Panhellenic audiences would have been familiar with heroes such as Achilleus and Odysseus through local, or "epichoric," traditions. The fully Panhellenic register of the ancient Greek epic tradition, which is represented by the *Iliad* and *Odyssey*, as well as the Hesiodic *Theogony* and *Works and Days*, thus coexisted with and came to transcend, at least in the manuscript tradition, epichoric versions of similar narratives, which were numerous, known to differing degrees in different parts of Greece, and often conflicting.

Though traditional, then, Panhellenic narratives respond to the emergence of arenas apart from the household (*oikos*) and community (*polis*), which provided the main ceremonial, cultic, and casual contexts in which ancient Greeks absorbed their native myths. Thus it appears that the canonical epics were composed for and in performance at festivals that drew elites from across Greece to display themselves, to engage in mock combat in the form of athletic competitions, and to celebrate a shared sense of Hellenicity. These festivals fostered the emergence of a Panhellenic perspective on the story that Greeks found best suited to articulate their shared identity, namely the Trojan War.

According to the model advanced here, Zeus serves to conceptualize Panhellenic narrative paths among epichoric and, as will be discussed momentarily, would-be Panhellenic accounts of the Trojan War. Approached this way, the association of gods with the plot is a common, perhaps universal, feature of traditional ancient Greek epic narratives generally; the identification of the plot with Zeus, on the other hand, represents a specifically Panhellenizing manifestation of this traditional theme.

The Homeric epics deploy a variety of strategies in order to establish common mythological ground for their Panhellenic audiences. To begin with, they draw on and synthesize themes, characters and stories that featured in a significant cross-section of epichoric contexts; thus for example the Homeric gods are those that were worshiped in some form in most or all Greek communities. In addition, the Homeric epics limit their engagement with epichoric themes by virtue of their settings, which are for the most part outside the confines of major population and cultural centers such as Athens, Sparta, Thebes, and Corinth. To be sure, the extent of this synthesis remains unclear, owing to the incomplete nature of the evidence for Homeric multiforms and for non-Homeric traditions. Nevertheless, I hope to demonstrate that the available evidence is sufficient to support the case that many of the *Odyssey*'s narrative choices are informed at least in part by the need to engage with competing myths about Odysseus that were attaining a measure of Panhellenic recognition as the Homeric account was taking shape.

The theoretical basis for these assumptions will be explained and defended presently. First, however, it will be useful to pursue this idea of engagement between Homeric and non-Homeric narrative traditions a little further in order to arrive at a concept that is fundamental to my model for the structure of the *Odyssey*. To begin with, mutual referentiality among heroic narratives appears to have led to general agreement among most or all traditions regarding the basic story-line of the Trojan War. While individual traditions remained heterogeneous, certain broad "facts" came to obtain across the tradition as a whole: Achilleus dies at Troy, Troy falls, Nestor returns, and so on. In the present case, the performance tradition out of which the *Odyssey* emerged appears to have arrived at a basic outline according to which Odysseus returns from the Trojan War after misadventures, defeats suitors who infest his household, and, as discussed in Chapters 3 and 4, leaves Ithake again after killing them. Deviation from these "facts" would presumably have elicited from an ancient Greek audience the critical response, "no, that is not how the story goes."

Within the epic narratives themselves, I shall be arguing, these "facts" are referred to as αἶσα, μοῖρα, μόρος, τὸ θέσφατον or τὸ πεπρωμένον, expressions commonly translated as "fate."[4] I hasten to observe that these terms are not restricted to this conceptual category; the *Iliad* and *Odyssey* also create an air of inevitability, and emphasize their own authority, by referring to what may be specifically Homeric versions of events as "fated."[5] Context is necessary to determine whether a given reference is to the larger tradition, or to the Homeric tradition specifically. In *Odyssey* 5, to take an example from Chapter 2, when Hermes tells Kalypso of Zeus' declaration that it is Odysseus' μοῖρα to return home (41; cf. 114), he refers to a "fact" that obtains throughout the tradition. When, on the other hand, the goddess Ino/Leukothea shortly

---

[4] The synonymy of the most common of these terms is clear from passages such as *Odyssey* 5.113-114, where it is Odysseus' αἶσα to escape death away from Ithake and μοῖρα for him to return. Literature on "fate" in the Homeric epics is extensive; I have consulted in particular Erbse 1986:259-293 and Kullmann 1985; for the *Iliad* specifically, Nagy1979:81-82 §25n2; Schadewaldt 1966:152-155; Whitman 1958:228-230; for the *Odyssey*, Danek 1998:74-75, 188-193; Hölscher 1988:199-202; Rüter 1969:64-76. Ehnmark 1935:74-85 evaluates "pre-Parry" views of the subject.

[5] M. Edwards's formulation (1987:136) covers the range of meanings: "fate, of course, is the will of the poet, *limited by the major features of the traditional legends*" (emphasis added). Cf. Richardson 1990:193-196.

thereafter describes Odysseus' stay with the Phaiakes as μοῖρα (345), the reference is not to a plot-line with universal currency, but to one followed only by the *Odyssey* and a subset of non-Homeric traditions.

The attraction of Zeus to the nexus of fate and narrative in *Odyssey* 5 is, I suggest, representative of the architecture of the narrative as a whole. It is Zeus who ensures that the actions of the characters follow the path ordained by the "facts" of Odysseus' larger heroic identity. This is not to limit the scope of Zeus' character to structural themes. In particular his identification with overall narrative structure seems also to have made his character a useful means to enforce upon the *Odyssey* what is often described as its distinctive "moral" viewpoint. In other words, my model does not rule out the possibility that Zeus serves in the *Odyssey* to define the relationship between gods and men in terms that are distinct from – though I would prefer "complementary to" – those that are emphasized in the *Iliad*.

In any case, my reading of the texts and the scholarship has led me to conclude that the "facts" of the Trojan War became established across epichoric traditions during the emergence of fully Panhellenic performance contexts. The *Iliad* and *Odyssey* do not define the larger epic tradition, but are defined by it, and the terms of that definition are observed within the narratives through the character of Zeus.

Zeus and narrative choices in the story of Odysseus

This book aims in particular to demonstrate that the artistic achievement, thematic unity, and Panhellenic fitness of the *Odyssey* derive in large part from its handling of three major narrative choices that emerge from the "facts" of Odysseus' story. At these inflection points in the *Odyssey*, Zeus plays a significant role in determining how the hero will proceed, which is to say, in establishing the Homeric "take" on Odysseus.

First, a choice is made between the two main paths for Odysseus' journey from Troy back to Ithake. One path leads through the "real world" of Greek geography, the other through an "enchanted world" that cannot be mapped onto "real" Greece. The returning Nestor, for instance, takes the former path, visiting Lesbos, Tenedos, and Euboia en route (*Odyssey* 3.157-192; cf. *Nostoi* 94 Bernabé, 108 Allen). Odysseus in the *Odyssey*, on the other hand, spends most of his return voyage in a world of witches and monsters that is unrecognizable to the Greeks (cf. 10.190-192), and therefore divorced from the countless "Odysseus slept here" myths that were part of the local mythology of many

Greek cities and regions. Significantly, as discussed in Chapter 2, it is Zeus who in Book 5 engineers Odysseus' transition back to the real world.

A second major choice in the narrative path of Odysseus-traditions concerns whether Odysseus triumphs over the suitors as the leader of an invasion force, or instead arrives on Ithake alone and employs deception in order to overcome the suitors' numerical superiority. The *Odyssey* of course chooses the latter path, but the former, as discussed in Chapter 3, seems to have been followed by many non-Homeric traditions. Nevertheless, the *Odyssey* betrays awareness of the road not taken, as when Nestor suggests that Odysseus may one day come and punish the suitors "alone or even all the Achaians [with him]" (ἢ ὅ γε μοῦνος ἐὼν ἢ καὶ σύμπαντες Ἀχαιοί, 3.216-217). Here again, it is Zeus who deprives Odysseus of the last of his crew so that he does in fact arrive on Ithake alone (12.415-419).

A third major inflection point comes after Odysseus kills the suitors. A number of non-Homeric realizations of this part of his story issue in what I shall describe as a "political" solution to the problem of the suitors' deaths, as a result of which Odysseus is driven from Ithake and undergoes another series of adventures. In the *Odyssey*, by contrast, Zeus devises a fantastic *deus ex machina* response to the problem and thereby denies the possibility of significant "post-*Odyssey*" adventures for the hero, though here again, as discussed in Chapters 3 and 4, the *Odyssey* alludes to non-Homeric options.

These narrative choices correspond to the three narrative sequences that scholars, employing a broad spectrum of methodologies, have distinguished in the *Odyssey*.[6] The aim of this book is to demonstrate how these narrative choices define the Panhellenic *Odyssey* against the backdrop of competing narratives, and how the coordination of these choices lends overall unity to the Homeric version of Odysseus' story.

Method and theory

It is perhaps due to the aforementioned tendency to dismiss the Odyssean divine apparatus that there has been no systematic treatment of Zeus' role in the *Odyssey* comparable to, for instance, Philippe Rousseau's Διὸς δ' ἐτελείετο βουλή: *Destin des héros et dessein de Zeus dans l'intrigue de l'Iliade*

---

[6] Representative arguments for tripartite structure in Louden 1999:1-25; Bowra 1962:43-44; Heubeck 1954:36-53; for other approaches to large-scale structures in the *Odyssey*, see Tracy 1997:365-379 and Thalmann 1984:51-56.

(Lille 1996).[7] However, the subject is not *tabula rasa* among students of the *Odyssey*. Klaus Rüter's *Odysseeinterpretationen*, for example, analyzes in detail the relationships among main divine agents in the first third of the poem; Jenny Clay's *Wrath of Athena* provides a detailed account of that goddess's role; and Erwin Cook's *The Odyssey in Athens* explores the theme of divine justice as it relates to narrative structures. At the same time, my methodological and theoretical approach to the text differs sufficiently from previous work to yield a substantially new reading, and therefore deserves special attention.

My overall position on the composition of the epics is "Unitarian." That is, like most modern critics, I approach the epics in the form we have them as coherent and integrated wholes. Unlike some critics, I understand the complementary relationship between the *Iliad* and *Odyssey* to be a consequence of the Homeric epics having emerged, not sequentially, but simultaneously and in a state of mutual awareness. In current critical parlance, my approach can be described as "intertextual," in the special terms that scholars have developed for the study of relationships among orally-derived texts. Pietro Pucci in particular has argued for a "specular" reading of the poems, by which he means that they each interpret and reinterpret the other, regardless of which if either was first to achieve canonical form.[8]

This approach can be extended to describe the relationship between Homeric and non-Homeric traditions. Thus Pucci also proposes that the *Odyssey* "acknowledges and limits its own literary territory by gestures of confrontation with the other poems and other heroic traditions from which it emerges, and by controversial acts of appropriation from these sources."[9] I note that this conclusion resembles in certain respects the one reached through the application of very different methodologies, namely "Analysis" and "Neo-Analysis," according to which the main themes of the Homeric poems derive from earlier Trojan War epics. Indeed, Pucci could have supported his

---

[7] Rousseau's work has been brought to a broader audience by Gregory Nagy; cf. 2002:63-66, where Nagy's own work on the *Dios boulē*, also mostly relating to the *Iliad*, is summarized. That work has informed my reading of the *Dios boulē* theme in the *Odyssey*; I note in particular Nagy's 1979:81 argument that "the Will of Zeus" is "the self-proclaimed 'plot' of our *Iliad*;" cf. 333-336, and similar argumentation in 2003:58-59, 1990b:15, 221-222.

[8] Pucci 1987:41-43, with the conclusion that, even were the priority of the *Iliad* or *Odyssey* established as historical fact, "the specularity of polemic gestures . . . would remain untouched . . . since by a sort of *après coup* the second text's reading would enforce this specularity on the earlier text." This approach echoes such earlier work as Conte 1986:40-95; Thalmann 1984:75-76; Ong 1982:132-135; and Nagy 1979:42-58, and has been developed by e.g. Cook 1995:3-4 and Lowenstam 1993:1-12.

[9] Pucci 1987:38-39.

argument for Homeric "confrontation and appropriation" by observing that such scholars as Reinhold Merkelbach, Alfred Heubeck and Wolfgang Kullmann have demonstrated conclusively that few of the themes that make up the Homeric epics can be considered exclusively Homeric.[10]

Pucci's synchronic explanation of features of the received texts that (Neo)Analysis interprets in terms of diachronic layers of sources and recipients is both less complicated and easier to reconcile with the oral background of Homeric poetry. For to trace the trajectories of allusions among epic traditions is to gaze down a hall of mirrors, given the feedback between performing poets, who presumably knew a variety of songs about the Trojan War, and their audiences, who were passionately devoted to various epichoric traditions. The mutual referentiality among early Greek epic traditions has been explored to great effect by Laura Slatkin. Borrowing a term from Mabel Lang, Slatkin focuses on instances of what she calls "reverberation," the deployment of "a constellation of themes that establish bearings for the poem as it unfolds . . . linking it continually to other traditions and paradigms and to a wider mythological terrain."[11]

Recent scholarship, however, has tended to maintain the basic source-and-recipient model advocated by (Neo)Analysis. Thus it is commonplace to argue that the influence travels in the opposite direction, in other words, to maintain that our evidence for non-Homeric epic, in particular the poems of the so-called Epic Cycle, is for the most part derivative of the *Iliad* and *Odyssey*.[12] Here again Pucci's model of confrontation and appropriation offers an alternative to a historical scheme that is speculative, better suited to texts composed with the aid of literacy, and dismissive of a body of evidence that has from antiquity enriched the understanding of Homeric composition.

The mutual referentiality advocated here is in sympathy with Gregory Nagy's distinction between canonical and non-canonical epic in terms of relative degrees of Panhellenicity. By Nagy's interpretation, "the degree of Panhellenic synthesis in the content of a composition corresponds to the degree of diffusion in the performance of this composition."[13] I shall, however, have occasion to reformulate Nagy's conception of non-Homeric evidence,

---

[10] For an overview of Analyst and Neo-Analyst achievements, cf. Kullmann 1991; Nagy 1996:133-134, 1990a:72; M. E. Clark:1986.

[11] Slatkin 1991:108, citing Lang 1983; cf. Lowenstam 1993:1-12; for a text-based approach see A. Edwards 1985:5-9.

[12] The range of critical opinion advocating this view of the Cycle is well represented by Carlier 1999:101-104; Dowden 1996:48; Latacz 1996:75, 89; Scaife 1995:171-172; Taplin 1992:85n4.

[13] Nagy 1990a:70.

such as the Epic Cycle, as consisting of "layering" that has been "sloughed off" by the Homeric tradition, a view that I believe overestimates the impact of Homeric authority on non-Homeric traditions.[14]

According to my approach, then, extant ancient references to Trojan War tradition, Homeric and non-Homeric alike, preserve a rough synchronic cross-section of the oral tradition in which the *Iliad* and *Odyssey* took shape. In practice, this means that I shall be using such relatively late sources as scholia, epitomes of lost early epics, historians, mythographers and geographers in order to approximate the kinds of traditions with which the *Odyssey* engaged as it was achieving Panhellenic status.[15] My analysis cannot of course exhaust the possible narrative twists and turns that are represented in the hundreds, even thousands of stories about and references to Odysseus that have survived from antiquity, let alone those that may await discovery on papyri, in unedited scholia, and so on. Rather, I shall focus on a select set of traditions that are relatively well represented in the extant evidence, and that can be traced to specific locales in ancient Greece. In diachronic terms, these epichoric traditions coexisted with the canonical Homeric traditions before, during and after written texts began to circulate, and together constituted a reservoir for the persistence of non-canonical versions in the face of Panhellenic Homeric authority.

Nagy's distinction between epichoric and Panhellenic traditions can be refined usefully with the introduction of another category, "proto-Panhellenic."[16] I shall use this term to refer to epic traditions, such as the Hesiodic *Catalog of Women* and the poems of the Epic Cycle, that never achieved the authority of the canonical epics, but that nevertheless appear to have been composed and performed for audiences familiar with diverse epichoric traditions. Thus the broadly-diffused canonical Homeric and Hesiodic epics are defined as fully Panhellenic, and stories such as those about local heroes and the foundation of individual *poleis* as epichoric; "proto-Panhellenic," on

---

[14] Presented most fully in Nagy 1990a:70-81.

[15] My reasons for accepting as largely accurate our most comprehensive testimony on the non-Homeric Trojan War epics, that of the probably fifth-century CE Neoplatonist, Proklos, are summarized in Marks 2005:13-14; for a more skeptical view, see e.g. Burgess 2001:26-27.

[16] Cf. Nagy's discussion (1996:50-56) of relative degrees of Panhellenicity in the context of comparative evidence for the diffusion of various Indic epic traditions; see discussion in Chapter 4. My terminology was developed independently of Malkin's 1998:117 "proto-pan-Hellenic" category; I note however that his application of the term to the Polis Bay site on Ithake (for which see also Chapter 4) complements on the level of cult my conception of the Cyclic narratives: in each case, local traditions transcend their origins, but fail to reach a truly broad constituency across the Greek-speaking world.

the other hand, describes a middleground between these two levels of diffusion and authority. A proto-Panhellenic narrative is however more akin to fully Panhellenic than it is to epichoric epic in the important respect that the "target audience" transcends the bounds of individual communities: such an epic would, therefore, have reason to incorporate the *Dios boulē* theme, while a fully epichoric epic would not.[17]

Although such categories are by nature artificial, it may be observed that the evolution of the concept of "Homer" in antiquity seems to acknowledge analogous distinctions. Not only the *Iliad* and *Odyssey*, but also the Cyclic epics, Homeric *Hymns*, and non-hexametrical *Margites* were attributed to Homer in the early biographical tradition. By the Hellenistic period, however, Homeric authority had become restricted to the *Iliad* and *Odyssey* (and sometimes only the former). Likewise, only the fully Panhellenic epics were preserved over the long run in the manuscript tradition. Thus the evolution of Homer into the author of the *Iliad* and *Odyssey* can be equated with the emergence of fully Panhellenic discourse, while at the same time proto-Panhellenic traditions became progressively distanced from the figure of Homer.[18] Nor need the differentiation of authoritative Homeric epic from non-Homeric epic be explained in purely aesthetic or literary-critical terms. For the emergence of authoritative texts seems also to have been part of a larger trend in the evolution of Greek cultural identity, and as such was equally influenced by such historical contingencies as the Persian and Peloponnesian wars, the nation- and empire-building of Philip II, Alexander and the his successors, and even the encroachment of Rome. From this perspective, the *Iliad* and *Odyssey* do not so much supplant as they survive proto-Panhellenic and epichoric epic traditions.

I should make clear at this point precisely what I mean by "tradition." In this book, "a tradition" is a narrative or practice that is the cultural possession of a self-constituted group of ancient Greeks. By the "ancient Greek epic tradition," on the other hand, I refer to the phenomenon of narrative poetry in its various epichoric, proto-, and fully-Panhellenic contexts, while "*Odyssey*-tradition" refers to the notional, though irrecoverable, sequence of compositions-in-performance through which the Homeric text evolved. "Odysseus-tradition," by contrast, refers to all potential versions of Odysseus'

---

[17] Note that the emergence of Panhellenic discourse can thus be explained as either the evolution of one epichoric tradition to a position of authority over others, or as the synthesis of parallel traditions in a Panhellenic context.

[18] For the evolution of ancient views of Homer, see Graziosi 2002:55-62, 193-200; M. West 1999.

story that were handed down in traditional contexts, including but not limited to written and oral performances as well as such sources as vase paintings. I should also apologize here in advance for a useful, though inelegant shorthand. It is in order to avoid assumptions inherent in using "Homer" as the agent responsible for the Homeric epics that I have recourse to such formulations as "the *Odyssey* engages with non-Homeric traditions," where "the *Odyssey*" to refers to the text as we have it.

The existence of a tradition of course assumes a constituency, and in the case of early Greek epic poetry, this means an audience. The demography of ancient Greek audiences cannot of course be recovered with precision, but the concept is indispensable to modern Homeric studies. For the purposes of this book, the "Homeric audience" refers to any hypothetical assembly of Greeks at Panhellenic festivals to hear performances of the epics as they were achieving the form in which we have them.[19] I shall in Chapter 6 review arguments that arenas for Panhellenic performance evolved gradually, and relatively late, toward the end of the Archaic period.

In arguing that the *Odyssey* engages with the expectations of the Homeric audience, however, I do not wish to raise the specter of naive auditors of Homeric poetry. It is difficult if not impossible to reconstruct the historical circumstances in which significant numbers of ancient Greeks were hearing Panhellenic discourse for the first time. For the purposes of this book, a crucial point is that the *Odyssey* was not the only, or necessarily even the primary, source through which ancient Greeks heard about Odysseus.

Chapter summaries

Part I of this book, Chapters 1-3, develops to a synoptic view of Zeus' role in the overall structure of the *Odyssey*. Zeus' appearances as a speaking character in the *Odyssey* are presented in a formalized way, in divine councils, which are a species of "type scene," and I consider each of these in turn; a typological analysis of these scenes is offered in Appendix 2. I find particular significance in the fact that the distribution of Odyssean divine councils correlates with the boundaries of the three narrative sequences, and to the *Odyssey*'s major narrative "choices," described above. I hope to demonstrate that Zeus' actions,

---

[19] My understanding of the "Homeric audience" has been informed in particular by Thalmann 1998:291-305; Stehle 1997:174-177; and Gentili 1988:3-23.

or rather words, in the council scenes define and connect these sequences – Telemachos' voyage, or, as ancient critics termed it, the *Telemachia*, Books 1-4; Odysseus' return, or *Nostos*, Books 5-13 (including the *Apologoi*, Odysseus' adventures in Books 9-12 that lie outside the main narrative); and Odysseus' killing of the suitors, or *Mnesterophonia*, Books 14-24.

In Chapter 1, "Oresteia and *Odyssey*," I argue that the germ of each of the *Odyssey*'s three major sequences is embedded in Zeus' account of Aigisthos, Agamemnon and Orestes, with which the main narrative of the *Odyssey* commences. I conclude that Zeus' account of the Oresteia provides a thematic template by prompting Athene to propose a plan based on character-equivalencies that align Agamemnon, Klytaimnestre, Aigisthos and Orestes with Odysseus, Penelope, the suitors, and Telemachos.

In Chapter 2, "Ogygie to Ithake," I examine how Zeus' interactions with Athene and Hermes in Book 5 program the final stage of Odysseus' return and motivate his *Apologoi*. Fulfillment of Zeus' plan for Odysseus is made to depend on the unwitting action of Poseidon, who like Athene is manipulated into serving the *Dios boulē*. At the end of this sequence, Zeus further uses Poseidon in order to establish the *Odyssey*'s relationship to epichoric traditions concerning the Phaiakes.

Chapter 3, "End(s) of the *Odyssey*," explores the settlement of the conflict between Odysseus and the suitors on Ithake. Here Zeus plays the crucial role of establishing narrative closure in a manner consistent with the *Odyssey*'s Panhellenic perspective. Zeus' answer to the problem of reciprocal violence on Ithake severs connections to epichoric traditions relating to Odysseus' "post-*Odyssey*" life, but it also emerges organically from themes introduced in the Oresteia-paradigm and reified throughout the plot. In the process, I offer what I believe to be a conclusive refutation of the argument that *Odyssey* 24 is non-Homeric.

Part II of this book, Chapters 4-6, seeks to identify the implications of and possible motivation for the construction of Zeus' role in the manner proposed in Part I. The relationship between non-Homeric Odysseus-traditions is examined from the perspective of arenas in which epichoric and proto-Panhellenic traditions may have arisen and interacted with one another, thereby giving rise to influential perspectives on Odysseus with which the canonical narrative was in a sense compelled to engage.

In Chapter 4, "After the *Odyssey*," I argue that a fundamental distinction between the *Odyssey* and non-canonical Odysseus-traditions is that the latter construct "real world" narrative options for the resolution of the conflict with the suitors, while the Homeric narrative relies on divine intervention as planned and orchestrated by Zeus. By comparing the *Odyssey*'s "false" visions of its hero's return with non-Homeric accounts, I make the case that west Greece was a locus of especially vigorous epichoric Odysseus-traditions. Specifically, I explore the possibility that a very non-Homeric Odysseus may have become familiar to many Greeks through performance traditions on Ithake, in Epirus, and at the Olympian festival in Elis, which traditions the Homeric account again confronts and attempts to de-authorize.

In Chapter 5, "Nestor's Nostoi," I analyze another *nostos*-narrative, the one told by Nestor in *Odyssey* 3. Nestor's Nostoi, I argue, betrays a traditional singer's way of thinking about epic composition, specifically about the relationship between a performable narrative and the larger epic tradition. Nestor emerges as an analog of the Homeric narrator, and hence of composers in the Homeric tradition. I conclude that Nestor organizes the Trojan War story into discrete narratives that bear comparison to the *Iliad* and Cyclic epics, and I devote particular attention to Nestor's deployment of a divine apparatus that is thematically equivalent to the one in the main narrative of the *Odyssey*.

In Chapter 6, "Divine Plan and Narrative Plan," I contextualize my findings about the relationship between Zeus and the plot of the *Odyssey* in terms of oral composition, the emergence of Panhellenic traditions, and the worship of Zeus in ancient Greece. Zeus' supremacy in the ancient Greek epic tradition, I propose, is an artifact of Panhellenic performances. Consulting the fundamental work of Albert Lord, I argue that the *Dios boulē* corresponds to large-scale structuring themes in South-Slavic and other oral traditions. In order to corroborate this assertion, I review concisely the evidence for Zeus-worship in pre-Classical Greece, and conclude that Zeus was uniquely suited to preside over Panhellenic narratives.

I hope to show that the unfolding of Zeus' divine plan creates a narrative plan through the controlled negotiation of narrative choices. Within the narrative, these choices are identified with the conflicting aims of gods who are, at least in the canonical epics, subordinate to Zeus. Choices authorized by the chief god align the narrative with, or distance it from, various traditions among which the canonical epics developed. Thus Zeus' harmonization of the conflicting aims of Athene and Poseidon in the *Odyssey* can be seen as a metaphor for the *Odyssey*'s own composition. In like manner as Zeus manipulates and cajoles others into making their aims coextensive with his own, the *Odyssey* finesses the competing claims of parallel traditions, according as much recognition and authority to each as its own thematics allow.

1

ORESTEIA AND *ODYSSEY*

THROUGHOUT THE *ODYSSEY*, the story of Agamemnon, Klytaimnestre, and Orestes is paradigmatic for that of Odysseus, Penelope, and Telemachos. The Odyssean "Oresteia," as the story will be referred to here, provides examples of the kinds of perils that could await Odysseus, and of the resources on which he can rely. A number of characters describe or refer to the death of Agamemnon, the treachery of Klytaimnestre and her consort Aigisthos, and the heroism of Orestes, the first being Zeus, whose speech on the subject opens the main narrative.

Much critical attention has been paid to the manner in which Zeus' Oresteia frames the theological, philosophical, and moral implications of Odysseus' return.[1] Less attention, however, has been paid to the narrative implications of Zeus' opening speech. Comparison with other versions in the *Odyssey*, and with non-Homeric versions, makes clear that his Oresteia is no bland recitation of the "facts," but a polemical casting of the tale in Homeric terms.[2] One facet of this polemic, I suggest, is a programmatic assertion of the god's own role in the *Odyssey*. Just as Orestes, who acts with Zeus' approval, suffers no retribution for killing Aigisthos, so Zeus will intervene at the end of the *Odyssey* to ensure that Odysseus will not suffer for killing the suitors.

---

[1] Such concerns dominate, for example, Olson's detailed analysis (1995) of Zeus' presentation of the Oresteia in the *Odyssey*, e.g. 26-28, 44-45, 69, 205-209, 217-218; representative of similar arguments are S. West *CHO* I:16-17 and Clay 1983:215-228. Lord 1960:159-160, on the other hand, proceeds from the perspective that the alignment of these tales in the *Odyssey* is "far from inconsistent with analogical thinking or associative thinking of oral poets everywhere." The reading advanced here draws particularly on, and occasionally reacts to, the arguments of Louden 1999:90-94; Cook 1995:21-37; Katz 1991:18, 27-37, 48-53 and Erbse 1986:237-241, in addition to those of Olson, West, Clay, and Lord.

[2] On the polemical nature of the story see e.g. de Jong 2001:12-13 and Olson 1995:26-27. Other references to the Oresteia in the *Odyssey* occur at 1.298-300, 3.253-275, 303-310; 4.512-537; 11.409-434; 24.24-34, 96-97, 199-200; for non-Homeric accounts see below and Chapter 5.

Zeus' Oresteia begins a divine council scene that is functionally equivalent to the scenes with Zeus and Thetis, then Zeus and Here, in Book 1 of the *Iliad* (493-611). In both cases, Zeus and a subordinate goddess forge, or reestablish, a connection with the hero of the epic that foreshadows the special favor the hero will receive in the course of the story. In the *Iliad*, Zeus begins at once to enact the plan that emerges from the initial Olympian scenes (2.3-5), and eventually describes it in some detail (e.g. 15.59-77).

I shall be arguing that the *Odyssey* shares this structural conceit, but that Zeus enacts his plan by transmitting it as it were subliminally to Athene. For although the plan for the hero's return that the gods enact at the beginning of the narrative will be called Athene's, its basic outline derives from Zeus' Oresteia. Further, the very distinctiveness of Zeus' account raises the specter of other versions of the well-known and ancient story, in which themes such as remorse and retribution complicate the hero's revenge. I begin by exploring character-equivalencies that link Zeus' Oresteia and Athene's plan for Odysseus and Telemachos.

Zeus, Athene and the opening of the *Odyssey*

It is in response to Zeus' speech that Athene first raises the subject of Odysseus (1.48-62). She proposes that he be sent home from Kalypso's island, and that his son Telemachos be sent in search of news about him:

> Ἑρμείαν μὲν ἔπειτα, διάκτορον Ἀργειφόντην,
> νῆσον ἐς Ὠγυγίην ὀτρύνομεν, ὄφρα τάχιστα   85
> νύμφηι ἐυπλοκάμωι εἴπηι νημερτέα βουλήν,
> νόστον Ὀδυσσῆος ταλασίφρονος, ὥς κε νέηται.
> αὐτὰρ ἐγὼν Ἰθάκηνδ' ἐσελεύσομαι, ὄφρα οἱ υἱὸν
> μᾶλλον ἐποτρύνω καί οἱ μένος ἐν φρεσὶ θείω,
> εἰς ἀγορὴν καλέσαντα κάρη κομόωντας Ἀχαιοὺς   90
> πᾶσι μνηστήρεσσιν ἀπειπέμεν, οἵ τέ οἱ αἰεὶ
> μῆλ' ἁδινὰ σφάζουσι καὶ εἰλίποδας ἕλικας βοῦς.
> πέμψω δ' ἐς Σπάρτην τε καὶ ἐς Πύλον ἠμαθόεντα
> νόστον πευσόμενον πατρὸς φίλου, ἤν που ἀκούσηι,
> ἠδ' ἵνα μιν κλέος ἐσθλὸν ἐν ἀνθρώποισιν ἔχησιν.
> Then let us send Hermes the runner, Argeiphontes,
> to the island of Ogygie, in order that quick as possible   85
> he may tell to the fair-tressed nymph our unerring plan,

the homecoming of firm-minded Odysseus, so that he may
   return.
But I myself will go to Ithake, so that his son
I may the more urge on and put might in his heart,
to call to assembly the long-haired Achaians   90
and denounce all the suitors, who always
slaughter his rich flocks and shambling crook-horned cattle.
And I will send him to Sparta and to sandy Pylos
to learn of his own father's return, if he may somehow hear,
and in order that he may have good repute among people.

Odyssey 1.84-95

And so it happens. Athene departs for Ithake at once, and Books 2 through 4 narrate Telemachos' public denunciation of the suitors and his quest for word of his father. Odysseus' story is taken up in Book 5, when the gods dispatch Hermes to Ogygie.

Athene's speech here in Book 1 serves a number of practical functions. It provides a table of contents, informing or reminding the audience of the overall outlines of the tale, and perhaps helps the performer to organize his subject matter.[3] At the same time, the speech supplies what is, by the conventions of ancient Greek epic, the requisite motivation for the events to follow, since it is the gods who explain and make coherent the series of coincidences and fantastic occurrences that attend Odysseus' return. Further, Athene's mention of Telemachos and the suitors foreshadows the conflict that is the main theme of the second half of the narrative, so that her initial speech helps to establish the dramatic unity of the three main sequences of the *Odyssey*, the *Telemachia*, *Nostos*, and *Mnesterophonia*.

The motivation behind the narrative of the *Odyssey* has generally been understood as a fairly straightforward process: the chain of causality in the Odyssean narrative begins with Athene.[4] And as the above quote shows,

[3] The "table of contents" speech is a Homeric topos; see de Jong 2001:15 ad 1.81-95
[4] See in particular Clay 1983, whose book is dedicated to the proposition that Athene's wrath is "a key to the structure of the entire *Odyssey*" that "demanded a radical restructuring of the story" (quotes from 51 and 53). Similarly, Murnaghan 1995:61: "Athene quickly emerges as the source and sponsor of the plot that follows;" Peradotto 1990:170, "[Athene is the] embodiment of the narrative impulse itself ... the prime mover of the action, the impetus who keeps it going ... and the force that brings it to its counterfeit conclusion;" S. West *CHO* 1:61, "She [Athene] controls the complex action almost as if the characters were marionettes and she the puppet master." Similar arguments by Lowe 2000:139-140; Maitland 1999:10n25; Pucci 1987:20; Erbse 1986:237; Burkert 1985:122; Austin 1975:240.

the plan for Books 1 through 13 is indeed articulated by the goddess. Yet Athene speaks up only in response to Zeus' account of the Oresteia, which I now quote in full:

> ὢ πόποι, οἷον δή νυ θεοὺς βροτοὶ αἰτιόωνται.
> ἐξ ἡμέων γάρ φασι κάκ' ἔμμεναι· οἱ δὲ καὶ αὐτοὶ
> σφῇσιν ἀτασθαλίῃσιν ὑπὲρ μόρον ἄλγε' ἔχουσιν,
> ὡς καὶ νῦν Αἴγισθος ὑπὲρ μόρον Ἀτρεΐδαο   35
> γῆμ' ἄλοχον μνηστήν, τὸν δ' ἔκτανε νοστήσαντα,
> εἰδὼς αἰπὺν ὄλεθρον, ἐπεὶ πρό οἱ εἴπομεν ἡμεῖς
> Ἑρμείαν πέμψαντες ἐύσκοπον Ἀργειφόντην,
> μήτ' αὐτὸν κτείνειν μήτε μνάασθαι ἄκοιτιν·
> ἐκ γὰρ Ὀρέσταο τίσις ἔσσεται Ἀτρεΐδαο   40
> ὁππότ' ἂν ἡβήσῃ τε καὶ ἧς ἱμείρεται αἴης.
> ὡς ἔφαθ' Ἑρμείας, ἀλλ' οὐ φρένας Αἰγίσθοιο
> πεῖθ' ἀγαθὰ φρονέων· νῦν δ' ἀθρόα πάντ'ἀπέτισε.

Alas, how indeed now men find fault with the gods.
For evils are from us they say; but they themselves
by their own reckless acts have sufferings beyond
        their portion.
So even now Aigisthos beyond his portion   35
courted the wedded wife of Atreus' son, and killed him
        when he returned,
although he knew it was sheer destruction, since we
        ourselves told him,
having sent Hermes, keen-sighted Argeiphontes,
to tell him neither to kill the man nor court his wife;
for from Orestes there would be payback for Atreus' son   40
whenever he came of age and longed for his land.
Thus spoke Hermes; but he did not persuade the mind of
        Aigisthos
for all his good intent; and now he has paid back all at once.

Odyssey 1.32–43

The broad thematic correspondences between this story and the main narrative of the *Odyssey* are well documented. Zeus' Aigisthos, for example, is comparable to the Kyklops, Odysseus' crew, the Phaiakes, and the suitors, all of whom suffer after failing to heed divine admonition. The heedless Aigisthos picks up the theme of the heedless crew in the proem, which theme

Athene will transfer to the heedless suitors. The thematic opposition between Aigisthos and Orestes will be recreated in that between the suitors and Telemachos when the setting moves to Ithake (cf. 1.114-117). Thus the view of divine justice with which Zeus frames his Oresteia can be seen to inform the narrative as a whole.

Here I should make clear that by "justice" I refer to the Odyssean conception of proper and improper behavior, and not to some enlightened universal conception toward which the Greeks were ostensibly groping.[5] Zeus does not defend the institution of marriage (nor would he be the most logical figure to do so), nor does he even decry murder. Stripped of its Olympian solemnity, Zeus is merely observing that those who offend a determined party are likely to suffer. As theology or ethics, such sentiments can hardly have seemed any more profound or revolutionary in Bronze or Iron Age Greece than they do today; and this very fact suggests that the Odyssean theme of justice may disguise the operation of a more utilitarian theme. In other words, though Zeus frames his story as a theodicy, the overt theme of justice may be subordinate to a less apparent but more essential theme.

Again, I draw attention to the fact that Zeus' speech does not simply prefigure the narrative, but is the first event within it. As such, it occurs at a critical juncture in the *Odyssey*'s chronology. First, Zeus' speech prompts Athene to raise the subject of Odysseus at a time when Poseidon, his divine antagonist, is absent from the assembly of the gods. As a result, the divine plan for Odysseus' return can be elaborated without the kind of rancor that often occurs when the gods disagree on the fate of a mortal, as for example when Here and Apollo clash over the treatment of Hektor in *Iliad* 24.[6] Second, Zeus' timing is equally significant on the terrestrial plane, in that he initiates the discussion that will issue in a plan for Odysseus' return at what the narrative constructs as the last possible moment. For Odysseus leaves Ogygie at the very end of the sailing season, and returns to Ithake as the suitors are about to devour completely his resources; most importantly, his wife is ready to remarry, according to his own instructions (18.269-270).[7] Postponement of his voyage to the next sailing season would result in a hollow and pointless return.

---

[5] See Chapter 3 n32.

[6] On Poseidon's absence at the beginning of the *Odyssey*, see e.g. Scodel 1999a:40; Cook 1995:20-21.

[7] Discussion of the lateness of the hour at which the *Odyssey* begins in Latacz 1996:138; Murnaghan 1995:69; Pedrick 1992:49; S. West *CHO* 1:15; Erbse 1972:122. In addition, Odysseus must return within the year if prophecies of his twenty-year absence are to be fulfilled (i.e. 2.175, discussed below).

Nevertheless, as noted, previous scholarship has tended to view the relationship between Zeus' Oresteia and the main narrative of the *Odyssey* as rather prefatory than essential to the plot.[8] In these terms, it would represent one of any number of possible devices that could motivate Athene. However, even allowing for the artificiality of epic conventions, this interpretation renders the scene almost comic upon examination. Athene sits around the Olympian agora, waiting until Zeus offers her a pretext to announce a plan for Odysseus and Telemachos. As the clock ticks toward the last possible moment any such plan could be successful, Zeus happens launch into a story that happens to contain a sweeping generalization about divine justice to which Odysseus is a glaring exception, and that, to anticipate my analysis below, happens to contain the seeds of the narrative itself.

Of course, epic always borders on melodrama, and such a scenario may have been conjured up in the minds of Homeric audiences. But the question of dramatic tone aside, the broader implications of an Athene-centric *Odyssey* are profound. Not only does the *Odyssey* thus conceived commence with a series of labored coincidences, but its divine apparatus also suffers from a kind of power vacuum compared to the hierarchical Olympos of the *Iliad*. Most critics conclude that Athene fills this vacuum, but over the course of her further interactions with Zeus the goddess will prove unequal to the task.

A minority of scholars has advanced a different interpretation of Zeus' speech. Alfred Heubeck suggested in passing that Zeus intends to provoke Athene to react as she does;[9] and Marilyn Katz has argued that references to the Oresteia generally represent "a dynamic force that gives direction to [the *Odyssey*'s] plot."[10] Pressing such insights further, I suggest that the *Odyssey* subtly but purposefully traces causation for the events in the main narra-

---

[8] Thus Lord 1951:76 argues that "We do not care to think of the [*Odyssey*] without [Zeus' opening] speech, which is so highly significant in our interpretation of Homeric thought and religion, but it is not essential to the story;" see Chapter 6 n9. (Neo-)Analytically-informed critics tend to fault Zeus' speech as ill-conceived in relation to the *Odyssey* as a whole; cf. S. West *CHO* 1:77 ad 1.32ff; Kullmann 1985:5-6; Fenik 1974:209-211; Schadewaldt 1958:17-20.

[9] Heubeck 1954:51; cf. Rüter's criticism (1969:83n52) of him for "wanting to attribute to the intention of characters what is in actuality the intention of the poet" [*Heubeck ... scheint der Absicht der handelnden Personen zuschreiben zu wollen, was in Wahrheit Absicht des Dichters ist*]. This is precisely my point: the character of Zeus serves as a projection into the narrative of the singer's intent.

[10] Katz 1991:29-48, quote from 18, though I view Zeus' opening speech as a generative paradigm, rather than "an alternative plot that threatens to attract the *Odyssey* into its orbit" (30). Olson's overview (1995:24-27) of the relationship includes a particularly full bibliography, to which may now be added Lowe 2000:140-141 and Thalmann 1984:163-165.

tive to the machinations of Zeus, in the first instance by having him prompt Athene to propose the plan that she does for Odysseus' return, and to do so at a specific dramatic moment. This interaction between the two gods is then paradigmatic for their further conferences in the *Odyssey*.

I note that no canonical account of the Oresteia attained the kind of authority that the *Odyssey* did over Odysseus' story. Through the Archaic and Classical periods, poets from Stesichoros to Pindar and the Athenian trage-dians produced Oresteias that differed not only in regard to the motivation and valorization of the characters, but even in dramatic setting.[11] The *Odyssey*, then, likely took shape and circulated against the backdrop of a divergent body of stories about Agamemnon and his son, any number of which may have been familiar to Homeric audiences.

In any case, the reciprocal relationship between the sets of characters in Zeus' Oresteia and Athene's proposal for Odysseus and Telemachos is unmis-takable. Zeus mentions Aigisthos (by name, 1.35, 42), Agamemnon (by patro-nymic, 35, 40), Klytaimnestre (as Agamemnon's wife, 36, 39), "we gods" (37), Hermes (by name, 38, 42), and Orestes (by name and patronymic, 40). Athene's proposal specifies Odysseus (by name, 83), Hermes (by name, 84), "we gods" (82 with 85), Kalypso (the "fair-haired nymph," 86), Telemachos (as Odysseus' son, 88), and the suitors (91), who by their very designation as "suitors" imply the object of their suit, Penelope.[12] Two of the characters named by Athene, Hermes and "we gods," are explicit in Zeus' Oresteia; the rest have close paral-lels with it. Agamemnon corresponds to Odysseus as the threatened Trojan War hero, and Aigisthos to the suitors (and to Kalypso as a threat to the hero's marriage); Klytaimnestre corresponds to the implied Penelope as the hero's wife, and Orestes to Telemachos as the hero's son (and to Odysseus as suitor-slayer).

The generative logic that links Zeus' Oresteia and Athene's proposal can thus be described as a series of equivalencies between similar character-types, for each of which Zeus supplies the predicate:[13]

---

[11] Surveyed by Prag 1985.

[12] For the extrapolation of Penelope, see de Jong 2001:13.

[13] Odysseus equates his own situation with that of Agamemnon at *Odyssey* 13.383-385. Representative arguments about the correspondences among the characters in Louden 1999:19; Doherty 1995:183-186; Lowenstam 1993:3-4; S. West *CHO* 1:16-17; Slatkin 1991:117; Clay 1983:217-219; Fenik 1974:160-161. I note the general observation of Bakker 1997:91 that "often the mentioning of a name, the verbalization of the theme of a hero, activates concepts and facts associated with this hero."

Character-type	Zeus' Oresteia	Athene's proposal
returning Trojan War hero	Agamemnon	Odysseus
hero's wife	Klytaimnestre	[Penelope]
hero's faithful son	Orestes	Telemachos
seducer of hero's wife	Aigisthos (of Klytaimnestre)	suitors (of Penelope) Kalypso (of Odysseus)
power opposing seducer	"we gods"	"we gods"
voice of opposing power	Hermes	Hermes

Athene thus responds to Zeus' cues in order to formulate a plan for Odysseus that embodies her own desires for her favorite.[14]

These character-equivalencies can be direct – as Aigisthos dies, so the suitors die – or antithetical – Agamemnon dies, Odysseus lives. Indeed, uncertainty about the polarity of the equivalencies injects a measure of suspense into the narrative. Such possible storylines as defeat for Odysseus at the hands of the suitors or Telemachos committing matricide can be exploited for dramatic effect even as they are revealed as impossibilities.[15]

Character-equivalency also results from gemination: the single figure of Orestes parallels both Odysseus and his son. The functional identity of Orestes and Odysseus as avengers is reinforced at a formulaic level when Athene applies the theme of "longing" to Odysseus (ἧς γαίης ὣ ἱμείρεται, 59), echoing Zeus' application of it to Orestes (ἧς ἱμείρεται αἴης, 1.41). The Orestes-Odysseus connection resonates further as the narrative progresses. Once Odysseus supplants Telemachos in the role of avenger, the two will be able to experience the shared father-son revenge-fantasy for which Agamemnon and Achilleus seem to yearn (*Odyssey* 11.454-461, 492-503). Lastly, as discussed in Chapter 3, the connection helps the *Odyssey* to justify Odysseus' extreme revenge.

I will now focus in greater detail on three of these character-equivalencies – those between Klytaimnestre and Penelope, Hermes and, so to speak, himself, and Orestes and Telemachos – in order to illustrate the polemical

[14] The test of the troops in *Iliad* 2 offers an analogy: as Agamemnon attempts to elicit protest against his own call for the Greeks to abandon the war, so Zeus elicits from Athene a protest against his assertions about divine justice; cf. Wilson 2002:72-73.

[15] Lord 1960:160 argues that the *Odyssey* initially exploits the possibility of an Oresteia-style "return story" pattern, while "later in the *Odyssey* Homer emphasizes [the] *differences* between the two stories. But in the opening of the song Homer is thinking of the parallels" (emphasis in original).

nature of Zeus' Oresteia and the significance of this polemic for the details of Athene's plan. In each case, Zeus' presentation of characters from the Oresteia either aligns the *Odyssey* with, or distances it from, non-Homeric accounts of Odysseus.

Klytaimnestre and Penelope

Recent scholarship has drawn attention to the suppression of Klytaimnestre in Zeus' Oresteia: Zeus refers to her only as "wife" (36, 39), while he names the other actors at least by patronymic.[16] And though Klytaimnestre's complicity in Agamemnon's murder, and her subsequent death, would reinforce the justice theme, Zeus represents her as almost a passive victim, in marked contrast with the active agency attributed to her by other Odyssean characters.

The downplaying of Klytaimnestre distracts attention from the fundamental difference between Agamemnon's situation and that of Odysseus as it will emerge in the *Odyssey*, namely, the extent to which the heroes can depend on their wives. Penelope's loyalty, however, was not the "fact" of Odysseus-tradition that the *Odyssey* would make it seem.

For in other accounts, Penelope's relationship with the suitors is analogous to Klytaimnestre's with Aigisthos. Thus, for example, some time in the second century CE the Greek travel-writer Pausanias was shown a landmark in Mantineia:

> ἐν δεξιᾶι τῆς ὁδοῦ γῆς χῶμα ὑψηλόν· Πηνελόπης δὲ εἶναι τάφον φασίν, οὐχ ὁμολογοῦντες τὰ ἐς αὐτὴν ποιήσει <τῆι> Θεσπρωτίδι ὀνομαζομένηι. ἐν ταύτηι μέν γ᾽ ἐστ᾽ τῆι ποιήσει ἐπανήκοντι ἐκ Τροίας Ὀδυσσεῖ τεκεῖν τὴν Πηνελόπην Πτολιπόρθην παῖδα· Μαντινέων δὲ ὁ ἐς αὐτὴν λόγος Πηνελόπην φησὶν ὑπ᾽ Ὀδυσσέως καταγνωσθεῖσαν ὡς ἐπισπαστοὺς ἐσαγάγοιτ᾽ ἐς τὸν οἶκον, καὶ ἀποπεμφθεῖσαν ὑπ᾽ αὐτοῦ, τὸ μὲν παραυτίκα ἐς Λακεδαίμονα ἀπελθεῖν, χρόνωι δὲ ὕστερον ἐκ τῆς Σπάρτης ἐς Μαντίνειαν μετοικῆσαι, καὶ οἱ τοῦ βίου τὴν τελευτὴν ἐνταῦθα συμβῆναι. τοῦ τάφου δὲ ἔχεται τούτου πεδίον οὐ μέγα, καὶ ὄρος ἐστὶν ἐν τῶι πεδίωι τὰ ἐρείπια ἔτι Μαντινείας ἔχον τῆς ἀρχαίας.

---

[16] Zeus' polemical presentation of Klytaimnestre is stressed by Olson 1995:26; Felson 1994:95; Zeitlin 1995:143; Rüter 1969:75. Agamemnon naturally emphasizes Klytaimnestre's role in his own death (cf. 24.200-202), but his account is largely confirmed by Nestor and Menelaos, the latter having obtained his information from a divine source (Proteus). Klytaimnestre's name is however suppressed in Nestor's first telling of the story; cf. de Jong 2001:82 ad 3.254-316, and discussion of 3.193-198 in Chapter 5.

> On the right of the road is a high mound of earth; and they [the Mantineians] say that it is the tomb of Penelope, not agreeing with the poem called the *Thesprotis*. In the poem, Penelope bears to Odysseus after he returns a child, Ptoliporthes; but the Mantineans' story says that Penelope was charged by Odysseus with having enticed men and brought them into their home, and was sent away by him, and that she went first to Lakedaimon, but later moved from Sparta to Mantineia, and there came to the end of her life. By the tomb is a plain of no great size, and there is a mountain on the plain where lie the ruins of old Mantineia.

Pausanias 8.12.5-7

As in many of Pausanias' reports, and Greek myths in general, a natural feature is connected to the story of a god, hero, or, in this case, heroine. Pausanias never makes clear precisely how he learns such stories; "the Mantineians say" (φασίν) could imply that he has interviewed an informant, read an inscription, or witnessed the performance of a poem or play in connection with the cult site.[17] In any case, a likely reservoir for such accounts would be epichoric traditions of oral narrative poetry. That is, the story could well have taken shape and been propagated in the context of performances commemorating the sacred space of Old Mantineia.

Epichoric accounts, as discussed, often disagree with each other and with Panhellenic and proto-Panhellenic versions. Thus Pausanias observes here that the story of Penelope's tomb told in Mantineia conflicts with a non-Homeric epic, the *Thesprotis*.[18] Pausanias does not contrast the faithless Mantineian Penelope with the Homeric Penelope; but since he cites the *Odyssey* frequently in other contexts, he was certainly aware of the difference, and presumably considered it obvious to his readers.

From the perspective established in the Introduction, Penelope's Mantineian tomb is representative of the kinds of traditions out of and in the face of which the *Odyssey*'s Panhellenic account emerged. For though Pausanias' report is itself relatively late, similar accounts can be traced back to

---

[17] The site itself has not been securely identified, though see Mazarakis-Ainian 1997:167-169 Malkin 1998:125 argues plausibly for the transmission of Odysseus-tradition in Arkadia (for which also cf. Pausanias 8.44.4) through "an independent, perhaps not even epic route with more emphasis on Penelope than elsewhere."

[18] *Thesprotis* may have been another name for the *Telegony*; see Chapter 4 n44.

the Classical period, and these in turn, as will be discussed momentarily, likely depend on still older traditions. Again, these are not stories one would expect to derive from the Homeric account. Such a source-and-recipient relationship would require a complete reorientation of a major Odyssean character proverbial for just the sort of behavior that the reorientation denies her. Such revalorization is precedented in iambic or parodic contexts; but the unfaithful Mantineian Penelope is an august figure, an apparent recipient of cult honors.

I accordingly propose that the *Odyssey* targets stories about an unfaithful Penelope for "de-authorization" – that is, targeted rejection from the canonical narrative. Suppression of Klytaimnestre in Zeus' speech signposts this program, which continues almost until the end of the *Odyssey* as various characters, human and divine, remark on Penelope's fidelity.[19] At the same time, the *Odyssey*, by the very act of de-authorization, acknowledges the existence of these stories. Indeed, the frequency with which characters refer to Penelope's unwavering resistance to the suitors suggests that they "protest too much," and thereby betrays awareness of versions in which the heroine's resistance weakens. The *Odyssey* has also a further motivation for alluding to the alternative version, since an unfaithful Penelope is one of the possibilities that, as mentioned above, can create dramatic tension in a well-known story. Thus for instance Athene disingenuously impresses on Telemachos the need for his immediate return to Ithake from Sparta with the warning that his mother's impending remarriage may deprive him of his standing and possessions (15.16-26).[20]

The potentially unfaithful Penelope is then an analog of Klytaimnestre, so that the story proceeds in part as if Odysseus and Telemachos are preparing to confront a conniving and homicidal wife and mother. Zeus' suppression of Klytaimnestre in his Oresteia is in this respect analogous to the suppression of this "other Penelope" by the *Odyssey* itself. In each case the narrative is streamlined and simplified by focus on the male characters; yet the question of the wife's fidelity is inherent in the paradigm, and Penelope's character is revisited whenever Klytaimnestre is mentioned.

---

[19] Penelope's fidelity is discussed by, for example, Antikleia (*Odyssey* 11.181-183), Agamemnon (11.443-446, 24.194-198), Athene (13.336-338, 379-381) and Telemachos (16.33-34, 73-77).
[20] See Felson 1994:82-83 on Athene's warning, and 128 for the conclusion that "Homer uses Penelope to keep his text fluid and changeable as long as possible. She, as a character, is pivotal to the opening up of the text." Similarly Murnaghan 1995:69-70.

Hermes

In contrast with the downplaying of Klytaimnestre in his Oresteia, Zeus places seemingly disproportionate emphasis on Hermes, whom he names twice in the nine lines of his account, once with a full array of epithets (*Odyssey* 1.38, 42). Hermes' function here, which can be classified as an instantiation of the common folktale motif of the "warner," is crucial for Zeus' assertion about human suffering. For Zeus' point is that what mortals perceive as suffering "beyond one's portion" (ὑπὲρ μόρον, 34) is in fact the result of proceeding with a course of action after having been warned of its dire consequences.[21]

Since this rhetorical point could be made with the simple statement that "we gods warned him," repetition of Hermes' name and function in Zeus' concise Oresteia seems conspicuous, even in a poetic tradition characterized by repetition. I suggest that Zeus' emphasis here is motivated by the analogous roles that Hermes, and Athene, will play in the plan that the goddess proposes for Odysseus and Telemachos. Specifically, Hermes' admonition of Aigisthos parallels the warning that the suitors receive in Book 2, and Hermes' own message to Kalypso in Book 5.

In the first case, Athene delivers the warning to the suitors through the medium of Telemachos, who at her prompting summons an assembly and calls on Zeus to visit the suitors with unrequited destruction if they do not cease to consume his family's goods (2.144-145; cf. 1.91-92).[22] Zeus lends his authority to Telemachos' threat by sending an omen (146-152), in which the seer Halitherses perceives the imminent return of Odysseus and the destruction of the suitors (161-176). As a consequence the suitors are, like Aigisthos, duly warned; their destruction is, like his, a matter of personal responsibility.[23]

Hermes' mission to dissuade Aigisthos from wooing Klytaimnestre (μήτε μνάασθαι ἄκοιτιν, 1.39) also recalls the role that he will play in Athene's plan, that of dissuading Kalypso from trying to make Odysseus her husband (cf. 1.15, λιλαιομένη πόσιν εἶναι). Significantly, though Hermes is by implication included among the assembly of "all the gods but Poseidon" during which his embassy to Kalypso is discussed, he says nothing to Kalypso about Athene.

---

[21] On the theme of the divine "warner" see Louden 1999:4-6, 109; Hölscher 1988:25-34; Fenik 1974:208-218.

[22] Telemachos' wish that the suitors perish without atonement (νήποινοι, 2.145) is realized in Zeus' settlement in Book 24; see Chapter 3.

[23] A point emphasized by Cook 1995:35 and G. Rose 1967:392-394.

Rather he attributes his mission to "Zeus' idea" (Διὸς νόον, 5.103; cf. 99), and warns her that failure to release Odysseus will invoke the μῆνις, 'wrath,' of Zeus (5.146-147).

Inclusion of Hermes in Zeus' Oresteia may also be significant in terms of the messenger god's connection with Odysseus and his family through kinship and cult. In the *Odyssey* itself, Hermes helps Odysseus to overcome Kirke (10.277-307), and is said to have bestowed skill in the criminal arts upon Autolykos, the hero's maternal grandfather, as a reward for practicing his cult (19.396-399).[24] The relationship is natural in that Hermes and Autolykos, like Odysseus, share the character-type of trickster. And, as often in Greek myth, formal similarity is expressed through kinship and broader thematic links. Thus, according to non-Homeric tradition, Hermes is himself the father of Autolykos (e.g. Hesiod *Catalog of Women* fr. 64 MW).

Hermes also plays a more sinister role in non-Homeric accounts of Odysseus' story. Specifically, he is among the alleged seducers of Penelope, with whom he fathers the god Pan.[25] One of the earliest references occurs in Herodotos:

Πηνελόπης, ἐκ ταύτης γὰρ καὶ Ἑρμέω λέγεται γενέσθαι ὑπὸ Ἑλλήνων ὁ Πᾶν ...

... Penelope, from whom, along with Hermes, it is said by the Hellenes that Pan was born ...

Herodotos 2.145.4

Another, more full account connects the story with the same region in which Pausanias found Penelope's tomb:

τινὲς δὲ Πηνελόπην ὑπὸ Ἀντινόου φθαρεῖσαν λέγουσιν ὑπὸ Ὀδυσσέως πρὸς τὸν πατέρα Ἰκάριον ἀποσταλῆναι, γενομένην δὲ τῆς Ἀρκαδίας κατὰ Μαντίνειαν ἐξ Ἑρμοῦ τεκεῖν Πᾶνα.

---

[24] On Hermes and Odysseus see S. West *CHO* I:78-79 ad 1.37ff. Thus Hermes' gift of *moly* to Odysseus in the Kirke episode (*Odyssey* 10.290, 304) could allude to compensation for seducing the hero's wife and/or to the family connection between them.

[25] In other versions, Pan derives from Penelope's copulation with "all" of the suitors; see Frazer 1921 v. 2:305n1, who catalogs, with "Apollodoros" *Epitome* 7.38-39, Cicero *De Natura Deorum* 3.22.56, Servius ad *Aeneid* 2.44, and Tzetzes *ad* Lykophron 772, but not the Herodotos passage. In other accounts, a daughter of Dryops is Pan's mother (e.g. *Homeric Hymn* 19.34).

And some say that Penelope was seduced by Antinoos and was sent away by Odysseus to her father Ikarios, and that when she came to Mantineia in Arkadia, she bore Pan by Hermes.

"Apollodoros" Epitome 7.38

Zeus' Oresteia constructs at the outset a "good Hermes," one who aids the gods in pointing out the negative consequences of seduction. As in the case of the competing versions of Penelope, Zeus' positive valorization can be seen as a programmatic act, as well as a tacit acknowledgment that stories of the "bad Hermes" had achieved a level of diffusion that would provoke de-authorization.[26] Members of the Homeric audience who were familiar with such traditions, perhaps Arkadians or worshippers of the god Pan generally could have found Hermes' prominence at the beginning of the *Odyssey*, and the choice of him to dissuade Kalypso from "cuckolding" Penelope, ironical or even humorous. At the same time, Zeus' casting of Hermes as an opponent of seduction in the Oresteia paradigm could also foreshadow the fact that the Odyssean Penelope will not be seduced by the god.[27]

Orestes and Telemachos

The warning issued to the suitors in Book 2 completes the first stage of Athene's proposal for Telemachos (1.90-91). The second stage, his journey to Pylos and Sparta (93), has little overt connection with the basic plot-line of Zeus' Oresteia. Again, however, apparently superfluous details in Zeus' account seem to anticipate Telemachos' journey. Thus Zeus states that Orestes is entering manhood, as is Telemachos, when he kills Aigisthos, and that he returns home from elsewhere, as Telemachos will do from the Peloponnesus in order to do so (again, ὁππότ' ἂν ἡβήσηι τε καὶ ἧς ἱμείρεται αἴης, 1.41).[28]

---

[26] Note that elsewhere in the *Odyssey* Hermes declares (in an inset narrative) his willingness to bed another's wife (8.339-342).

[27] That is, Penelope will not be seduced by a god either openly, or in disguise—she will not play Alkmene to Hermes' Zeus. Hence, in part, her frequent epithet περίφρων, which is used exclusively of positively valorized female characters: in the *Odyssey*, Penelope, Eurykleia (e.g. 19.357) and Arete (11.345); in the *Iliad* Diomedes' wife Aigialeia (5.412); see discussion of the epithet by Felson 1994:6, 16-19, 41-42. Likewise, the *Iliad*'s description of Aigialeia as περίφρων could similarly be intended to de-authorize non-Homeric traditions in which she is seduced by Kometes, the son of her husband's charioteer Sthenelos (Mimnermos fr. 22 W), or is among the spouses of Trojan War heroes whom Nauplios, father of Palamedes, convinces to commit adultery ("Apollodoros" *Epitome* 6.9); see Chapter 5 for Diomedes' *nostos*.

[28] So also Hesiod fr. 23(a) 29 MW: ὅς [Orestes] ῥα καὶ ἡβήσας ἀπε[τείσατο π]ατροφο[ν]ῆα.

Predictably, as the narrative proceeds Orestes is in turn set up as a role model for Telemachos; thus Athene, and later Nestor, exhort him to action with the example of the universal acclaim that Orestes secured by avenging his father (1.298-300, 3.203-204).

The details that Zeus provides about Orestes, then, have specific relevance to Orestes' role as a counterpart to Telemachos, for they reveal the two as age-mates on the threshold of manhood. From an anthropological perspective, Zeus' Oresteia presents Orestes in the context of an initiatory pattern that applies to Telemachos as well, and is in fact widespread in Greek myth and ritual. This "withdrawal and return" pattern is broad – the youth leaves home and returns after an ordeal to claim full membership in his family and community – and only broadly does it fit both Telemachos and Orestes: one is away for days, the other for years; one obtains information about his father from Trojan War heroes, the other from an oracle; and so on.[29] Nevertheless, when the Oresteia is mapped onto the *Odyssey*, the figure of Orestes points to a significant role for Telemachos in the story of his father's return, a role that could include even assertion of his hereditary rights through matricide. And, since Telemachos must withdraw in order to return, the gods can in this respect be said to plan the *Telemachia*. Orestes represents for Telemachos one possible path to immortalization in song (e.g. 3.204); only later will the *Odyssey* reveal the possibility that he can share the revenge-fantasy with a living father.[30]

By my interpretation, then, Athene in responding to Zeus' speech constructs Telemachos' journey as a kind of substitute initiation into the heroic world, a process undergone by Orestes as well in his quest for vengeance. And while the itinerary that Athene proposes for Telemachos – Pylos and Sparta – cannot be derived from Zeus' speech, it is nevertheless the case that Nestor and Menelaos, as Odysseus' closest living peers, are natural figures to take his place in performing Telemachos' initiation.[31] The Pylians and Spartans among whom Telemachos acquires the confidence to take control of

[29] On withdrawal and return generally, see Sowa 1984:95-121, 212-235 with bibliography; for initiation, Burkert 1985:260-264. For Telemachos specifically, see G. Rose 1967.
[30] Lord 1960:160-161 supports his case for multiple possible realizations of Telemachos in the ancient Greek epic tradition with comparative evidence: "In the South Slavic tradition the role of the son is highly variable," while "only in the Agamemnon type [of return song] is the son a necessary element."
[31] Diokles of Pherai (*Odyssey* 3.488-489=15.186-187; cf. *Iliad* 5.542-549) may also be counted among the peers of Odysseus contacted by Telemachos on his quest.

his household are thus thematically analogous to the Athenians who prepare Orestes for his return home to kill Aigisthos (*Odyssey* 3.307).[32]

As noted above, Zeus' concise telling omits a theme that is central to most non-Homeric accounts of the Oresteia, and that will be central to the *Odyssey* itself, namely the further cycle of vengeance that the avenger brings upon himself. For all that the *Odyssey* says about Orestes' life after killing Aigisthos is that he enjoyed wide fame. Any sense of guilt, as personified by the Erinyes in archaic vase-paintings as well as dramatic representations of the Oresteia is absent from the Homeric version of the story. Nor, as noted at the beginning of the chapter, is there any mention of the prosecution of Orestes by the kin of his victims that features in other accounts.[33] This simplification of the Oresteia, I shall argue in Chapter 4, has a significant parallel in the *Odyssey*'s account of the aftermath of Odysseus' revenge.

Nostoi and *Odyssey*

The focus on Aigisthos in Zeus' Oresteia is also explicable in terms of the overall chronology of the ancient Greek epics that describe the Trojan War.[34] For the *Nostoi*, a Cyclic epic that told the story from the sack of Troy up to the main narrative *Odyssey*, concluded with an account of the Oresteia:

ἔπειτα Ἀγαμέμνονος ὑπὸ Αἰγίσθου καὶ Κλυταιμνήστρας ἀναιρεθέντος ὑπ᾽ Ὀρέστου καὶ Πυλάδου τιμωρία καὶ Μενελάου εἰς τὴν οἰκείαν ἀνακομιδή. Μετὰ ταῦτά ἐστιν Ὁμήρου Ὀδύσσεια.

---

[32] In other accounts Orestes returns from Phokis; see S. West *CHO* I:180 ad 3.307. Agamemnon shade asks Odysseus if he has seen Orestes in Orchomenos, *Pylos,* or *Sparta* (*Odyssey* 11.459-460) which could suggest that a version of Orestes' story included visits to these sites, and thu an even closer relationship between the main narrative of the *Odyssey* and its version of th Oresteia.

[33] The *Odyssey*'s silence on this point was noted in antiquity; cf. scholia to Euripdes *Orestes* 164 1647. According to one account, Orestes is prosecuted by his maternal grandfather Tyndareu ("Apollodoros" *Epitome* 6.25), whose role would in Telemachos' case be assumed by Ikarios (c *Odyssey* 2.133). On the prosecution of Odysseus, see Chapter 4.

[34] Thus Lord 1960:160: "allusion to the return of Agamemnon [at the beginning of the *Odysse* points...to the scope of tales in the tradition of ancient Greece." cf. Schadewaldt 1958:1 Similarly, the death of Aigisthos is the last event in Nestor's account of the *nostoi* (cf. 3.193-20 303-312); further discussion in Chapter 5.

Then Agamemnon is killed by Aigisthos and Klytaimnestre, and [there is] the vengeance of Orestes and Menelaos' return to his household. After these things is the *Odyssey* of Homer.

Proklos *Chrestomathy* 95.17-19, 100 Bernabé, 109.1-6 Allen

The amount of time that is imagined to separate the killing of Aigisthos from the main narrative of the *Odyssey* is unclear.[35] Zeus frames his Oresteia, "so even now" (ὡς καὶ νῦν, 1.35), and Nestor says that Menelaos' recent (νέον, 3.318) return to Greece occurred on the day Orestes performed Aigisthos' funeral feast (αὐτῆμαρ, 3.311); but this information is insufficient to establish the timeline. Nestor provides a *terminus post quem* when he states that Orestes' revenge took place in the eighth year after Aigisthos seized power ([Aigisthos] κτείνας Ἀτρείδην . . . ἑπτάετες δ' ἤνασσε . . . τῶι δέ οἱ ὀγδοάτωι κακὸν ἤλυθε δῖος Ὀρέστης . . . κατὰ δ' ἔκτανε πατροφονῆα, 3.304-307). Troy falls ten years before the *Odyssey* begins, and Agamemnon requires an indeterminate amount of time to return. His route takes him near Cape Maleia on Crete, where he is blown off course in a storm to "the end of the land," where dwells, oddly enough, Aigisthos (4.517-518).[36] At any rate, Agamemnon proceeds home from this place under a favorable wind (4.520), and it is difficult to see how his entire voyage from Troy to Mykene can have lasted the three years that would be required to make Aigisthos' seven years of rule end as the *Odyssey* begins. As a consequence, it appears that events Zeus refers to as having occurred "even just now" and Nestor as "recent" transpired some two or three years previously.[37]

---

[35] For the *Odyssey*'s opening chronology, see Lowe 2000:130-134; Olson 1995:91-119; Pedrick 1992:50-54; Austin 1975:85-89; Stanford 1965:ix-xii; Schadewaldt 1958:28-29.

[36] In some accounts, Aigisthos' father Thyestes is banished to the island Kythera off Cape Maleia from Mykene after mistakenly dining on his son Pelops (e.g. "Apollodoros" *Epitome* 2.15), and it was perhaps with this myth in mind that ancient scholars (e.g. Andron *FGrH* 10 F 11 and HP scholia to *Odyssey* 4.517) identified Kythera as "the end of land where Thyestes lived" (ἀγροῦ ἐπ' ἐσχατιὴν ὅθι δώματα ναῖε Θυέστης//τὸ πρὶν ἀτὰρ τότ' ἔναιε Θυεστιάδης Αἴγισθος, 4.517-518). S. West *CHO* 1:224-225 ad 4.514-20 and Merkelbach 1951:47-48 resort to interpolation to explain perceived difficulties with the *Odyssey*'s account of Agamemnon's return. It is however possible that the *Odyssey* references a parallel tradition; other returning Greek heroes, including Odysseus, experience storms off Maleia.

[37] The chronological issues are well explored by de Jong 2001:11 ad 1.29-31 with Appendix A; cf. S. West *CHO* 1:181 ad 3.318. Cunliffe s.v. νῦν (3) translates the particle at *Odyssey* 1.35 as "looking back to an occurrence in the past, now," citing e.g. *Iliad* 1.445 and 506.

It is of course unlikely that traditional singers of the *Odyssey* intended to convey, or that their audiences expected to hear, a precise chronology of these events. Nevertheless, there is an important point to be made concerning the relationship between Zeus' Oresteia and the opening of the *Odyssey*. Zeus' choice to speak of the death of Aigisthos cannot be understood as a commentary on events that he and the other gods have observed recently. From the perspective of the character Zeus, then, his Oresteia either represents an arbitrary rumination on events now several years past, or is motivated by some other factor. One such factor, I suggest, is the boundary that emerged through a process of negotiation between *Nostoi*- and *Odyssey*-traditions; another is the desire on the part of the latter to juxtapose the stories of Odysseus and Agamemnon in a significant way.

Chapter conclusions

Proceeding from the well-documented parallels between the story of Agamemnon, Klytaimnestre, and Orestes on the one hand, and the *Odyssey*'s account of Odysseus, Penelope and Telemachos on the other, I have argued that the Oresteia as Zeus presents it foreshadows the relationships among the *Odyssey*'s characters and the path that the narrative will take. Working from the assumption that Homeric composition was in part a synthetic process, a goal of which was to elaborate a Panhellenic narrative that drew on, harmonized, and transcended parallel traditions, I have proposed that the *Odyssey* exploits such traditions in order to deepen its own characterizations and to heighten dramatic tension. Thus the polyvalent figures of Penelope and Hermes are constructed in implicit contrast with their very different roles in non-Homeric contexts. Moreover, the very boundaries of the Odyssean narrative suggest a process of negotiation with the larger epic tradition, so that Zeus' Oresteia recalls the *Odyssey*'s junction with the Cyclic *Nostoi*.

The polemical presentation of Zeus' Oresteia, I conclude, involves manipulation of virtually every character and theme. Thus the very arbitrariness of the Oresteia-*Odyssey* relationship points to the significance of Zeus' role in the plan that Athene formulates for Odysseus. Zeus defines the thematic parameters of both stories, so that all Athene must (or can) do in order to come up with a plan for Odysseus is to make obvious connections between his story and Agamemnon's. As discussed in subsequent chapters, the kinds of interactions to which I have drawn attention in the first divine council remain prominent in further planning sessions among the gods. In Chapter 2, I find particular significance in the fact that, the next time Athene and Zeus take up the subject of Odysseus, what is called "Athene's plan" is dictated explicitly by Zeus.

2

OGYGIE TO ITHAKE

WHEN ODYSSEUS HIMSELF enters the main narrative of the *Odyssey* in Book 5, he is, as at the beginning, trapped on Kalypso's island in the middle of the sea. This is the world of the hero's divine antagonist Poseidon, from which he will escape in accordance with the plan that Athene puts forward in the first divine council scene in Book 1. As discussed in Chapter 1, her plan calls for Hermes to instruct Kalypso to release the hero (1.85-87). In Book 5, it is Zeus who actually charges Hermes with this mission, and his orders elaborate a detailed plan that coordinates the efforts of a number of divine and mortal characters so as to program the main narrative through Book 13. It is Zeus who declares that Odysseus will land back on Ithake unharmed and fabulously wealthy, and who specifies the time and place for the *Apologoi*, the hero's retrospective account of his journey from Troy to Kalypso's island of Ogygie that occupies Books 8 through 12.

Although Poseidon is absent from Olympos in Book 5 as he is in Book 1, he plays a crucial role in fulfilling the plan that Zeus puts forth in his instructions to Hermes. Poseidon's actions in Book 5, despite their consequences, are intended to frustrate the gods' plan for Odysseus, and in a second and final appearance, in Book 13 near the end of the Ogygie-to-Ithake sequence, the sea god confronts Zeus face-to-face. Contrary to expectations raised by both Zeus and Poseidon, the Odyssean Olympos remains untouched by the kind of strife that often characterizes such scenes in the *Iliad*. Poseidon has then one more task to perform, and as the main narrative leaves his world, he is in the process of tying up one of the *Odyssey*'s loose ends, namely the fate of the Phaiakes, the audience for Odysseus' *Apologoi* who are at the same time the subject of a politically charged body of non-Homeric traditions.

The interactions between Zeus and the subordinate gods Athene and Poseidon in Books 5 and 13 clarify and expand the picture of the divine apparatus that emerges in Book 1. The concerns of the subordinate gods are limited to engagement with one facet of the central character Odysseus: he is the object of Athene's care and Poseidon's hatred. The perspective of Zeus, on the other hand, transcends the aims of either god, and his plan for Odysseus harnesses both. In like manner, the *Odyssey* itself seeks to transcend, through selective inclusion, de-authorization and programmed ambiguity, the mass of epichoric and proto-Panhellenic myths that were connected with the returning Odysseus.

The "second" Odyssean divine council (*Odyssey* 5.3-43)

The divine council scenes at the beginnings of *Odyssey* 1 and 5 seem to narrate two parts of what is conceptually a single scene. This interpretation is consistent with a compositional tendency known as "Zielinski's law," which describes one of the ways ancient Greek poets – tragic as well as epic – responded to the problem of narrating events that unfold simultaneously in different settings.[1] A narrative constructed in accordance with this law follows events as they transpire in one setting, and then switches to another setting, at the same time rewinding the clock, often without any explicit notice of the fact, to the point at which events began in the first setting. The divine council scenes at the beginnings of *Odyssey* 1 and 5 occur in a context in which Zielinski's law is often operative in Homeric narrative: two emissaries are dispatched from Olympos. A comparable example is the simultaneous dispatch, and sequential account, of Iris to restrain Poseidon from helping the Greeks in battle, and of Apollo to restore the Trojan leader Hektor, in *Iliad* 15 (151-262).[2]

Audiences seem to have been cued to the operation of this convention by the repetition of a paradigmatic scene at the points where the narrative strands diverge. Thus at the beginning of Book 5 as at the beginning of Book 1, the Olympian gods, again excepting Poseidon, sit in assembly (5.3; 1.27); again, Zeus and Athene are the only speakers; and again, the topic of discussion is Odysseus and his son. This discussion assumes, and completes, Athene's proposal in Book 1: as she has sent Telemachos on his journey to Pylos and Sparta, so Hermes will send Odysseus from Ogygie to his home on Ithake.

---

[1] Zielinski 1899-1901; the phenomenon was noted earlier by Kirchoff 1879:196. Among those who favor the application of this "law" to *Odyssey* 1 and 5 are Scodel 1999a:42-43; Hainsworth *CHO* 1:251-252; S. Richardson 1990:90-92 and, by implication, Olson 1995:116-118; critical of its application here are Latacz 1996:142 and, by implication, de Jong 2001:124 and Louden 1999:104-122. See Rüter 1969:74 for discussion of Analytic arguments that attribute the two councils to different poets.

[2] N. Richardson *IC* 6:284 ad 24.77-119.

The exchange between Zeus and Athene in Book 5, then, seems to rewind the narrative clock so that Telemachos' and Odysseus' adventures proceed simultaneously. But it does so in a self-conscious way, in comparison with scenes such as the dispatch of Iris and Apollo in *Iliad* 15, where the divergence and rejoining of the parallel narrative strands go unremarked. Athene initiates the "second" discussion of Odysseus by expressing despair that the hero remains on Ogygie, and that the suitors are preparing to ambush Telemachos (5.11-19). The self-consciousness becomes apparent when Zeus responds with surprise to Athene's words:

> τέκνον ἐμόν, ποῖόν σε ἔπος φύγεν ἕρκος ὀδόντων.
> οὐ γὰρ δὴ τοῦτον μὲν ἐβούλευσας νόον αὐτή,
> ὡς ἤτοι κείνους Ὀδυσεὺς ἀποτίσεται ἐλθών;
> Τηλέμαχον δὲ σὺ πέμψον ἐπισταμένως, δύνασαι γάρ,
> ὥς κε μάλ᾽ ἀσκηθὴς ἣν πατρίδα γαῖαν ἵκηται,
> μνηστῆρες δ᾽ ἐν νηὶ παλιμπετὲς ἀπονέωνται.

> My child, what a word has escaped the barrier of your teeth.
> For did not you yourself plan this idea,
> so that indeed Odysseus will come and exact payback from
>   those men?
> As for Telemachos, send him on with care, for you have the
>   power,
> so that he may fully unscathed reach his paternal land,
> and the suitors in their ship return back home.

> *Odyssey* 5.22-27

Athene's forgetfulness – conspicuous for the goddess of *mētis* – and Zeus' response to it seem to acknowledge, perhaps ironically, the temporal distortion caused by the operation of the convention that Zielinski's law describes. Zeus then bids Athene to see to the completion of Telemachos' journey (she actually does so at 13.440, as the *Telemachia* and *Nostos* sequences feed into the *Mnesterophonia*), and himself instructs Hermes to see to Odysseus' return.

Ironical or not, the exchange between Athene and Zeus in Book 5 invites the external audience to reflect on the conventions by which the narrative operates. Attention is directed, not just to the management of narrative time, but also to the mechanics of the divine apparatus. For Athene's claim of *aporia* calls into question her competence to transform her plan into a coherent course of events. If the "idea" (νόος, 5.23) is hers, as Zeus claims, she has not made it practicable.

It will be useful to anticipate the next chapter here briefly in order to adduce a comparable scene in Book 24, where Zeus poses the same possibly wry question (5.21-24=24.477-480) under similar circumstances, when Athene finds herself unable to resolve the *Mnesterophonia* sequence. In that scene, Zeus himself steps in to dictate the terms by which Odysseus' power over his household and Ithake will be made secure. In both scenes, Zeus downplays his own role in the formulation of a workable plan by declaring Athene to be the guiding force, even as he takes control of the situation. Yet there is no indication that the goddess considers Zeus' contributions in Books 5 and 24 a usurpation of her plans. Thus Zeus enacts his own plan as it were under the aegis of Athene.

That plan in Book 5 maps out Odysseus' path from Ogygie to Ithake in detail, specifying when, where, and how the voyage will take place, and whom the hero will encounter en route. According to Zeus' instructions, Hermes is to tell Kalypso of the gods'

> νημερτέα βουλήν,
> νόστον Ὀδυσσῆος ταλασίφρονος, ὥς κε νέηται,
> οὔτε θεῶν πομπῆι οὔτε θνητῶν ἀνθρώπων·
> ἀλλ' ὅ γ' ἐπὶ σχεδίης πολυδέσμου πήματα πάσχων
> ἤματι εἰκοστῶι Σχερίην ἐρίβωλον ἵκοιτο,
> Φαιήκων ἐς γαῖαν, οἳ ἀγχίθεοι γεγάασιν·   35
> οἵ κέν μιν περὶ κῆρι θεὸν ὣς τιμήσουσι,
> πέμψουσιν δ' ἐν νηὶ φίλην ἐς πατρίδα γαῖαν,
> χαλκόν τε χρυσόν τε ἅλις ἐσθῆτά τε δόντες,
> πόλλ', ὅσ' ἂν οὐδέ ποτε Τροίης ἐξήρατ' Ὀδυσσεύς,
> εἴ περ ἀπήμων ἦλθε, λαχὼν ἀπὸ ληίδος αἶσαν.   40
> ὣς γάρ οἱ μοῖρ' ἐστὶ φίλους τ' ἰδέειν καὶ ἱκέσθαι
> οἶκον ἐς ὑψόροφον καὶ ἐὴν ἐς πατρίδα γαῖαν.

> . . . unwavering plan,
>   the homecoming of firm-minded Odysseus, so that
>   he may return,
>   neither under gods' escort nor that of mortal men,
>   but on a raft of many fastenings, suffering woes,
>   on the twentieth day he may reach fertile Scherie,
>   the land of the Phaiakes, who are close to the gods.   35
>   These people will honor him like a god greatly in
>   their hearts,
>   and will send him on a ship to his own paternal land,

after giving him bronze and gold in abundance and clothing,
so many things as Odysseus would never have taken out of
  Troy,
had he come unmolested with his portion of plunder.   40
For thus his fate is to see his own people and to reach
his high-roofed house and his paternal land.

Odyssey 5.30-42

To repeat, Zeus has asserted that the plan for Odysseus and Telemachos is Athene's (5.23); and she herself later refers to the plan for Odysseus' return specifically as "mine" (ἐμῆι βουλῆι τε νόωι τε, 13.305). Whether or not the audience is to imagine that Athene is aware of the fact, Zeus has in effect taken control of the narrative: this time, in contrast with the parallel scene in Book 1, the "table of contents" speech is his. His instructions to Hermes, then, translate Athene's general desire for Odysseus' return into a workable plan, which is enacted over the course of Books 5 to 13. And, whereas Athene is apparently unable to manage other characters' responses to her vague ideas for Telemachos and Odysseus, Zeus by contrast brings together with his specific plan the actions of a series of characters, many of whom act in ignorance of the chief god's broader goals.

As mentioned in the Introduction, Hermes, in carrying out Zeus's instructions, tells Kalypso that she must send Odysseus on his way lest she incite Zeus' wrath, because "it is in no way possible that another god get alongside or frustrate the *Dios noos* (mind of Zeus)" (5.103-104~137-138). The expression *Dios noos* seems to echo *Dios boulē* (cf. ἐβούλευσας νόον, e.g. 5.23=24.479). Kalypso for her part recognizes the operation of a plan that, if unfair, must nonetheless be followed by herself and the other gods (5.118-140). Her predictable compliance unleashes the hero, allowing his role in the narrative at last to unfold.

Zeus' instructions to Hermes in Book 5 are also crucial for the shape of the Odyssean narrative in that they create the opening for Odysseus' performance of his *Apologoi* (Books 9-12) by placing him among the Phaiakes. The choice to begin the narrative *in medias res* – which again is linked to Zeus' decision to ruminate on the Oresteia when he does – demands that the *Apologoi* adventures, which are promised in the proem (1.3-4), take the form of flashbacks. I note that the *Odyssey* suggests other points at which the *Apologoi* could attach to the main narrative, for instance during Odysseus' stay with Aiolos (10.14-16) and his reunification with Penelope (23.310-342).

In contrast with the main narrative, the events in the *Apologoi* are not made to depend on the gods. Rather, Books 8-12 are structured according to a different set of organizing principles, in particular self-contained chiastic patterns that take the Phaiakes' promise to Odysseus of gifts and return (11.333-384) as the central point, around which are arranged thematically related episodes.[3] The diminished role of the gods in the *Apologoi* is in part a consequence of the fact that the story is told by a mortal narrator, Odysseus. This narrative situation has a subtle and far-reaching effect on the flow of information, since mortal narrators become aware of divine activity only by direct witness or report, a phenomenon commonly referred to as "Jørgensen's law." That is, the Homeric narrator and divine characters are as a rule aware of the divine agent responsible for any given act or circumstance in the narrative. Human characters, by contrast, remain ignorant of the actions of specific gods unless they are informed by a divine character or, in the case of seers and singers, possess special powers. Thus mortals employ the generic terms θεός, δαίμων, or "Zeus" in a generalizing sense to describe divine activity. Odysseus, for example, attributes his exceptional knowledge of an exchange between Zeus and Helios in Book 12 (389-390) to the goddess Kalypso, who was herself informed by Hermes, who in turn is an assumed participant at divine councils, as can be seen in Book 5.[4]

The scene in Book 12, Zeus' one speaking appearance outside the main narrative in the *Odyssey*, is the exception to the chief god's disengagement from the *Apologoi* that proves the rule. Helios complains to the gods about the slaughter of his cattle by Odysseus' men and threatens to shine among the dead in Hades if he does not receive satisfaction (12.374-390; cf. 19.275-276). Zeus ignores the threat and defuses the situation with mollifying words, including a declaration that he will himself destroy the offenders (385-388). Here the underlying themes of divine justice and Olympian comity can be seen to obtain in inset narratives as they do in the main narrative. Likewise, the actions of Zeus at both narrative levels always have significance for the overall course of events. Thus it is with the fulfillment of the promise to Helios that the *Apologoi* sequence merges with the main narrative: Zeus' destruction of Odysseus' last ship and crew lands the hero alone on Ogygie (12.415-425

---

[3] The arrangement of themes in the *Apologoi* and their continuity with the main narrative is explored by Burgess 1999:183-202 (citing analogous themes in *Gilgamesh*); Louden 1999:27-29; Tracy 1997; Cook 1995:65-92, especially 74-76; Vidal-Naquet 1986:20-24; Whitman 1958:288-289; Heubeck 1954:44-46; Merkelbach 1951:175-198.

[4] Jørgensen 1904; cf. Danek 1998:81-83; Cook 1995:179; Clay 1983:21; Erbse 1972:12-13; Dodds 1951:11; Calhoun 1940:268-274; de Jong 2001:310 ad 12.374-90 on the scene with Zeus and Helios. For Nestor as a significant exception, see Chapter 5.

with 7.244-297).[5] Zeus' absence from the remainder of the *Apologoi*, then, is motivated by Odysseus' limitations as a narrator, which reflect the *Odyssey*'s decision to frame these adventures in a manner that insulates them from epichoric tradition, and from significant consequences for the main narrative. The "facts" dictate that Odysseus will survive his return from Troy; Zeus' only concern, from the *Odyssey*'s perspective, is to ensure that his return be consistent with Odyssean themes.

That concern is emphasized in the detailed program that Zeus elaborates at the beginning of Book 5, most notably in his time-line for Odysseus' return. Zeus tells Hermes that Odysseus will land on Scherie after twenty days at sea (5.34). Hermes immediately departs Olympos for Ogygie, and the day on which Zeus issues the instructions ends with Odysseus and Kalypso in bed and reconciled to his departure (5.1-2 with 225-228). The next morning, Odysseus begins constructing the raft on which he will leave Ogygie, a task that takes four more days to complete. On the fifth day after Zeus issues his instructions, Odysseus puts to sea (263), and, aided by a favorable wind from Kalypso (268), sails uninterrupted for eighteen days until he spies the Phaiakes' island of Scherie (279).[6]

At precisely this moment, Poseidon catches sight of Odysseus and raises a storm in order to destroy his raft. The goddess Ino/Leukothea (333-353), an unnamed river god (441-453), and Athene (427, 436-437) all help Odysseus to remain alive through two days afloat and at last to escape the sea (280 with 453-457). The hero thus comes ashore on Scherie exactly twenty days after setting out from Ogygie.

Zeus' chronology, then, takes into account that a day will pass before Odysseus begins work on his raft; that he will, with the aid of technology that Kalypso will provide (234-235, 246-247), require four days to build it; that he will be shipwrecked after eighteen days' smooth sailing; and that finally, with the aid of various divine agents, he will after two days come ashore. The instructions to Hermes in this respect amount to a transparent exposition of the *Dios boulē* as a narrative plan:

[5] I note that the scene with Helios, though not part of the main narrative, represents another point at which Zeus is attracted to a boundary between the *Odyssey* and non-Homeric Odysseus-traditions: "Thrinikia" was identified in antiquity as "Trinakria," i.e. Sicily (e.g. *Aeneid* 3.440; Strabo 6.2.1; Eustathios 1717.25 ad *Odyssey* 12.127), a fact that could underly Helios' reference to Hades, to which Sicily was a supposed portal; cf. Ovid *Metamorphoses* 5.347.

[6] Interestingly, Gilgamesh's journey to the Underworld also takes 18 days (Tablet X iii 49); cf. M. West 1997:406 and 411, who notes the same "time-formula" in reference to a journey on land (IV i 4-5), and attributes its cross-cultural occurrence to coincidence; the formula also describes another interval in the *Odyssey* (5.278-279~24.63-65).

Zeus' instructions to Hermes (5.30-42)	Realization in the main narrative
(1) Odysseus is to travel without escort	5.269-281
(2) on a "stoutly built raft"	5.247-257
(3) under difficult conditions	5.291-493
(4) for 20 days	5.278, 388
(5) to Scherie	5.453-457
(6) where the Phaiakes will honor him	Books 6-13; cf. 23.338-339
(7) and send him to Ithake on a ship[7]	13.70-125
(8) more enriched than when he left Troy	13.10-15, 137-138

Any composer of a narrative has the power to generate coincidences and fulfill prophecies. Thus an interpretive question similar to the one faced in assessing the emphasis on Hermes in Zeus' Oresteia arises here regarding the extent to which apparently gratuitous details should be understood as functional, rather than as by-products of the repetitive and formulaic style of Homeric narrative. It is therefore significant that the care taken to fulfill in detail Zeus' predictive instructions in Books 5 to 13 is exceptional. Thus for example Telemachos' voyage in Books 2 to 4 at first proceeds through a series of nights and days, but the passage of time becomes less clear once he reaches Sparta. Similarly, the internal chronology of the *Iliad*, though not particularly complex, requires some effort to deduce even from a written text. The novelty, then, of the precise temporal details of Books 5-13 thus appears designed to attract attention.

The exchange between Zeus and Hermes in Book 5 expands the picture of the Odyssean divine apparatus that begins to emerge in the "first" divine council. In the first council scene, I proposed in Chapter 1, Athene is introduced as the divine patron of Odysseus and ostensible author of the narrative plan for his return, though the narrative offers clues that she is not the guiding force. Here in Book 5, the impression fostered by these clues is strengthened: Athene is unable to manage the course of events, and "her" plan is assimilated

---

[7] Note that at 13.121 the Homeric narrator attributes the Phaiakes' return of Odysseus διὰ μεγάθυμον Ἀθήνην, despite the fact that this part of the return plan is specified by Zeus at 5.34-42.

to a plan of Zeus.[8] The same, as we shall now see, can be said of Zeus' dealings with Poseidon, the other subordinate Olympian who plays a major role in the *Odyssey*.

Poseidon's attack on Odysseus in *Odyssey* 5

When the *Odyssey* opens, Poseidon is feasting with the Aithiopes, the "most remote of men" (ἔσχατοι ἀνδρῶν, 1.23), which is to say those furthest from the geographic and cultural "center" represented by Olympos for the gods and by mainland Greece for human characters.[9] Thus, as mentioned in Chapter 1, a consequence of the timing of Zeus' Oresteia is that the ensuing discussion of Odysseus takes place when Poseidon is unable to complicate matters. Zeus from the outset is represented as being aware of the difficulties posed by Poseidon's hostility to Odysseus, and of the reasons for it; he even suggests portentuously that the angry god will have to be forced to submit (1.68-79).

Yet though the plan for Odysseus' return is elaborated in Poseidon's absence, it is made to depend on his active participation. Specifically, were it not for a storm that Poseidon unleashes against him, Odysseus would not make landfall on Scherie, as Zeus specifies in his instructions to Hermes (5.34-35). For Odysseus when he approaches the island after eighteen days' sailing from Ogygie (278-280) shows no sign of weariness, and he has been provisioned amply by Kalypso (265-267). Moreover, had Odysseus decided to land on Scherie without the impetus of the storm, his voyage from Ogygie would have taken eighteen days, not the twenty specified by Zeus. Poseidon contributes to the fulfillment of Zeus' plan without renouncing his hostility to Odysseus, and without being asked to act or to refrain from action by Zeus or any other. In other words, Poseidon is allowed to pursue his own agenda, but, rather like a tragic hero, in doing so he furthers a larger design that conflicts with his own interests.

Poseidon perceives the effect of the divine council scenes in Books 1 and 5 when, returning from the Aithiopes, he sees Odysseus approaching Scherie (282-284). The god reacts with surprise and indignation:

> ὢ πόποι, ἦ μάλα δὴ μετεβούλευσαν θεοὶ ἄλλως
> ἀμφ' Ὀδυσῆϊ ἐμεῖο μετ' Αἰθιόπεσσιν ἐόντος·

---

[8] On the programmatic nature of this speech, see Hainsworth *CHO* 1:256 ad 5.22-7 and Rüter 1969:108; on its relationship to the divine council in Book 1, see M. Clark 1997:206-209.

[9] Odysseus is similarly remote, in the middle of nowhere on Kalypso's island (ὀμφαλὸς θαλάσσης, *Odyssey* 1.50), as are the Phaiakes (ἔσχατοι, 6.205).

καὶ δὴ Φαιήκων γαίης σχεδόν, ἔνθα οἱ αἶσα
ἐκφυγέειν μέγα πεῖραρ οἰζύος ἥ μιν ἱκάνει.
ἀλλ᾽ ἔτι μέν μιν φημὶ ἄδην ἐλάαν κακότητος.

Well now, certainly indeed the gods altered their plan
about Odysseus while I was with the Aithiopes;
and now there he is near the land of the Phaiakes, where it is
his fate
to escape the great cord of misery that has come upon him.
But still I think I shall give him his fill of wretchedness.

Odyssey 5.286-290

Poseidon's anger in *Odyssey* 5 results from his perception that a plan has been reformulated by the gods (μετεβούλευσαν ἄλλως, 286) so as to grant Odysseus his return, which is fated (αἶσα) to proceed without incident once he reaches the Phaiakes (288-289). It is in order to reverse the effects of this ostensible reformulation of the divine plan that Poseidon sends the storm that wrecks Odysseus' ship and precipitates his landing on Scherie, twenty days after leaving Ogygie.

Thus it turns out that Zeus' plan, though it will benefit Odysseus in the long run, does not disregard Poseidon's desire that the hero suffer. Rather, the plan "budgets" two days for Poseidon's attack. Again, Zeus' engagement with Poseidon can be traced to the opening divine council scene, where he observes that Poseidon is angry with Odysseus for blinding his son, the Kyklops (1.68-70). The blinding is in turn central to the *Odyssey*'s explanation for Odysseus' protracted return. Near the end of the *Kyklopeia* portion of the *Apologoi*, set during the first year of Odysseus' wanderings, long before the main narrative begins, the Kyklops prays to Poseidon that, if Odysseus cannot be destroyed (9.532),

ὀψὲ κακῶς ἔλθοι ὀλέσας ἄπο πάντας ἑταίρους
νηὸς ἐπ᾽ ἀλλοτρίης, εὕροι δ᾽ ἐν πήματα οἴκωι

May he return late and miserably, having lost all
companions,
on the ship of another, and find troubles at home

Odyssey 9.534-535

When the *Odyssey* opens, Odysseus is already "late," has already endured much misery, has already lost his companions, and his "troubles at home" are already a matter for discussion on Olympos (1.91-92; 5.11-12). By stipulating

45

in his instructions to Hermes that Odysseus reach Ithake in a Phaiakian ship (5.37), Zeus fulfills the final element in the Kyklops' prayer, that Odysseus travel "on the ship of another."

But while Zeus can thus be seen to bring to fulfillment the letter of the Kyklops' prayer, he is less concerned with its intent. When the Kyklops asks that Odysseus return "on the ship of another," his desire is presumably that the hero arrive home in a state of humiliating penury. In accordance with Zeus' plan, however, Odysseus returns in comfort and in possession of fabulous wealth. And this state of affairs is a direct result of his shipwreck by Poseidon. For were Odysseus to reach Scherie as he left Ogygie, on a sturdy raft amply stocked with provisions, he would have no need for "the ship of another," nor room for fabulous gifts.

Nevertheless, while Zeus exploits Poseidon as an unwitting tool for the return and enrichment of Athene's favorite, he at the same time grants the concession that Poseidon be allowed to inflict two days of misery upon him, and thereby to exact some measure of vengeance for the blinding of the Kyklops. Indeed, since Odysseus will "escape misery" once he lands on Scherie (5.288-289), and since Teiresias provides him with instructions for lifting the Kyklops' curse (11.121-131), the voyage in Book 5 represents Poseidon's last chance to torment the hero. Poseidon then can take pleasure in the suffering he visits on Odysseus; but the fact that his storm ends up enriching the hero he wishes to make suffer, and rendering anticlimactic the complete fulfillment of the Kyklops' prayer, threatens to rekindle his hostility.

The relationship between Zeus and Poseidon is then in important respects analogous to that between Zeus and Athene. In each case, the subordinate god acts, without opposition, to further a limited agenda, Athene as Odysseus' patron, Poseidon as his antagonist. And in each case the limited agenda is tempered, coordinated, and, I suggest, motivated by Zeus. Athene guides Odysseus to his fated return to home and throne in terms that Zeus dictates. It is representative of Zeus' transcendent perspective, over and above both Athene and Poseidon, that these terms include elements, most obviously Odysseus' shipwreck and two days of suffering at sea, that the goddess would not have incorporated into a plan that was truly her own. Poseidon, by comparison, helps his favorite the Kyklops to exact retribution that is intended to make Odysseus' fated return as wretched as possible. But in the event, though Poseidon's storm pushes the hero to the limits of his endurance, it brings about a homecoming for the hero in comfort and in possession of wealth for a lifetime, terms most agreeable to Athene.

The overall pattern of divine interactions in the *Odyssey*, then, applies to Poseidon as well as to Athene, and for that matter to Helios: Zeus orchestrates the progress of the story through the medium of subordinates, who pursue their own relatively narrow aims, even as they bring about fulfillment of Zeus' all-embracing plan. Significantly, however, Zeus confers with Athene before a course of events is initiated, while he incorporates Poseidon and Helios into his plan after events are already in motion. Poseidon thus behaves as a partially informed, over-literal, and reactionary "reader" of Zeus' intent. His lack of subtlety allows, or causes, him to function more as a pawn of Zeus than does Athene, an informed, if still also to a significant degree unwitting, "reader."

Anticlimax: Zeus and Poseidon in *Odyssey* 13

After the Phaiakes convey Odysseus to Ithake, the narrative shifts again to Poseidon, who observes their ship on its homeward voyage and makes an angry inquiry into the "plan of Zeus" (Διὸς δ᾽ ἐξείρετο βουλήν, 13.127). Although returned from the Aithiopes, Poseidon remains absent from Olympos while Odysseus is with the Phaiakes, and the scene in Book 13 is his only encounter with his fellow Olympians in the main narrative of the *Odyssey*.[10] Again, Poseidon's absence forestalls objections to the plan for Odysseus' return as it is elaborated in the divine council scenes in Books 1 and 5. Also as mentioned, Zeus in Book 1 creates the expectation that Poseidon's animosity toward Odysseus will at some point issue in conflict among the gods (1.77-79). Poseidon's approach to Zeus in Book 13 therefore brings with it the expectation of the divine showdown toward which the narrative has been building.

Yet no confrontation materializes. Poseidon proves less refractory than Zeus' characterization of him in Book 1 and his own statements in Book 5 suggest that he will be, and Zeus takes pains to accommodate him. Of course, since Odysseus' return is a *fait accompli* by the time Poseidon realizes that the storm in Book 5 did not have the intended effect, his declaration of

---

[10] All the gods have palaces on Olympos (*Iliad* 1.606-608), though it is not clear where Poseidon is at the beginning of *Odyssey* 13. After sending the storm against Odysseus in Book 5, he departs for Aigai (5.38), his frequent residence when away from Olympos (*Iliad* 8.203, 13.21; *Homeric Hymn* 22.3). For the passage of narrative time here, see de Jong 2001:xii and 321 ad 13.125-38.

allegiance to Zeus here (e.g. σὸν αἰεὶ θυμὸν ὀπίζομαι ἠδ' ἀλεείνω, 13.148) is in part a virtue of necessity; here as in Book 5 Poseidon accepts that Odysseus' return is fated (13.131-133; 5.288-289).[11] Nevertheless, we might expect at least some criticism of the gods for having "planned otherwise" (Odyssey 5.286) in Poseidon's absence.

The anticlimactic encounter between Poseidon and Zeus is on the one hand explicable in dramatic terms. Here, at the midpoint of the epic, focus is about to shift to the growing tension on Ithake, which will, unlike the conflict of interests on Olympos, issue in violence. Olympian comity is maintained when Poseidon takes the opportunity to direct his anger away from the gods toward the mortal world in which it originated. The brunt of this violence is to fall on the Phaiakes, who are no longer of use to the plot. The *Nostos* sequence thus resolved, a new source of dramatic tension will emerge, namely anticipation of the violence that Odysseus will unleash in Ithake.

Poseidon's complaint takes the form of an *a fortiori* argument framed, like Zeus' Oresteia, in terms of the relationship between gods and men. If mere mortals dare to defy him, the god asserts, the other immortals will surely scorn him:

Ζεῦ πάτερ, οὐκέτ' ἔγωγε μετ' ἀθανάτοισι θεοῖσι
τιμήεις ἔσομαι, ὅτε με βροτοὶ οὔ τι τίουσι,
Φαίηκες, τοί πέρ τε ἐμῆς ἔξεισι γενέθλης.   130
καὶ γὰρ νῦν· Ὀδυσῆα φάμην κακὰ πολλὰ παθόντα
οἴκαδ' ἐλεύσεσθαι - νόστον δὲ οἱ οὔ ποτ' ἀπηύρων
πάγχυ ἐπεὶ σὺ πρῶτον ὑπέσχεο καὶ κατένευσας -
οἳ δ' εὕδοντ' ἐν νηὶ θοῆι ἐπὶ πόντον ἄγοντες
κάτθεσαν εἰν Ἰθάκηι, ἔδοσαν δέ οἱ ἄσπετα δῶρα,   135
χαλκόν τε χρυσόν τε ἅλις ἐσθῆτά θ' ὑφαντήν,
πόλλ', ὅσ' ἂν οὐδέ ποτε Τροίης ἐξήρατ' Ὀδυσσεύς,
εἴ περ ἀπήμων ἦλθε, λαχὼν ἀπὸ ληίδος αἶσαν.

Father Zeus, no longer will I myself among the
    immortal gods
be held in honor, since mortals in no way honor me,
the Phaiakes, who are of my very own kin.   130

---

[11] Thus Danek 1998:266: "Poseidon also distinguishes a possible from an 'impossible' alternative: the *nostos* itself was guaranteed by Zeus, which tallies with the fact that the tradition allowed no version in which Odysseus does not come home" [*Poseidon unterscheidet also eine mögliche von einer ,unmöglichen' Alternative: Der νόστος selbst war durch Zeus gesichert, was damit übereinstimmt, daß die Erzältradition keine Version zuließ, in der Odysseus nicht heimkehrte*].

And so now: I thought that Odysseus, after suffering
   many evils,
would come home, and I never took away his homecoming
entirely, after you first promised and gave your nod –
but they led him asleep over the sea in their swift ship
and deposited him on Ithake, and gave him innumerable
   gifts,   135
bronze and gold in plenty and woven clothing,
lots of it, such things as Odysseus would never have
   taken from Troy
even if he had come unscathed having drawn his portion
   from the plunder.

                                         Odyssey 13.128-138

Apparently, the Phaiakes should have recognized that the storm that landed Odysseus on their island was sent by Poseidon, and therefore should not have treated the hero quite so well. And indeed the effects of Poseidon's storm in Book 5 have been reversed in almost every detail: Odysseus arrives on Scherie after twenty days awake,[12] but he reaches Ithake asleep, "having forgotten such things as he had suffered" (λελασμένος ὅσσ' ἐπεπόνθει, 13.92). Shipwreck is not even a possibility on the voyage to Ithake, since the Phaiakes' ships are guaranteed calm seas (7.317-320). During the storm Odysseus loses the splendid garments Kalypso had provided (5.264, 343, 372), but he arrives on Ithake in possession of "fine woven clothing" (13.136; cf. 218).

    Yet despite his indignation, Poseidon prefaces his complaint with a declaration of allegiance to Zeus' "promise and nod."[13] Zeus responds to Poseidon's deferential tone in kind:

οὔ τί σ' ἀτιμάζουσι θεοί· χαλεπὸν δέ κεν εἴη
πρεσβύτατον καὶ ἄριστον ἀτιμίῃσιν ἰάλλειν.
ἀνδρῶν δ' εἴ πέρ τίς σε βίῃ καὶ κάρτει εἴκων
οὔ τι τίει, σοὶ δ' ἔστι καὶ ἐξοπίσω τίσις αἰεί.
ἔρξον ὅπως ἐθέλεις καί τοι φίλον ἔπλετο θυμῷ.

---

[12] Odysseus apparently cannot sleep while he sails (*Odyssey* 5.271), and of course cannot while he swims.

[13] Whether or not Poseidon is understood as referring at *Odyssey* 13.133 to an "actual" nod given by Zeus, the theme itself suggests the same level of narrative organization implied by Poseidon's surmise that the gods have "altered their plan" (5.286). Cf. the significance of Zeus' nod in the *Iliad* (e.g. 1.514, 524).

In no way do the gods dishonor you; and a harsh thing
    would it be
to visit the eldest and best with dishonor.
As for men, if indeed any yielding to force and strength
fails to honor you in some way, payback will ever be yours
    afterward.
Do as you wish and your heart desires.

Odyssey 13.141-145

By asserting Poseidon's continued honor among the gods and his freedom
to dispose of human affairs as he sees fit, Zeus reaffirms the lesser god's
prerogatives. There also may be a note of criticism here, however, in that, by
crediting Poseidon with broad freedom of action, Zeus may also imply that
Poseidon himself shares responsibility for the situation, in like manner as
he tells Athene that the state of affairs in Books 5 and 24 is a consequence of
"your own plan."

It will be useful to discuss a pair of comparable Iliadic scenes in order
to establish a broader context for Zeus' conciliatory strategy. In the first,
Poseidon complains to Zeus about the Greeks' failure to offer sacrifices when
constructing their fortifications (*Iliad* 7.454-463). As in *Odyssey* 13, the god
seeks to compel mortals to observe divine prerogatives (ὅς τις ἔτ' ἀθανάτοισι
νόον καὶ μῆτιν ἐνίψει; 447) and appears preoccupied with his own personal
standing (451-453). Also as in *Odyssey* 13, Zeus responds to Poseidon with the
familiar theme of surprise (455=*Odyssey* 13.140; cf. *Odyssey* 5.22), but reassures
him in fulsome terms and sets forth a plan to achieve his wishes (456-463; cf.
Iliad 12.17-33).[14]

A complementary view of the relationship between the two gods emerges
from Zeus' response to Poseidon's defiance of his ban on divine participation in
the Trojan War (*Iliad* 15.158-219). Here Zeus bolsters his demand that Poseidon
quit the battlefield with an assertion of preeminence in might and birth (σεό
φησι βίηι πολὺ φέρτερος εἶναι/καὶ γενεῆι πρότερος, *Iliad* 15.181-182; cf. *Iliad*
13.355). Poseidon protests that, to the contrary, he, Zeus, and Hades each have
an "equal share of honor" (τριχθὰ δὲ πάντα δέδασται ἕκαστος δ' ἔμμορε τιμῆς,
15.189).[15] Against the background of this exchange, Zeus' statement in *Odyssey*

---

[14] Maitland 1999:3 and van Wees 1992:111-112 see irritation in Zeus' words in *Iliad* 7, though the
absence of such animus from the Odyssean passage may argue against this interpretation.

[15] For the terms of this exchange see Muellner 1996:28-31; Lowenstam 1993:75-76, 77n45; Janko *IC*
4:245 ad 15.165-7. The B scholiast to *Odyssey* 13.142 proposes that the superlative πρεσβύτατον
refers not to age but to honor (οὐ καθ' ἡλικίαν ἀλλὰ τιμιώτατον), citing in support *Iliad* 4.59
(see next note).

13 that Poseidon is "eldest and best" is revealed as, not a platitude rooted in mythological "fact," but a rhetorical strategy keyed to the significance of Poseidon's role in the narrative. For the "facts" allow for any Olympian to be described as older or younger than Zeus, who is conceived last, but does not, like his brothers and sisters, endure ingestion by Kronos *post partum* and subsequent rebirth through regurgitation.[16]

Zeus' assertion of authority based on primogeniture in *Iliad* 15 is part of his strategy to enforce his own plan by taking charge of the battlefield. By contrast, Zeus is more disinterested in *Odyssey* 13, where Poseidon no longer can oppose the gods' plan for Odysseus, and *Iliad* 7, where Zeus has no overt interest in the destruction of the Greek wall. Thus Zeus can be seen to advance alternative perspectives on his kin relationship to Poseidon that correspond to different narrative situations. When he is confronting Poseidon's attempt to wrest control of the narrative in *Iliad* 15, Zeus himself is older; when he is co-opting an already neutralized Poseidon in *Odyssey* 13, the latter is the elder. A general trend thus emerges. Decisions that require engagement with the boundaries of Homeric narrative – the extent of the Phaiakes' story in *Odyssey* 13, the relative future in the case of *Iliad* 7 – invoke as if by reflex the authority of Zeus. Open hostility, however, is reserved for instances in which the progress of the narrative itself is threatened, as in *Iliad* 15.

In *Odyssey* 13, Poseidon no longer represents a threat to Odysseus. The irony generated by Poseidon's ignorance of the larger context of his own actions in the *Odyssey* is made conspicuous by the inclusion in his complaint in Book 13 of three *versus iterati* from Zeus' instructions to Hermes in Book 5 (13.136~5.38; 13.137-138=5.39-40), which describe the gifts the Phaiakes bestow on Odysseus as exceeding in value the plunder the hero obtained at Troy. Thus Zeus' prescription for Odysseus' enrichment, which he in Book 5 makes a by-product of Poseidon's storm, recurs verbatim in Poseidon's own complaint about that enrichment. To be sure, verse repetition is common in orally-derived texts; and here eight books separate Poseidon's unwitting "quotation" from Zeus' "original." However, the encounter with Poseidon is Zeus' first appearance in the main narrative since instructing Hermes and Poseidon's first since sending the storm. Thus, Poseidon's "quotation" can be seen as

---

[16] For the birth story, see Hesiod *Theogony* 453-497; cf. "Apollodoros" *Bibliotheke* 1.1.5-2.1. The other Olympians' double status is exploited in a similar manner in the *Homeric Hymn to Aphrodite*, which describes Hestia as both eldest and youngest of gods "on account of the plan of Zeus" ('Ιστίηι ἣν πρώτην τέκετο Κρόνος ἀγκυλομήτης/αὖτις δ' ὁπλοτάτην βουλῆι Διὸς αἰγιόχοιο, 22-23; cf. *Theogony* 454). Here's claim in the *Iliad* to be eldest of Kronos' daughters (με πρεσβυτάτην τέκετο Κρόνος, 4.59) can be validated on similar grounds.

a part of a structural ring that embraces the *Nostos* (and embedded *Apologoi*), the termini of which are marked by the coordinate actions of the two gods. In other words, the *versus iterati* are part of a self-conscious link between Books 5 and 13 that a Homeric audience could reasonably be expected to perceive.[17] In the economy of the Odyssean narrative, this structural feature is exploited in order to characterize, seemingly with some humor, the relationship between Zeus and lesser Olympians.

Poseidon and the Phaiakes

The irony generated by Poseidon's unwitting participation in Zeus' plan is also tragic, or at least threatens to be so, for the Phaiakes, despite, indeed because of, their kind treatment of the hero. An attack on them by the Poseidon is not unforeseen, since Odysseus' arrival on Scherie is linked to a prophecy long known to the Phaiakes concerning their own destruction. Alkinoos tells how:

> τόδ' ὥς ποτε πατρὸς ἐγὼν εἰπόντος ἄκουσα
> Ναυσιθόου, ὃς ἔφασκε Ποσειδάων' ἀγάσασθαι
> ἡμῖν οὕνεκα πομποὶ ἀπήμονές εἰμεν ἁπάντων·
> φῆ ποτε Φαιήκων ἀνδρῶν εὐεργέα νῆα
> ἐκπομπῆς ἀνιοῦσαν ἐν ἠεροειδέι πόντωι
> ῥαίσεσθαι, μέγα δ' ἡμῖν ὄρος πόλει ἀμφικαλύψειν.

> This once I thus myself heard my father saying,
> Nausithoos, who used to say that Poseidon was offended
> at us because we are effortless escorts of all men.
> He said that one day a well-wrought ship of Phaiakian men
> returning from an escort on the misty sea
> would be struck, and a great mountain would cover our city.

> *Odyssey* 8.564-569

This prophecy in Book 8, which Alkinoos repeats nearly verbatim after Poseidon does strike the ship (13.173-177), foreshadows the proposal that

---

[17] M. Clark 1997:206-211 analyzes the repeated elements in Zeus' instructions to Hermes. The 5.38-40/13.136-138 repetition is partly formulaic (cf. *Odyssey* 16.231, 23.341), but at three lines is one of the longer groupings of exact *versus iterati* outside the context of messages that are dictated and then delivered. My approach here is informed by that of Lowenstam 1993:9, who argues that "a significant detail, a pattern of events, or a series of narrative details might be repeated within a work to present a comparison or contrast with the preceding material or to foreshadow an upcoming event;" cf. Nagler 1974:200-201. On the significance of Homeric ring-structure see Louden 1999:1-3, 43-45; Lohmann 1970, esp. 12-40.

Zeus solicits from Poseidon in Book 13 when he offers him free rein to "do as you wish and your heart desires" (145). As in Book 5, where Poseidon's storm fulfills conditions that are specified in Zeus' instructions to Hermes (5.34) as well as foretold to the sea goddess Ino/Leukothea (345), what is "dear to Poseidon's heart" in Book 13 is consistent with what is "fated," though Poseidon is apparently unaware of the fact. In any case, Poseidon tells Zeus:[18]

> νῦν αὖ Φαιήκων ἐθέλω περικαλλέα νῆα
> ἐκ πομπῆς ἀνιοῦσαν ἐν ἠεροειδέϊ πόντωι
> ῥαῖσαι, ἵν' ἤδη σχῶνται, ἀπολλήξωσι δὲ πομπῆς
> ἀνθρώπων, μέγα δέ σφιν ὄρος πόλει ἀμφικαλύψαι.

> Now then I want to strike the Phaiakes' very beautiful ship
> as it returns from the escort [of Odysseus] on the misty sea,
> so that they are then held back, and cease from the escort
> of people, and I want a great mountain to cover their city.

> *Odyssey* 13.149-152

What happens next is one of the enduring cruxes of Odyssean scholarship. Zeus approves Poseidon's plan:

> ὡς μὲν ἐμῶι θυμῶι δοκεῖ εἶναι ἄριστα·
> ὁππότε κεν δὴ πάντες ἐλαυνομένην προΐδωνται
> λαοὶ ἀπὸ πτόλιος, θεῖναι λίθον ἐγγύθι γαίης
> νηὶ θοῆι ἴκελον, ἵνα θαυμάζωσιν ἅπαντες
> ἄνθρωποι, μέγα/μετὰ/μὴ δέ σφιν ὄρος πόλει ἀμφικαλύψαι.

> 158μέγα Ω; μετά Β; μή Σ Η to *Odyssey* 13.152

> This is how it seems best to me in my heart:
> whenever all catch sight of the ship as it is driven
> all the people from the city, make [the ship into] a stone near
>   the land
> like a swift ship, so that all may wonder
> all people, and with a great mountain cover their city.
>   (reading μέγα)

---

[18] Peradotto 1990:78 observes apropos of the Book 13 passage that "Poseidon's pleasure is precisely to fulfill the terms of Nausithous's prophecy"; similarly Cook 1995:123-127; Friedrich 1989:396. The blinding of the Kyklops also fulfills a prophecy revealed by a seer (9.507-512), and Odysseus is himself unaware that he is the instrument of its fulfillment.

> and afterward with a mountain cover their city.
> (reading μετά)
> but not with a mountain cover their city. (reading μή)
>
> *Odyssey* 13.154-158

The crux concerns Zeus' articulation of the second part of Poseidon's proposal, his wish to "cover" the Phaiakes' city with a mountain and thereby destroy it.[19] After this exchange with Zeus, Poseidon departs immediately for Scherie, and when the Phaiakes' ship nears the shore, he strikes it with his hand and turns it to stone; "and he was gone" (ὃ δὲ νόσφι βεβήκει, 13.164), not to appear again in the *Odyssey*. The Phaiakes react to the petrifaction of the ship – here Alkinoos repeats Nausithoos' prophecy – and are last seen attempting to propitiate Poseidon with sacrifices and prayers (184-187a), at which point the narrative cuts away in mid-line to Odysseus as he awakens on Ithake. Zeus has already granted Poseidon freedom of action with regard to the Phaiakes, but it seems clear that Poseidon will do as Zeus proposes, in like manner as Athene in Book 5 allows Zeus to shape "her" plan for Odysseus, and as Helios in Book 12 backs down from his threat to shine among the dead. So Zeus here in Book 13 shapes Poseidon's proposal into narrative, and he expands on it in at least one respect by adding a dramatic touch: the people will witness the petrifaction of the ship just as it nears land.

The fate of the Phaiakes, then, hinges on Zeus' words at 13.158. The manuscripts read μέγα 'great' or μετά 'later'. By either of these readings, Zeus tells Poseidon to carry out his plan to destroy the Phaiakes' city. The departure of Poseidon at 164 is not necessarily inconsistent with these readings, for he could return later to complete his punishment, perhaps once he has fetched a mountain. An interpretation of destruction deferred rather than averted is perhaps responsible for the reading μετά, which can account for an interval between the petrifaction of the ship, which occurs within the narrative, and the covering of the city with a mountain, which is projected outside it.

A different outcome, however, was apparently known to ancient Homeric scholars:

---

[19] Cunliffe ἀμφικαλύπτω s.v. (3), citing only passages relating to Poseidon's attack on the Phaiakes (*Odyssey* 8.569, 13.152, 158, 177, 183), deduces the meaning "to put around (something) so as to isolate (it)," in which case the Phaiakes could be said to survive, even reading μετά or μέγα. However, the closest parallel for this meaning in other contexts is "cover to protect" in descriptions of Ajax' shield (*Iliad* 8.331=13.420); and the mountain is not protection. Other Homeric uses of this verb, on the other hand, involve destruction: death "covers" warriors (e.g. *Iliad* 5.68); the Trojan *polis* "covers," i.e. accepts within its walls, the Trojan horse (*Odyssey* 8.511).

Ἀριστοφάνης δὲ γράφει, μὴ δέ σφιν. ἀντιλέγει δ᾽ ἐν ὑπομνήμασιν Ἀρίσταρχος.

Aristophanes writes, "and do not [cover] their [city with a mountain]." But Aristarchos argues against this in his commentary.

H Scholion to *Odyssey* 13.158[20]

That is, at least one distinguished critic, Aristophanes, either proposed or adopted μή, according to which reading Zeus modifies Poseidon's proposal by telling him not to cover the city. Another distinguished critic, Aristarchos, apparently defended the "vulgate" manuscript reading. The crux cannot be settled on straightforward philological grounds, since all three variants are consistent with Homeric meter and diction. Debate about which reading should be considered correct continues to the present day.[21]

The Phaiakes' destruction is certainly consistent with the justice of Zeus as established in the first divine council and realized as the narrative proceeds. Their failure to heed the will of the gods, as communicated through Nausithoos' prophecy, aligns the Phaiakes' fate with those of Aigisthos, the Kyklops, Odysseus' crew, and the suitors; and the destruction of Troy, another event prophesied but not realized within Homeric narrative, demonstrates that wholesale destruction of sympathetic characters is not "un-Homeric." Moreover, the thematically related divine council scene in Book 12, in which Helios like Poseidon complains to Zeus about human disregard for divine prerogatives, issues in the destruction of Odysseus' crew.[22] From a different perspective, destruction of the Phaiakes has the benefit of de-authorizing traditions in which Telemachos abandons Ithake – in contrast with the fate suggested for him at the end of the *Odyssey* – in order to wed the Phaiakian

---

[20] The lemma for the scholion is 13.152, the nearly identical line from Poseidon's proposal; but since it would be out of place for Poseidon to propose *not* to do something, the emendation to 158 adopted by Nauck and von der Mühll is certain.

[21] Representative modern arguments in support of the received text in Peradotto 1990:78-80 and Erbse 1972:145-148; in support of Aristophanes' reading, Dougherty 2001:155; Cook 1995:124n36; Louden 1999:144n103; Friedrich 1989; Hoekstra *CHO* 2:173 ad 13.125-87 is agnostic. For an earlier perspective, see Eustathios 1737.20-30. M. West 1997:424, following Gordon 1962:110-111, 232, notes a striking parallel with a Middle Egyptian (ca. 2000 BCE) folktale in which the sole survivor of a seastorm is marooned on an island, from which he escapes with the help a friendly serpent; afterward, the island is prophesied to turn into water.

[22] A point emphasized by e.g. Louden 1999:20-25; Cook 1995:123-127; Clay 1983:230; Erbse 1972:24.

princess Nausikaa.[23] Lastly, if the Phaiakes are spared, this is apparently the one instance in all of traditional early Greek epic, or even ancient Greek literature generally, in which a prophecy goes unfulfilled.[24]

On the other hand, however, the *Odyssey* could simply depart from the conventional role of prophecy to the extent of proving Nausithoos' prophecy partially incorrect: the ship is turned to stone, but the city is not engulfed by a mountain. From a theological perspective, sparing the Phaiakes would be consistent with Zeus' tempering of angry subordinate deities to the benefit of mortals. In like manner as Zeus will put a stop to the Ithakans' civil war by quelling the bloodlust of Athene in Book 24 (539-540; see Chapter 3), he could reduce the severity of the penalty Poseidon exacts from the Phaiakes.

It remains an open question whether readings attributed to Aristophanes represent educated guesses or evidence drawn from now lost manuscripts.[25] Here at least, I suggest, Aristophanes' source does not matter; and in this lies a possible resolution of the crux. For, conjecture or not, μή could recreate a traditional reading. However we explain the load that the verse we know as *Odyssey* 13.158 is made to carry, traditional singers would presumably not have missed the fact that, in the midst of a narrative bound tightly together by multiple agents and causes, the issue of the Phaiakes' fate could be altered so simply, and without affecting the flow of the main narrative, by substituting one metrically equivalent expression for another.

Approached this way, the multiple readings at *Odyssey* 13.158 could represent, in the context of the textual tradition, a locus of multiformity that arose in the context of the performance tradition.[26] Thus, if destruction of the Phaiakes would not offend the sensibilities of a given audience, a singer might exploit it in order to emphasize the inevitability of prophecy and the consequences of failure to heed it, to generate shock and pathos, to engage

---

[23] Eustathios (1796.40-42) cites Aristotle and Hellanikos as sources for a version of "post-Odyssean" events in which Telemachos marries Nausikaa. If Telemachos relocates to Scherie, this tradition may be connected with "Apollodoros'" Thesprotian version, since it can explain why Odysseus returns to Ithake to find Poliporthes in charge; see Chapter 4 n12.

[24] This argument is made by Erbse 1972:145-148 and criticized by Friedrich 1989:396n6. To be weighed against the latter's privileging of the fact that the prophecy is not actually fulfilled within the narrative are instances where the fulfillment of plans discussed but not narrated is assured, such as the aforementioned destruction of Troy and the pacification of Ithake at the end of the *Odyssey*.

[25] Aristophanes' methodology is discussed by Nagy 2004:110-128. Among Alexandrine scholars, Aristophanes may have been rather conservative; Pfeiffer 1968:173-174 and n8, for instance, contrasts Aristophanes' concern with παλαιὰ γραφή with Zenodotos' penchant for διόρθωσις.

[26] Nagy 1979:43: "Any theme is but a multiform, and not one of the multiforms can be considered a functional 'Ur-form'."

with extra-Odyssean traditions, or any combination thereof. Under different performance circumstances, before audiences that might find the Phaiakes' destruction objectionable, a singer could have Zeus intercede for them in the face of the elemental hostility of Poseidon.

The play of μή, μέγα and μετά at *Odyssey* 13.158 is not, then, the deconstructionist's inherent linguistic ambiguity, or not that only. Rather, the crux is, I suggest, exemplary of the narrative choices over which Zeus presides in Homeric epic. In this case, the final decision remained contingent on performance circumstances. In other words, the crux is no crux at all, but rather the textual artifact of a kind of narrative "switch" that regulated, during each performance of *Odyssey* 13, both the tenor of interactions between mortals and immortals and the interface between Homeric and epichoric tradition.

To be sure, this interpretation is no more capable of proof than arguments for one or another reading. It does however derive at least some support from the prominence of the Phaiakes in epichoric traditions. For at least by the Classical period Homeric Scherie was identified with the historical Greek settlement of Corcyra on the Adriatic.[27] Geographic features supported the link: Corcyra was, like Scherie, a colonial foundation situated on an island (cf. *Odyssey* 5.280-281, 6.4-10, though the description could apply to a peninsula), and the harbors on either side of the Phaiakes' city (λιμὴν ἑκάτερθε πόληος, 6.263) are consistent with the Hyllaic harbor and "harbor of Alkinoos" located on either side of the headland on which the Corcyrean acropolis was constructed. Moreover, the latter harbor features a large rock, for which the petrified ship in *Odyssey* 13 offers an *aition*.[28]

Since historical Greeks often traced their families back to mythical forebears, obliteration of Scherie would problematize any claim to Phaiakian heritage by the citizens of historical Corcyra. And because the island was powerful and strategically significant throughout the Archaic and Classical periods, there is reason to suspect that its epichoric traditions might exert an influence on a Panhellenic text like the *Odyssey*.

---

[27] E.g. Thucydides 1.25.4, 3.70.4; among later authors, cf. Kallimachos *Aitia* fr. 12; *Aeneid* 3.289-293 (in which it is not made clear whether the *aerias Phaeacum arces* are inhabited); Strabo 7.3.6. The link between the Phaiakes and Corcyra is discussed by Malkin 1998:111-112, 190, 195; Hoekstra in *CHO* 2:174 ad 13.157-8; Peradotto 1990:79-81. Some ancient writers located Scherie nearer Italy; see Wolf and Wolf 1968:82-89.

[28] The double harbor on Scherie is not unique in the *Odyssey*: the suitors lay their ambush for Telemachos at a place called Asteris, which is described as having λιμένες δ' ἔνι ναύλοχοι αὐτῆι/ἀμφίδυμοι (4.846-847).

According to Thucydides, Corcyrans of his day were proud that

ναυτικῶι δὲ καὶ πολὺ προύχειν ἔστιν ὅτε ἐπαιρόμενοι καὶ κατὰ τὴν
Φαιάκων προενοίκησιν τῆς Κερκύρας κλέος ἐχόντων τὰ περὶ τὰς
ναῦς.

... in naval affairs they were by far preeminent, sometimes boasting
about the previous habitation of the Phaiakes, who had renown[29] for
things having to do with ships.

Thucydides 1.25.4

The Corcyrans do not here claim direct descent from the Phaiakes, since
they were bound by the historical fact that their *polis* began as a Corinthian
colony.[30] Nevertheless, the Corcyrans believed that "previous habitation"
(προενοίκησις) by the Phaiakes conferred on them something like a claim of
autochthony: the outstanding characteristic of the site's "original," mythical
past, nautical prowess, had been reproduced in them, its present inhabitants.
Just how Corcyrans conceived of their relationship with the Phaiakes is
unclear, and likely varied within the community and over time. It does appear
that the association with Scherie was institutionalized in Corcyra in the
form of a hero-cult of Alkinoos, to whom was dedicated the harbor with the
conspicuous rock, as well as a precinct of the *polis*, an honor shared jointly
with, interestingly enough, not Poseidon but Zeus.[31]

The historical relationship between Corcyra and its mother city Corinth
offers a ready explanation for why Corcyrans might wish to construct their
identity in part around local myths. For it is in the context of Corinthian
complaints about the lack of respect paid them by their colony that Thucydides
cites the Phaiakian pride of the latter. According to tradition, the two cities
fought the first Greek naval battle (Thucydides 1.13.4-5), and their relation-
ship remained tempestuous into the Classical period.[32] For the Corcyrans,
then, the Scherian connection offers a claim to cultural status wholly inde-
pendent of their mother-city. Moreover, the Homeric past offered little for

[29] Note Thucydides' use of the term κλέος, which suggests a medium through which such tradi-
tions were likely preserved, namely, epic poetry (cf. *Iliad* 9.189).
[30] The historical and mythical strands are interwoven in Strabo 6.2.4; see also Pausanias 2.5.2. For a
historical perspective on myths about Corinth's foundation of Corcyra, see Salmon 1984:65-70.
[31] Thucydides 3.70.4, describing a Corcyran accused of cutting stakes ἐκ τοῦ τε Διὸς τοῦ τεμένους
καὶ τοῦ Ἀλκίνου. As Malkin 1998:102n47 observes, Thucydides seems to view the cult as well-
established.
[32] Salmon 1984:270-280.

the Corinthians to exploit.[33] Thus the Phaiakes may have formed part of an ongoing discourse about Corcyrean identity that developed soon after the foundation of their *polis*, probably in the late eighth century.

As a consequence, the fate of the Phaiakes, even if they were based "originally" on a wholly different people, for instance the Phoenicians, represents a significant choice in performances before people with connections to the powerful and influential Greek communities of Corcyra and Corinth. The narrative decision to have Zeus spare the Phaiakes may have played well before audiences favorably disposed to Corcyra, and/or to factions within Corcyra seeking to exploit family claims to Phaiakian descent. The choice for destruction, on the other hand, may have appealed to Corinthians and their allies. Indeed identification of Corcyra with Homeric Scherie is doubly unflattering for Corinthians, since it not only allows their daughter-city to downplay its debt to them, but also implicitly relates the Corinthians themselves to the "arrogant Kyklopes" who compel the Phaiakes to abandon their original home for Scherie (*Odyssey* 6.4-10).

At the same time, the Corcyrans' care not to claim direct inheritance from the Phaiakes may reflect awareness of the tradition represented by the vulgate manuscript reading at *Odyssey* 13.158. By articulating their claims to Phaiakian heritage without alleging direct descent, the Corcyrans were in a position to exploit Homeric authority, as well as the recurrent topos in Greek historical and ethnographic thought that a land shapes its inhabitants (e.g. Herodotos 9.122.3).

If these arguments are valid, the textual crux at *Odyssey* 13.158 is incapable of resolution because it reflects a narrative decision that Odyssean tradition made only in the context of a specific performance.[34] If the *Odyssey* did as discussed emerge in the context of the Panathenaia, singers might base their narrative choice about the Phaiakes in part on current trends in Athenian policy regarding its frequent political opponent and economic competitor, Corinth. All of the attested readings are from this perspective equally "authentic," which is to say, all may have been current in the performance tradition throughout the Archaic and into the Classical period.

My purpose here is not to suggest that the *Odyssey* is a political manifesto of Athens or any other Greek state. Rather, I offer this interpretation of Zeus

---

[33] Corinth is mentioned only twice in Homeric epic (*Iliad* 2.570, 13.664); see Malkin 1998:133-134 for Odysseus in Corinthian tradition.

[34] Note also that the outcome of Odysseus' interaction with the Phaiakes in the *Odyssey* is positioned to supersede or at least to complicate traditions that make them hosts to the Argonauts and coinhabitants with Colchians (e.g. *Naupaktia* 145-149 Davies; Apollonios 4.1176-1222).

and Poseidon in *Odyssey* 13 as an example of how dramatic narrative moments could have become associated with highly-charged issues in contemporary Greek society. These issues transcend the narrowly political arena, for the overriding aim of a Panhellenic synthesis is to direct audiences away from local observances and beliefs and toward those common to a significant proportion of Homeric audiences. In this respect, Zeus' covert assignment of responsibility for the Phaiakes' fate to Poseidon can be seen as a metaphor for the relationship between the *Odyssey* and epichoric traditions. The figure of Zeus is deployed to articulate the extent of Homeric authority, that is, to establish the bounds of the narrative plan. The *Odyssey* then leaves only a slender thread to which the potentially thorny epichoric issues surrounding the Phaiakes' fate can be attached.

Again, Poseidon's perspective can be seen as analogous to an epichoric perspective within the *Odyssey*: he is not ignored, but is rather subordinated to the plan of Zeus. The *Dios boulē* theme, by emerging at pivotal points in the narrative, provides a matrix for controlled variation in the progress of the plot, ensuring that, whatever the outcome, Zeus' authority is the decisive factor. In the case of the connection between Homeric Scherie and historical Corcyra, singers could negotiate the controversial intersection between Odyssean and "Scherian" tradition at a single position in a single line, with the thematic and structural coherence of the song guaranteed for each of the available choices.

Chapter conclusions

Odysseus' voyage from Ogygie to Ithake offers a valuable window into the structure of the *Odyssey* as whole, for in this sequence the relationship between divine plan and narrative plan is revealed more clearly than anywhere else in the poem. Themes introduced in the opening divine council scene in Book 1 are developed further in the complementary council in Book 5, as Athene's plan for Odysseus is revealed to be dependent on Zeus. Under the guise of merely fleshing out her plan, Zeus implements a plan of his own that goes far beyond Athene's in detail and scope, in particular because it incorporates the actions of the hero's divine antagonist, Poseidon. Yet this plan does grant Poseidon the opportunity to attack Odysseus, and in a further council in Book 13, Zeus displays the same ostensibly conciliatory and disinterested attitude toward Poseidon that he does toward Athene.

Zeus' strategies in his dealings with Athene and Poseidon in the *Odyssey* are paralleled in the *Iliad*, though only under certain circumstances. In both poems, Zeus shows deference to subordinate deities when his control over the narrative is not threatened, as is the case with Poseidon's complaints in *Iliad* 7 and *Odyssey* 13. It is when Zeus' control over the narrative is challenged, as in *Iliad* 15, that he threatens violence, though such situations do not arise in the *Odyssey*. Thus the Odyssean divine apparatus can be seen as analogous to that of the *Iliad*, and distinct only in its more complete suppression of divine conflict.

Because the *Odyssey* sets most of the return-adventures described in Books 5-13 in a region separate from "real" Greek geography, the narrative is able to avoid engagement with many non-Homeric Odysseus-traditions. Where the *Odyssey* does confront such a tradition, in the case of the Phaiakes, it deploys Zeus to mediate the relationship between Homeric and non-Homeric accounts. Zeus' strategy here is to co-opt Poseidon again, granting the subordinate god apparent freedom to follow his own desires but covertly guiding his actions. In Zeus' crucial speech on the subject, a narrative "switch" seems to have allowed the manipulation of Poseidon to play out in different ways in response to different constituencies in the Homeric audience. When Odysseus does return to the "real world," however, the *Odyssey* is forced into overt and comprehensive engagement with parallel traditions, as will be explored in the next chapter.

3

THE END(S) OF THE *ODYSSEY*

REGARDING THE ODYSSEY'S THREE MAIN NARRATIVE SEQUENCES, then, I have argued that Zeus provides a kind of blueprint for the *Telemachia* and *Mnesterophonia* with his Oresteia, and that he orchestrates the *Nostos* overtly. The latter sequence, as discussed in the previous chapter, comes under Zeus' control in Book 5, when Athene appears unable to implement the plan she has formulated for Odysseus' return in Book 1. Thus, whether or not Athene's plan is, as I have argued, prompted by Zeus, she feels compelled to turn to him in order to manage the *Nostos*. In this chapter I make an analogous argument about the *Mnesterophonia*.

It is true that Zeus remains aloof from the actual planning and execution of Odysseus' attack on the suitors, apart from sending favorable omens (20.102-121, 21.413).[1] Yet it is Zeus who introduces the theme of Odysseus exacting *tisis* 'payback' from the suitors (5.24, 24.480); Athene, by contrast, at first focuses only on their conflict with Telemachos (1.91-92). The reference to *tisis* is another of the details that Zeus attributes to Athene's plan. As discussed in the previous chapter, he in so doing uses language that recurs in their last encounter in Book 24 (οὐ γὰρ τοῦτον μὲν ἐβούλευσας νόον αὐτή, ὡς ἤτοι κείνους Ὀδυσεὺς ἀποτίσεται ἐλθών; 5.23-24=24.479-480).

Zeus' low profile in Books 14-23 can, I propose, be explained in terms of the absence of significant differences among traditional accounts of the immediate consequences of Odysseus' return. For it is one of the "facts" of Odysseus' story that he always defeats the suitors. Complications arise, however, after

---

[1] As mentioned in Chapter 1, Zeus' eagle also approves the killing of the suitors at the Ithakan assembly (2.145-156), and he may be the implied author of the two other, uncredited, eagle omens in the *Odyssey*, at 15.160-178, interpreted by Helen as portending the deaths of the suitors, and at 20.241-247, convincing the suitors to abandon their plot against Telemachos. All eagle omens in the *Iliad* are explicitly from Zeus. For the significance of the omens, cf. Nagy's (2003:59) description of the one in *Odyssey* 20 as a "clarification of the Will of Zeus," and Foley's (1998:171) suggestion that Zeus' omens generally "denote . . . the ambient tradition."

Odysseus carries out his revenge. In a last divine council scene, Athene finds it necessary to make another appeal to the authority of Zeus, after the dead suitors' kin have united behind a leader, taken up arms, and are about to engage in battle with Odysseus and his partisans.

At this point, less than a hundred lines from the end of the poem, Zeus elaborates a settlement that resolves the narrative in a manner consistent with the themes he lays out in the opening scene. In order to effect this *deus ex machina* resolution, Zeus again assimilates Athene's plan to his own. Here too, I suggest, Zeus is invoked to establish a boundary between the *Odyssey* and non-Homeric Odysseus-traditions. Specifically, I shall be arguing that Zeus de-authorizes a family of traditions that told of a very different outcome to the *Mnesterophonia*, one in which the suitors' families seek vengeance and drive Odysseus into exile, rendering his victorious return temporary and hollow. The Odyssean Zeus, by contrast uses supernatural means to dispel the thirst for vengeance that overcomes the Ithakans, so that the *Odyssey* can end, almost literally, "happily ever after" (αἰεί, 24.483).

The authenticity of *Odyssey* 24

It must be observed that the received ending of the *Odyssey*, to which I attach such importance in my interpretation, has been criticized as abrupt, forced, superfluous, and generally non-Homeric. Some scholars have even maintained that all of *Odyssey* 24 is a late and clumsy epilogue. This view may go back to antiquity: according to one interpretation, the last line of Apollonios' *Argonautika*, ἀσπασίως ἀκτὰς Παγασηίδας εἰσαπέβητε (4.1781), was modeled on *Odyssey* 23.296, ἀσπάσιοι λέκτροιο παλαιοῦ θεσμὸν ἵκοντο, in order to hint at a contemporary belief that this is the "true" end of the *Odyssey*, and the remainder of the vulgate text but a massive interpolation. Likewise, scholia to *Odyssey* 23.296, and Eustathios (1948.48-49), report that Aristophanes and Aristarchos (the Alexandrine scholars who took opposing positions on the Phaiakes' fate) agreed in identifying this point as the τέλος and πέρας of the *Odyssey*, usually taken to mean the end, though perhaps rather something more like the dramatic climax.[2]

In modern times, Analytic and Neoanalytic critics have adduced an imposing array of ostensible linguistic, syntactic, formulaic, and thematic

---

[2] On Apollonios, Aristophanes and Aristarchos see Seaford 1994:38-42, 72-73, 178; Kullmann 1992:293; Heubeck *CHO* 3:342-345 ad 23.297; Moulton 1974:153-157; detailed analysis of earlier arguments in Erbse 1972:166-244.

anomalies that they believe establishes Book 24 as an accretion to the *Odyssey*'s Homeric core.[3] Unitarians, not surprisingly, have argued that supposed anomalies of theme, syntax and so on are often in the eye of the beholder, and, citing their own litany of indubitably Homeric themes and usages in the disputed passage, have insisted on the incompleteness of any *Odyssey* that would end at 23.296. As the Unitarian position has become dominant in Homeric studies in the wake of Parry and Lord, acceptance of *Odyssey* 24 as authentic has emerged as the *opinio communis*, even among Neoanalytically-inclined scholars.[4]

It would therefore be otiose to mount another elaborate defense of the received ending of the *Odyssey*. But I do note that my interpretation of Book 24 builds on and extends arguments regarding its authenticity; for one product of the debate has been a nuanced appreciation of the themes that connect the closing scenes to the narrative as a whole, and to the deployment of these themes in other contexts. Thus my understanding of the place of Book 24 in the Odyssean narrative has been informed by, for example, analyses of the structural similarity between the divine council scenes in *Odyssey* 24 and at the beginning of *Iliad* 4, and by the manner in which divine council scenes in *Iliad* 1 and 24 form a structural ring that contributes to that poem's dramatic unity.[5]

In order to establish what I believe to be at stake when Zeus intervenes in *Odyssey* 24, I shall first examine the manner in which the claims and counterclaims of Odysseus and the suitors are articulated. The theme of *tisis* 'payback', I suggest, sets up a kind of feedback loop of reciprocal violence that threatens from the outset to frustrate both the justice of Zeus and narrative closure. Thus Odysseus rejects the suitors' attempt to negotiate a settlement, and a significant portion of the suitors' families feels compelled to demand blood for blood. When Zeus once again intervenes at Athene's request, his settle-

[3] E.g. S. West 1989:132-133; Schadewaldt 1970:70, 74; Lesky 1967:130-132; Kirk 1962:248-251; Page 1955:101-136; Merkelbach 1951:142-155. Erbse 1972:177-229 provides an exhaustive discussion of linguistic anomalies.
[4] Representative Unitarian arguments in Moulton 1974; Lord 1960:177-185; Erbse 1972:166-244; Neoanalysts: Kullmann 1992:291-304; Heubeck *CHO* 3:342-345 ad 23.297; 1954:44.
[5] As Heubeck *CHO* 3:411-412 *ad loc* and 1954:44 observes, Athene's words at 24.475-476 (ἢ προτέρω πόλεμόν τε κακὸν καὶ φύλοπιν αἰνὴν/τεύξεις ἢ φιλότητα μετ' ἀμφοτέροισι τίθησθα), parallel Zeus' at *Iliad* 4.15-16 (ἢ ῥ' αὖτις πόλεμόν τε κακὸν καὶ φύλοπιν αἰὴν/ὄρσομεν ἢ φιλότητα μετ' ἀμφοτέροισι βάλωμεν). See also Hölscher 1988:77-80 and Moulton 1974:164-166. Ring composition in the *Iliad*: Silk 1987:38-39; Whitman 1958:97; the *Odyssey*: Louden 1999:1, 133; *Odyssey* 1-5: above Chapter 2; the non-Homeric *Kypria*: Marks 2002:6-12; South Slavic epic: Lord 1991:30-32. Objections to the *Odyssey* 24 divine council in Kirk 1962:238-239, 260-261; Page 1955:101-136. Defenders include: Danek 1998:457-458; Kullmann 1992:303-304; Moulton 1974; Pfeiffer 1968:175-177; Stanford 1965 2:428; Heubeck 1954:37-54.

ment turns out to rely on supernatural effects, so that only one more citizen must die in order for Ithake to enjoy peace and prosperity ever after, and for the *Odyssey* to impose a terminus on its hero's adventures.

Compensation or revenge

Zeus' settlement in *Odyssey* 24 brings together themes that run through the narrative and come to the fore in the *Mnesterophonia*. A key passage in the *Odyssey*'s justification and contextualization of its hero's actions is a speech Odysseus delivers after killing the first of the suitors, Antinoos (22.35-41). These men, Odysseus says, have acted against him with neither fear of the gods nor regard for the *nemesis* 'righteous indignation' of mortals (οὔτε θεοὺς δείσαντες...οὔτε τιν' ἀνθρώπων νέμεσιν κατόπισθεν ἔσεσθαι, 39-40), and therefore they must all die (41; cf. 61-64).

Eurymachos, after Antinoos the leading suitor, takes up the case for the defense (45-59). While admitting that he and his fellows are guilty of *atasthala*, acts of "wanton disregard" (47),[6] Eurymachos claims that they were only following Antinoos, who is αἴτιος πάντων 'responsible for everything' (48), and now conveniently dead. As Eurymachos would have it, Antinoos courted Penelope and plotted against Telemachos for political reasons, "in order that he might rule the people of well-built Ithake" (ὄφρ' Ἰθάκης κατὰ δῆμον ἐυκτιμένης βασιλεύοι, 52).[7] Now that Antinoos' coup has failed (or, as Eurymachos puts it, "Zeus did not bring these things to fulfillment for him," τά οἱ οὐκ ἐτέλεσσε Κρονίων, 51), Eurymachos exhorts Odysseus to "spare his people" (σὺ δὲ φείδεο λαῶν/σῶν, 54-55).

Eurymachos' rhetoric assimilates the suitors to the *dēmos*, the citizen body of Ithake, in a way that simultaneously excludes Odysseus and his *oikos* from it.[8] Odysseus is cast as an invader, with whom Eurymachos negotiates terms of surrender for the defeated community. Thus he proposes *timē* 'recompense': each suitor is to gather bronze and gold "among the people"

---

[6] On the suitors' guilt and the thematics of *atasthala* in the *Odyssey*, see de Jong 2001:12 ad 1.32-43; Cook 1995:23-24; Flaig 1995:377.

[7] The social and political implications of Eurymachos' charge against Antinoos are discussed by Wilson 2002:77; Thalmann 1998:187-188; Felson 1994:115-118; van Wees 1992:288-291; Murnaghan 1987:66-67. Nagy 1990a:237-239 discerns juridical force in Homeric αἴτιος.

[8] Haubold 2000 argues that "sparing the people" is a theme central to Homeric social dynamics. The authoritative Athene/Mentor also speaks of the culpability of the Ithakan δῆμος in the suitors' acts (*Odyssey* 2.239-41).

Chapter Three

(κατὰ δῆμον, 55) in order to satisfy Odysseus' desire for retribution (57-59).[9] Eurymachos, in other words, denies the suitors' collective guilt on the capital charge of lèse-majesté, while he simultaneously makes the *dēmos* collectively responsible for paying back Odysseus for the suitors' ostensibly less serious *atasthala*. And his is no mean offer: the bronze and gold, to the value of 20 oxen per suitor, times 108 (or 107, subtracting Antinoos) suitors, amounts to over 2000 oxen-worth of precious metals.[10] With this offer on the table, Eurymachos attempts to turn the *nemesis*-theme back on Odysseus: the latter's "righteous indignation" is understandable and justifiable, he asserts, but only until the offer of *timē* is made (πρὶν δ' οὔ τι νεμεσσητὸν κεχολῶσθαι, 59).

This understanding of damage and compensation is not merely the product of Eurymachos' self-serving rhetoric, but has been rehearsed for Odysseus and the external audience in the song of Ares and Aphrodite (8.267-366), another narrative built around the question of compensation. In this inset narrative Hephaistos, like Odysseus, suffers an assault on his marriage, exacts a measure of revenge, and is then offered recompense, in this case "all things such as are right" (αἴσιμα πάντα, 348; cf. 22.46). Despite his anger, Hephaistos yields, declaring that to refuse compensation "is neither possible nor seemly" (οὐκ ἔστ' οὐδὲ ἔοικε, 358). The *Odyssey* thus allows for the possibility of a negotiated settlement in circumstances at least superficially similar to those in Book 22. As a consequence, the exchange between Odysseus and Eurymachos represents, in dramatic terms, though not in terms of the "facts" of Odysseus-tradition, a real choice. Were Odysseus to follow the example of Hephaistos and accept recompense, the conflict between his *oikos* and the Ithakan people would cease, and the *Odyssey* could draw to a (rather unsatisfying) close.

But of course Odysseus is implacable, and not because Eurymachos' terms are insufficiently generous. Rather, Odysseus refuses compensation in any amount (22.41, 61-64) because he rejects the terms in which Eurymachos frames the conflict; the relative culpability of individual suitors is for him irrelevant. Odysseus acts instead in a manner consistent with a different

---

[9] Wilson 2002 deduces from compensation themes in the *Iliad* "a fixed system [that] grants [the leader] the power to assess goods from his subjects to fund his largess on behalf of the community;" this system she describes as "*timē*-based," in which *timē* often refers to the war plunder that reflects a hero's status (quote from 52; see in particular 54-55, 77, 91, 189n46). Cf. Muellner 1996:28-29 and van Wees 1992:69-77.

[10] Flaig 1997:22 describes this as *une somme colossale*. Telemachos enumerates the suitors at *Odyssey* 16.246-253.

compensation-paradigm, namely the Oresteia. Orestes' goal is also *tisis*, not a settlement with Aigisthos' regime (cf. 1.40), and the futility of negotiation in this context is underscored further by the gods' rejection of Aigisthos' attempts to regain divine favor through costly sacrifices (3.273-275).

Looking beyond the *Odyssey*, Odysseus' implacability aligns him thematically with Achilleus in the *Iliad*.[11] The latter's personal feud leads him to disregard, at least at first, any thought of the community as a whole; he even expresses willingness to see all combatants perish, Greeks and Trojans alike (*Iliad* 16.98-99). In a sense, the Odyssean Odysseus is bound even more tightly to the revenge theme than is the Iliadic Achilleus. For while the latter at least directs his efforts back toward the good of his fellows when to do so coincides with his own thirst for personal vengeance, Odysseus will remain disinclined to "spare his people" until he is compelled by Zeus to relent.

The *Odyssey*, then, entertains, but rejects, the possibility of a negotiated settlement between Odysseus and the suitors. Eurymachos' "Nuremberg defense," and his attempt to identify the suitors' cause with that of the people, run counter to the *Odyssey*'s core themes, and indeed point to an outcome unrealized in Odysseus-tradition. Yet Odysseus in the event proves unable to achieve total victory over the anti-Odysseus faction, which regenerates under new leadership almost immediately after the suitors' deaths. As Eurymachos predicts and Odysseus himself has foreseen, the hero incurs *nemesis* for failing to spare his people despite thematic justification and the fact that he acts, like Orestes, with the approval of the gods.

From revenge to vendetta

After burying their own dead and sending the remaining bodies home, the kin of the Ithakan suitors assemble in the agora (24.413-421).[12] Here Antinoos' father Eupeithes emerges as the not unlikely leader of the suitors' kin. Motivated, according to the Homeric narrator, by ἄλαστον πένθος, "pain that

---

[11] On the parallelism between Odysseus at the end of the *Odyssey* and Achilleus, see Cook 1995:150-151; Nagy 1979:317-318.

[12] For the constituency of this assembly see Flaig 1997:13-18 and van Wees 1992:148. The significant point for the present argument is that it seems to be conceived as a broad cross-section of the Ithakan populace (though only 12 of the suitors are Ithakan; *Odyssey* 16.251).

cannot be forgotten" (423),[13] Eupeithes exhorts the Ithakans to vengeance against Odysseus:

> ὦ φίλοι, ἦ μέγα ἔργον ἀνὴρ ὅδε μήσατ' Ἀχαιούς·
> τοὺς μὲν σὺν νήεσσιν ἄγων πολέας τε καὶ ἐσθλούς
> ὤλεσε μὲν νῆας γλαφυράς, ἀπὸ δ' ὤλεσε λαούς,
> τοὺς δ' ἐλθὼν ἔκτεινε Κεφαλλήνων ὄχ' ἀρίστους.
> ἀλλ' ἄγετε, πρὶν τοῦτον ἢ ἐς Πύλον ὦκα ἱκέσθαι   430
> ἢ καὶ ἐς Ἤλιδα δῖαν, ὅθι κρατέουσιν Ἐπειοί,
> ἴομεν· ἢ καὶ ἔπειτα κατηφέες ἐσσόμεθ' αἰεί.
> λώβη γὰρ τάδε γ' ἐστὶ καὶ ἐσσομένοισι πυθέσθαι,
> εἰ δὴ μὴ παίδων τε κασιγνήτων τε φονῆας
> τισόμεθ'· οὐκ ἂν ἔμοιγε μετὰ φρεσὶν ἡδὺ γένοιτο   435
> ζωέμεν, ἀλλὰ τάχιστα θανὼν φθιμένοισι μετείην.
> ἀλλ' ἴομεν, μὴ φθέωσι περαιωθέντες ἐκεῖνοι.

Friends, surely this man has devised an enormity against
  the Achaians:
some he led in ships, many and good men,
and he destroyed the hollow ships, and utterly destroyed
  the people.
And others he has come and killed, far the best of the
  Kephallenians.
But come, before this man makes his way quickly either
  to Pylos   430
or even to godly Elis where the Epeioi rule,
let us go; or even later shamed we will be always.
For these things are an outrage, even for men to come
  to learn of,
if we do not seek vengeance from the killers of our sons
  and brothers;
as for me myself there would be no pleasure in
  my heart   435

---

[13] Chantraine s.v. ἀλάστωρ derives ἄλαστος from λανθάνω (root *-lēth-), though as he observes other etymologies have been proposed. Compare the argument of Slatkin 1991:95-96 that, in the *Iliad*, Thetis' ἄλαστον πένθος (24.105) bestows on her "the same ominous character as that of her son." As mentioned in Chapter 1, this "second" Ithakan assembly picks up themes from the assembly in Book 2; thus, for instance, the fact that the suitors will go unavenged is signposted in Telemachos' vision of their deaths "without payback," νήποινοι (2.145; cf. ἀνάποινον at *Iliad* 1.99); cf. Heubeck *CHO* 3:405-406 ad 24.413-548, 415 ad 516-27; Erbse 1972:139-140.

in living, but with a quick death would I join those who have
  perished.
But come, let us go, lest they get ahead of us making their
  escape.

Odyssey 24.426-437

Here the *Odyssey* at last confronts the problem that has from the start
threatened to render the killing of the suitors a false climax to its hero's story.
Eupeithes asserts that the deaths of the suitors will occasion *lōbē* '[a sense of]
outrage' or 'cause for reproach' in future generations if their survivors do not
exact *tisis* 'payback' (433-435). In doing so, he reveals the potential for the
revenge-fantasy to degenerate into a self-perpetuating cycle of reciprocal
violence, which is also to say its potential to spawn countless sequels. For
the *tisis*-theme, at least in the *Odyssey*, is asserted to the exclusion of *timē*
'recompense' such as is offered by Eurymachos in the pursuit of a negotiated
settlement. Odysseus has rejected the offer of *timē* out of hand in Book 22, and
Eupeithes does not even mention the possibility in Book 24. In other words,
just as Odysseus' demand for *tisis* leaves the suitors no option but battle, so also
Eupeithes' demands suggest that that battle will be a fight to the death (435-
436). Thus his first concern is to prevent Odysseus from fleeing to another city
(430-431), an outcome that Odysseus himself entertains but rejects (23.118-
120), though it does form the basis for a number of non-Homeric Odysseus-
traditions, as discussed in Chapter 4.

The *tisis* that all strands of Odysseus-tradition agree the hero exacts
from the suitors cannot but generate *nemesis* and *lōbē*, which must in turn
be expunged through a reciprocal act of violence directed back at the hero.[14]
The Ares and Aphrodite scenario is thus revealed as a red herring, since the
immortal gods do not (as a rule) bear immortal grudges. From the first, the
justice of Zeus builds into the narrative an apparently irresolvable contradic-
tion: if the cycle of retribution is allowed to run its course, human suffering
will not be measured, as Zeus insists that it is with his Oresteia, but rather
boundless. Odysseus, traditionally and in accordance with the justice of Zeus,

[14] Wilson 2002, especially 23-25, 61, 89-96, demonstrates that Iliadic compensation themes tend
to follow one of two paths, toward either a "pay-off" in material goods, *apoina*, or toward
"payback," *poinē* or *tisis*, usually exacted as "harm" (though in the *Odyssey tisis* is on occasion
associated with the *apoina* path; cf. 2.76, 8.348); the theme of *lōbē* 'outrage' attaches to the latter
option. Odyssean *lōbē* is associated almost exclusively with the suitors: Athene spurs them to
lōbē (18.347-348 and 20.285); Eurykleia thus describes their treatment of the disguised Odysseus
(19.373); and Penelope warns Telemachos he will incur *lōbē* if he fails to protect the disguised
Odysseus from them (18.223-225). On Homeric *lōbē* see further Nagy 1979:255-264.

must kill the suitors, but Homeric society is sufficiently realistic that revenge remains inseparable from that universally-attested and enduring human institution, the vendetta.

Scholarship on the deployment of these themes in epic has focused largely on the *Iliad*, and while Iliadic and Odyssean usage is in most respects equivalent, there is an important difference. For where the *Iliad* betrays anxiety about the consequences of the unrestrained pursuit of *tisis*,[15] the *Odyssey* refuses to allow the destabilizing implications of the theme to cloud the revenge-fantasy. Thus, though construction of *tisis* as non-negotiable appears to make the vendetta-scenario inevitable, a vendetta militates against the Homeric, Panhellenic impulse to impose closure on the hero's story.

Again, Zeus' Oresteia introduces the theme in the *Odyssey*, where Hermes warns Aigisthos that Orestes will exact *tisis* (1.40), an act that is made synonymous with destruction (αἰπὺν ὄλεθρον, 37).[16] Yet Zeus, and the *Odyssey* in general, suppress any negative consequences of Orestes' revenge. So also, when Zeus goes on to describe the *Mnesterophonia* as *tisis* (ἀποτίσεται, 5.24) in the "second" divine council scene, no acknowledgment is made of the violent response that the killings will unleash. Zeus' uncluttered view of the revenge-fantasy is echoed by Athene, for whom the Orestes-paradigm offers to Telemachos only the possibility of glory (κλέος, 1.298). Similarly, when Teiresias maps Odysseus' fate onto a grid of mutually exclusive options, one fixed point is that the hero will exact *tisis* by killing the suitors (11.118-120), with no option of negotiation or of failure either to defeat the suitors or to manage the consequences of victory.

Herein, I submit, resides a telling internal contradiction. The suitors' *lōbē* demands from Odysseus and his partisans absolute *tisis*, which in turn casts on the suitors' kin *lōbē* that demands more absolute *tisis* (24.435-436). Odyssean themes limit the perspective of Eupeithes and his faction, as they have that of Odysseus, so that only two outcomes remain possible: destruction or more *tisis*. These thematic constraints threaten to impinge as well on Zeus' theodicy: in order for his assertions about human suffering to be credible, some force must stop the self-regenerating cycle of reciprocal violence. And in purely practical terms, the vendetta threatens to render hollow Odysseus' triumphant return: since the hero has already, as Eupeithes observes, been responsible for the

---

[15] Wilson 2002:32-34 cites Iliadic scenes in which "ambivalence about *tisis*" is revealed through its association with "profoundly savage conduct," namely, cannibalism.

[16] Cf. the destruction that attends Helios' demand for *tisis* for his cattle (*Odyssey* 12.382), and Zeus' affirmation of Poseidon's right to *tisis* against the Phaiakes (13.144).

destruction of one generation of Ithakan *aristoi* at Troy, and another with the *Mnesterophonia*, eradication of the Ithakan opposition in *Odyssey* 24 would seem to leave him little more than the lord of his own *oikos* and a depopulated town.

The impossibility of compromise or negotiation under such circumstances becomes apparent as the second Ithakan council proceeds. Eupeithes' call for *tisis* moves the crowd to pity (οἶκτος, 24.438),[17] but his assessment of the situation is contested immediately by two of Odysseus' partisans. Medon, a herald spared by Odysseus during the *Mnesterophonia*, gives eyewitness testimony that Odysseus acted with divine aid (443-449), and Halitherses then declares that the Ithakans' own baseness (ὑμετέρηι κακότητι, 455), and the suitors' *atasthala* (458), specifically their consumption of Odysseus' goods and diminution of his wife's *timē* (ἀτιμάζοντες ἄκοιτιν, 459), foredoom the proposed action against Odysseus to issue in "self-inflicted evil" (ἐπισπαστὸν κακόν, 462). These speeches are not entirely ineffective, but such apparently incontrovertible arguments that the pursuit of *tisis* will prove self-destructive fail to dissuade a significant portion of the people (ἡμίσεων πλείους, 464)[18] from following Eupeithes' lead and preparing for battle outside the city (467-468).

Thus neither the culpability of the victim, the justification of the avenger, nor divine approval of the vengeance attenuate the impetus of the themes of *lōbē, nemesis,* and *tisis.* Failure to avenge his son's killing will compromise Eupeithes' position in the community now and in the future. From this perspective, although Medon's and Halitherses' warnings ensure that Eupeithes' impending death conforms to the parameters of Zeus' theodicy, Eupeithes is nevertheless distinct from other *spretores deorum* in the *Odyssey,* for his admonition comes too late to allow for any real options. Other characters who disregard divine warnings have greater latitude: Aigisthos and the suitors are not compelled to engage in their unlawful marriage suits; the Kyklops is not forced to eat Odysseus' men; they in turn could have refrained from eating Helios' cattle; and even the Phaiakes might have fulfilled the demands of *xenia* without turning Poseidon against themselves.

---

[17] However, οἶκτος alone does not precipitate action: Telemachos in the first Ithakan council elicits οἶκτος from the crowd (*Odyssey* 2.81), but no remedy for his complaints; cf. Finley 1965:94-95.

[18] Eupeithes' position is adopted by the greater part of the Ithakans if οἱ δ' at 24.463 and σφιν at 465 refer to Eupeithes' followers and τοὶ δ' at 464 to those whom Halitherses convinces; thus Heubeck *CHO* 3:410 ad 24.463-6, Erbse 1972:241, Stanford 1965 v.2:427. However, the pronouns could equally indicate that a minority follow Eupeithes; thus Benardete 1997:139 and Ameis-Hentze-Cauer *ad loc.*; further arguments are catalogued by S. West 1989:129, who concludes sensibly that "the passage is genuinely ambiguous."

The economy of *nemesis, lōbē,* and *tisis* in the *Odyssey,* then, overwhelms the institutions of the Homeric agora.[19] The court scene on Achilleus' shield (*Iliad* 18.497-508) demonstrates that these institutions are capable of taking on complicated issues regarding the value of life and death, but the actions of both Odysseus and the suitors complicate matters by their very magnitude (cf. *Odyssey* 23.118-122). From a practical standpoint, the involvement of the entire Ithakan polity and the surrounding region points to the difficulty of securing impartial judges who might negotiate a settlement, a point to which I shall return in the following chapter. And even if a judge could be found, other Homeric parallels, along with non-Homeric accounts of the *Mnesterophonia,* suggest that the punishment inflicted on Odysseus would be exile, a circumstance that, as we shall see in the next chapter, breeds *epigonoi,* who are likely to instigate yet another round of violence.

The only possible end to the Ithakan conflict, therefore, appears to be the eradication of one faction by the other. But eradication of a family, let alone a faction, is generally impossible in Greek myth as it is in Greek (or any) history. A figure can always be found to perpetuate old conflicts and claim the right to vengeance, whether in mythic Thebes, archaic Athens, or modern Palestine. Thus the momentum of *tisis* toward complete victory for one side and abject defeat for the other issues most naturally in the impasse of a self-perpetuating cycle of violence, a vendetta.

The last Odyssean divine council

The potential for reciprocal violence is not lost on the hero himself. The night before killing the suitors, Odysseus tells Athene that, as serious as is the danger they represent,

> πρὸς δ' ἔτι καὶ τόδε μεῖζον ἐνὶ φρεσὶ μερμηρίζω·
> εἴ περ γὰρ κτείναιμι Διός τε σέθεν τε ἔκητι,
> πῆ κεν ὑπεκπροφύγοιμι; τά σε φράζεσθαι ἄνωγα.

> There is something still more important I am pondering in
>   my mind:

---

[19] Flaig 1997:29 argues that Homeric institutions for resolving conflicts are generally weak, and describes the Ithakan council in *Odyssey* 24 as an *assemblée pervertie* (24). For a more positive assessment of the Homeric agora, see Hölkeskamp 1994 and Morris 1986:101-104. In any case, even modern political systems often prove unequal to the task of resolving internal conflicts that kill or displace large numbers of citizens.

for if I should actually do the killing, Zeus and yourself
willing,
where and how[20] would I make my escape? I ask you to
consider this.

Odyssey 20.41-43

Clearly, Odysseus fears reprisal if he proceeds as planned. Athene's answer
seems a little off-point:

σχέτλιε, καὶ μέν τίς τε χερείονι πείθεθ' ἑταίρωι,
ὅς περ θνητός τ' ἐστὶ καὶ οὐ τόσα μήδεα οἶδεν·
αὐτὰρ ἐγὼ θεός εἰμι, διαμπερὲς ἥ σε φυλάσσω
ἐν πάντεσσι πόνοις. ἐρέω δέ τοι ἐξαναφανδόν·
εἴ περ πεντήκοντα λόχοι μερόπων ἀνθρώπων
νῶϊ περισταῖεν, κτεῖναι μεμαῶτες Ἄρηι,
καί κεν τῶν ἐλάσαιο βόας καὶ ἴφια μῆλα.

Harsh one, a person could trust in a worse companion,
one who is mortal and does not know as many stratagems;
but I myself am a god, who protects you all the way through
in all your toils. And I will tell you plainly:
even if fifty mortal men in ambush
should encircle we two, eager to kill us in combat,
even then would you drive off their cattle and fat sheep.

Odyssey 20.45-51

The goddess comforts the hero with a keen grasp of the obvious: with a divinity
like her on his side, no mortal can stand before him. However, Odysseus
expresses reservations, not about the outcome of the battle, but rather about
the consequences of victory. He may very well by defeating the suitors earn
the right to drive off their herds; but he will not be able to drive them far if
he expects to remain in control of Ithake. The scenario Athene constructs is
Iliadic, one befitting an invader of a foreign territory, rather than an isolated
king at war with his own subjects. Athene in sum appears unable or unwilling
to see beyond the revenge-fantasy, and before Odysseus can press her on the
issue, she puts him to sleep (20.54).

---

[20] Homeric πῇ means "how" or "where" (Cunliffe s.v., citing this line in the latter sense); here the
senses merge (cf. *Odyssey* 12.287).

Athene's obtuseness here is the more remarkable in that she is a goddess whose primary associations with wisdom and the community – hence for instance her epithets *polyboulos* 'she of many plans' (e.g. *Iliad* 5.260) and *erysiptolis* 'guardian of the city' (e.g. *Homeric Hymn* 11.1) – would seem to make her a natural figure to diagnose Ithake's political ills. And not only does the goddess fail to anticipate the response of the Ithakans before the fact, she also apparently remains oblivious to the danger even after the suitors have been killed. For while Odysseus immediately afterward takes measures at least to delay the re-formation of the opposition (23.117-140, 361-365), Athene does nothing until the opposition is arming for battle against the hero.

At this moment (24.472), as the two factions prepare for the final showdown, the scene shifts for the last time to Olympos (488), where the gods have apparently been observing events on Ithake. Athene turns to Zeus and voices a familiar complaint, cited already in the context of previous divine councils, and elicits a familiar response:

> "ὦ πάτερ ἡμέτερε Κρονίδη, ὕπατε κρειόντων,
> εἰπέ μοι εἰρομένηι· τί νύ τοι νόος ἔνδοθι κεύθει;
> ἢ προτέρω πόλεμόν τε κακὸν καὶ φύλοπιν αἰνὴν   475
> τεύξεις, ἦ φιλότητα μετ' ἀμφοτέροισι τίθησθα;"
> τὴν δ' ἀπαμειβόμενος προσέφη νεφεληγερέτα Ζεύς·
> "τέκνον ἐμόν, τί με ταῦτα διείρεαι ἠδὲ μεταλλᾶις;
> οὐ γὰρ δὴ τοῦτον μὲν ἐβούλευσας νόον αὐτή,
> ὡς ἤτοι κείνους Ὀδυσεὺς ἀποτίσεται ἐλθών;   480

> "Our father, son of Kronos, utmost of the powerful,
> tell to me who asks: what idea does your mind now
>   hide?
> Will you establish further war and evil and awful
>   battle-noise,   475
> or will you cause mutual attachment between both
>   sides?"
> And her did cloud-gathering Zeus address in answer:
> "My child, why do you ask and enquire of me about this?
> For was this not the idea you yourself planned,
> that Odysseus would come and exact *tisis* from
>   those men?"   480

> > *Odyssey* 24.473-480

As noted in Chapter 2, this exchange resembles closely that between the two gods in Book 5: Athene is distressed about Odysseus' situation, and Zeus reminds her that she is herself responsible for it (24.477-480~5.21-24).[21] Here it is as if Athene's "pre-*polis*," and pre-Homeric, function as protector of hereditary rulers resurfaces in the insensitivity of her Odyssean incarnation to the community over which her favorite rules.[22] Unable to appreciate the complexities of life beyond the palace walls, Athene must seek a broader perspective in order to reintegrate the heroic ruler back into the community. At the same time, the *Odyssey* through Athene seems to reinforce an elite perspective on, or rather elite fantasy of, the relationship between ruler and ruled.[23] The highly ranked hero is to be accorded maximum personal autonomy, which is to be curbed grudgingly, and only when it threatens the survival of the community – and therefore the hero's very status as ruler.

Athene's initial question does however suggest an alternative to the *tisis* theme and its impetus toward vendetta, that of peace and love (476). Yet she does not consider bringing about this outcome herself, but rather implies with her question that such could only proceed from Zeus. In other words, Athene's question to Zeus in Book 24 seems to acknowledge that Zeus is the figure charged with resolving the *Odyssey*'s internal contradiction so that the story may achieve dramatic closure.

Again, the theme of *tisis* seems poised to frustrate any attempt to make the *Mnesterophonia* the dramatic climax of Odysseus' return. Here the power of Zeus over the *Odyssey*'s main themes becomes manifest, for the settlement he puts forward as a "fitting" (481) coda to "Athene's" plan simply circumvents the *tisis* theme altogether:

> ἔρξον ὅπως ἐθέλεις· ἐρέω δέ τοι ὡς ἐπέοικεν.
> ἐπεὶ δὴ μνηστῆρας ἐτίσατο δῖος Ὀδυσσεύς,
> ὅρκια πιστὰ ταμόντες ὃ μὲν βασιλευέτω αἰεί,
> ἡμεῖς δ' αὖ παίδων τε κασιγνήτων τε φόνοιο
> ἔκλησιν θέωμεν· τοὶ δ' ἀλλήλους φιλεόντων   485
> ὡς τὸ πάρος, πλοῦτος δὲ καὶ εἰρήνη ἅλις ἔστω."

[21] Note that, like Poseidon in Book 13, Athene here seems to assume that Zeus has already formulated some sort of plan (24.474 with 13.127).

[22] Burkert 1985:139-143 analyzes Athene's association with hereditary rulers.

[23] On the Homeric elite perspective, see Morris 2000:171-176; for an alternative view, cf. P. Rose 1992:89-91. There is of course room for subtlety in such analysis; A. Edwards 1993:54-59, argues for "subideologies" that run counter to the dominant ideology; similarly Thalmann 1998:298-302.

> Do as you wish; but I will tell you what seems fitting
>   to me.
> Since Odysseus has obtained *tisis* from the suitors,
> let them swear oaths, and let him be king always;
> and let us ourselves, as regards the killing of children
>   and brethren,
> impose forgetfulness; and let them love one another   485
> as before. And let there be prosperity and peace in
>   abundance.

Odyssey 24.481-486

Zeus' language here echoes that of treaties between historical Greek communities.[24] His roadmap to peace, however, relies on a condition that is beyond the reach of human dispute-resolution, namely the imposition of *eklēsis* 'forgetfulness' (485), on the opposing factions.[25] The importance of this supernatural element for Zeus' settlement can hardly be overstated. For without *eklēsis*, oaths can always be violated,; nor is it clear how later generations are expected to endure the inherited *lōbē*.

This supernatural solution is not entirely ad hoc, at least insofar as Zeus' ability to render the Ithakans *tabula rasa* is consistent with his larger mythological identity as the origin of memory, through his daughters the Muses (e.g. Hesiod *Theogony* 54-55, 915-917). Moreover, memory is a key concept in oral traditions generally. It is for the characters a recreation of an event, as it is for the performer of an epic; forgetfulness, by contrast, means the loss of an event and with it a way of thinking about the past. From this perspective, I suggest, Zeus' power to impose forgetfulness on the Ithakans, and thereby to silence reciprocal demands for *tisis*, represents one facet of the *Odyssey*'s claim to Panhellenic authority. For one implication of Zeus' *eklēsis* is that Odysseus will be secure in his home despite the violence through which he reclaimed it. The hero therefore will not suffer the exile alluded to by Eupeithes and Odysseus himself. As a consequence, the *Odyssey* effectively de-authorizes traditions

---

[24] For example, a sixth-century treaty between the citizens of Sybaris and the Serdaioi (*SEG* xxx 424, xxxi 357 = Meiggs and Lewis 10): ἁρμόχθεν οἱ Συβαρῖται κ' οἱ σύνμαχοι κ' οἱ Σερδαῖοι ἐπὶ φιλότατι πιστᾶι κ' ἀδόλοι ἀείδιον. αἰεί in fifth-century treaties: Meiggs and Lewis 63 and 64; Thucydides 4.63.1.

[25] The etymological root for this concept, -*lāth*-, is shared by "Lēthē," the river of forgetfulness in the underworld; cf. Bakker 2002:67-68; Flaig 1994:382-383; Heubeck *CHO* 3:413 ad 24.485. Interestingly, in the *Odyssey*, the verb from which *eklēsis* directly derives, ἐκλανθάνεσθαι, is associated with figures who die, namely Elpenor (10.557), and the suitors (3.224) and the slave-women who pleasure them (22.444); cf. *Iliad* 6.285.

that build on the social and political consequences of the suitors' deaths, but that lack Panhellenic currency.[26]

These traditions are the subject of the following chapter. In the context of *Odyssey* 24, erasure of the Ithakans' memory can be seen as a substitute for destruction of the Ithakans themselves. There does remain something of a paradox: the future Ithakans whom the *Odyssey* constructs will be unacquainted with the *Odyssey* itself, which preserves the memory of the *Mnesterophonia*. This is perhaps to be over-literal, but such considerations serve to remind the modern reader that enforced forgetfulness is for a primarily oral culture something akin to book-burning. In terms of contemporary information technology, then, tampering with memory in the manner that Zeus proposes would involve decisions about which songs will be sung.

Significantly, the manipulation of memory elsewhere in the *Odyssey* can also be linked to the poem's relationship to other traditions. Thus Helen's drugs[27] (*Odyssey* 4.222-232) suppress memories associated with other epics so that memories of thematic significance to the *Odyssey* can surface, namely her and Menelaos' stories of Odysseus at Troy. While under the influence, Menelaos and Peisistratos forget the deaths of their brothers (events narrated in the Cyclic *Nostoi* and *Aithiopis*, respectively); and perhaps as an after-effect, or sign of continued dosage, Telemachos nearly forgets that he is in the *Odyssey* (cf. 15.10-23). However, Helen's drugs eventually wear off: Agamemnon's death remains a cloud over Menelaos' post-Trojan War life, and Peisistratos will continue to grieve over the dead Antilochos (cf. 3.112, 4.186-188). Of those anaesthetized by Helen in *Odyssey* 4, only Telemachos will, thanks to Zeus, know the peace of forgetting permanently the effects of the Trojan War, for his Ithake will be "as before" (ὡς τὸ πάρος, 24.486).

The last divine council in the *Odyssey*, then, serves the crucial function of bringing closure to the narrative in terms that are consistent with the themes that are introduced in the first divine council and reinforced throughout the narrative, and that are at the same time inconsistent with non-Homeric traditions. As in previous council scenes, Zeus in Book 24 affects a pose of cooperative disinterest toward the subordinate deity most concerned with the hero's

[26] Thus Danek 1998:505 interprets *eklēsis* here as "the citation of a dead end, into which the plot would have veered, if Zeus had not provided another solution" [*das Zitat einer Sackgasse, in die die Handlung geriete, wenn Zeus nicht eine andere Lösung vorhergesehen hätte*]. The *Odyssey* may also be denying the authority of exile-traditions when Odysseus himself entertains but rejects the idea of flight into exile (23.118-120).

[27] Kirke's drugs, by contrast, do not affect the mind (10.240), though her wiles do cause Odysseus to forget his homeland and fate, as his crew "reminds" him (μιμνήσκεο, 472).

progress, but nevertheless insinuates himself into the process of determining the hero's fate. This he does by telling Athene, as he has Poseidon, "do as you wish; but this is what seems best to me" (24.481; cf. 13.145, 154).

Criticism of the *Odyssey*'s happy ending as ill-suited to the gravity of the issues involved notwithstanding,[28] Zeus' settlement is then prepared for by, and designed to engage with, themes that run through the narrative. Achievement of closure, however, is made to rely on a variation on the *deus ex machina* device, as the supernatural power of Zeus constrains Odysseus within the bounds of a Panhellenic framework, and at the same time makes possible the elite fantasy of a bloodless counter-revolution – or a nearly bloodless one.

A last, decisive death

After the last divine council, Athene departs Olympos in order to implement "her" plan, and arrives on Ithake as Eupeithes' and Odysseus' factions meet (24.488-501). Assuming the form of Mentor, the goddess takes her place amid Odysseus, Telemachos, and Laertes, but makes no attempt to avert the coming battle. Instead, she exhorts Laertes to hurl his spear, and he does so, felling the ringleader of the anti-Odysseus faction, Eupeithes (513-525). At this cue Odysseus' partisans attack with such force that they are on the point of destroying the rest of the opposition (καί νύ κε δὴ πάντας ὄλεσαν καὶ ἔθηκαν ἀνόστους, 528).[29]

Only now does Athene attempt to follow Zeus' instructions and disengage the combatants. Apparently doffing momentarily the guise of Mentor, she cries aloud:

> ἴσχεσθε πτολέμου, Ἰθακήσιοι, ἀργαλέοιο,
> ὥς κεν ἀναιμωτί γε διακρινθῆτε τάχιστα.

> Hold back from harsh war, Ithakans,
> so that bloodlessly you may be separated forthwith.

Odyssey 24.531-532

Her epiphany fills the Ithakans with terror; they drop their weapons and turn to flee (533-536).

---

[28] Thus for instance Danek 1998:504-505; Thalmann 1998:231-232; Kullmann 1992:303-304; S. West 1989:133-134; Rutherford 1985:144-145.

[29] Heubeck *CHO* 3:415 ad 24.516-27 compares Athene's exhortation of Laertes to her prompting of Pandaros to break the truce in *Iliad* 4 (92-103; Haubold 2000:69-70 adduces *Iliad* 11.758-759, where Athene "turns back the people" at the inflection point in Nestor's "Pylian epic".

Odysseus, however, continues to press the attack. Not only does Athene make no effort to restrain him, but she even seems herself to have become caught up in the blood-lust, for the thunderbolt that Zeus then hurls to punctuate the call to cease hostilities falls at her feet (539-540).[30] Thus admonished, Athene convinces Odysseus to stand down, and as the narrative closes the combatants are swearing the oaths specified by Zeus.[31] The *eklēsis* is at hand.

There is a satisfying dramatic symmetry to these closing scenes. Thus, for instance, as Eustathios (1969.31-35) observes, grandfather revels in the sight of father exhorting grandson; grandfather proceeds to kill the father of the suitor who plotted to kill the grandson and who died at the hands of the son. Perhaps the symmetry can be extended: the suitors die to a man so that Odysseus may reclaim his position; now Eupeithes alone dies so that the rest of the suitors' kin may preserve their own positions. There is also the satisfaction that the hero and his people will at last have peace after twenty years of suffering, and the comfort that the gods are shown as something other than spiteful, capricious, or disengaged. Some critics go further, and read into the *Odyssey*'s closing lines the groping of Archaic Greeks toward the enlightened civilization that they supposedly achieved in the Classical period.[32]

There are however some disturbing aspects to the *Odyssey*'s closing scenes. For one thing, the hero's last act in the narrative is to attack an unarmed and retreating crowd of his own fellow citizens. Second, Athene shows herself somewhat loose with the facts: what she describes as a "bloodless" (ἀναιμωτί, 532) end to the conflict comes after Eupeithes receives a spear through the head (523-525). And again, both the goddess and the hero need to be restrained by Zeus' thunderbolt from committing what even in antiquity would presumably have been reckoned an atrocity.

The Homeric epics of course generally endorse the slaughter of weaker or defenseless opponents and the viciousness of avenging divinity. Here at the end of the *Odyssey*, however, the violent themes identified with the hero and his patron deity persist even when the goal toward which they are directed has already been obviated by Zeus. I suggest that the emergence of these

---

[30] On this detail see Moulton 1974:166; Page 1955:113-114; Eustathios 1969.60-65.

[31] As Heubeck 1954:44 observes, Zeus' call for ὅρκια πιστά (483) in *Odyssey* 24 inverts his actions in *Iliad* 4, where he causes the combatants in the Trojan War to defy sworn oaths (ὑπὲρ ὅρκια, 4.72) so that the narrative may continue.

[32] Thus for instance Heubeck *CHO* 3:412 ad 24.482-485 sees Zeus' settlement as being "of the greatest importance in the history of ideas: it means nothing less than the abolition of the law of the blood-feud;" similarly Erbse 1972:140. Yet the simple fact that Zeus' scheme is in its stated terms impracticable without the supernatural element suggests that Homeric society was meant to recall a time when resources for managing such conflicts were limited.

apparently contradictory themes here betrays the operation of an organizing principle in the context of which the implacability of Odysseus and Athene, and the death of Eupeithes, are on some level necessary.

Eupeithes' unique culpability has been remarked on above: he leads the anti-Odyssean faction and has sired the most egregious suitor. He is in addition guilty of rank ingratitude, having himself on an earlier occasion sought and obtained Odysseus' protection from an Ithakan mob (16.424-430).[33] Eupeithes' sins, then, are over-determined. The *Odyssey* seems to imply that, even with the *eklēsis*, Ithakan society will be better without him. Or perhaps the crucial point is that the one character described as possessed of "pain that cannot be forgotten" (ἄλαστον πένθος, 423) has been forcibly excluded from Zeus' settlement.

That Eupeithes is made detestable, and that his death represents the last moment of violence before the community is restored to harmony, are details that seem to align him with the traditional figure of the scapegoat. The scapegoating ritual, which has been documented in many cultures, in ancient Greece involved the promotion of a debased individual to elevated status, followed his expulsion from the community amid verbal and physical abuse. In a number of cases, myths trace the ritual back to an original sacrifice on behalf of the community.[34]

Among the themes in *Odyssey* 24 that bear comparison to scapegoating rituals in ancient Greece is the path Eupeithes travels. He first appears in the center of the community, the agora (24.420), and then proceeds beyond the perimeter of the *polis* (πρὸ ἄστεος, 468), where he is killed. Similarly, in Athens, Chaeronea, and Massilia, for example, the scapegoat was led in procession from the public hearth through and out of the city.[35] Also, Eupeithes, like sacrificial victims in general, proceeds willingly to his doom.[36] Further, his death (like those of the suitors) occurs during or soon after a year-end festival of Apollo, with which may be compared scapegoating in the Attic year-end festival of

---

[33] Since this incident in Book 16 constructs Odysseus and Eupeithes as guest-friends, *xenoi* (cf. Eustathios 1807.10; Nagy 1979:233), the latter can further be said to transgress institutions presided over by Zeus Xenios, on which see Chapter 6.

[34] For the scapegoat theme see Seaford 1994:130-131; 312-318; Burkert 1985:82-84; Bremmer 1983 with extensive ancient references. To be sure, Eupeithes lacks some common features of ancient Greek scapegoats: his status is compromised neither by his looks or his birth; he dies by the hand of a single man, rather than the collective violence of the crowd; nor is he beaten about the genitals with the branches of an *arbor infelix*.

[35] Bremmer 1983:312-315; Burkert 1979:64-67.

[36] Cf. Bremmer 1983:307-308; Burkert 1983:137-138.

Apollo known as the Thargeleia.[37] Lastly, Zeus' stipulation of "wealth in abundance" for the Ithakans (486) suggests the main purpose of the ritual, that of ensuring the future harvest and the prosperity of the community generally.[38]

Though not culpable to the degree that their leader is, the rest of the suitors' kin are nevertheless guilty for their failure, first to restrain their sons' unlawful behavior, and second to heed the warnings of Halitherses and Medon against seeking *tisis*. Parallels with the crew, the Phaiakes, and their own children imply that the suitors' kin should also perish to a man. Their survival can perhaps in this respect be understood as having been purchased through the death of Eupeithes, on whom collective guilt is cast.

In ancient Greek ritual, scapegoating preserves the memory of past reciprocal violence by making it part of the ritual calendar and channels the economy of *tisis* into an act of restoration, rather than fragmentation, for the community as a whole. I note however that, while the ending of the *Odyssey* may draw on themes associated with scapegoating rituals, the narrative distances itself from any aitiological implications by opting for a solution that does not appear to require maintenance through cult. For Zeus' *eklēsis*, rather than transmuting reciprocal violence into ritual violence, instead redirects it into another vessel, Panhellenic epic. Figuratively speaking, antithetical Odysseus-traditions are sacrificed so that Homeric authority may live forever.

Chapter conclusions: the End(s) of the *Odyssey*

I hope to have demonstrated in this chapter that Zeus' role at the end of the *Odyssey*, far from being non-Homeric, awkward, or ad hoc, brings to a culmination themes that have run through the narrative. The theme of reciprocal violence at the end of the *Odyssey* is deployed in order to maintain dramatic tension, which is resolved by supernatural means. Further, the limited perspectives that are evinced by Athene in Books 1 and 5, and by

[37] On scapegoat ritual in the Thargeleia, see Bremmer 1983:318-319. On the Apollo festival as the context for the *Mnesterophonia*, see Cook 1995:150-152; Austin 1975:239-253; Murray 1934:211-212. It may be significant that the scapegoat's expulsion during the Attic Thargeleia took place on the supposed anniversary of the fall of Troy, for the ritual calendar may have suggested thematic parallels between Odysseus' taking of both Troy and Ithake by stratagem; thus Bremmer *loc. cit.*, citing Hellanikos *FGrH* 4 F 152a and Damastes *FGrH* 5 F 7.

[38] Cf. Burkert 1985:82-84; Bremmer 1983:301-303. Another, less compelling parallel may be mentioned here: the Ithakans' turning back toward the city (πρὸς δὲ πόλιν τρωπῶντο, 536) when Athene intervenes may suggest the custom of returning to the community without looking back after expulsion of the victim; see Bremmer 315, citing Lot's wife in Genesis and Aischylos *Choephoroi* 98.

Poseidon in Books 5 and 13, are again brought into alignment with Zeus' overarching perspective, which defines the contours of the Odyssean narrative in part by limiting or re-channeling the subordinate gods' partisan desires to inflict massive suffering on mortal characters. In this respect, Eupeithes' death could be seen as a concession by Zeus to Athene, analogous to Poseidon being "allowed" to send the storm in Book 5 and to petrify the Phaiakes' ship in Book 13. Zeus' ability to control human memory and divine behavior, I suggested, has meaningful analogies in the functions performed by singers of epics like the *Odyssey*.

Though I defer my broader conclusions about the overall *Dios boulē* in the *Odyssey* until Chapter 6, it will be useful to anticipate one of them here. The relationship between Zeus' last speech in Book 24 and "post-Odyssean" events can be seen as analogous to that between his first speech and the "pre-Odyssean" killing of Aigisthos in Book 1, which in part frame the *Odyssey* with respect to non-Homeric *Nostoi* traditions. That is, in like manner as Zeus abstracts Odyssean thematics from the Oresteia-paradigm in order to establish the beginning of the narrative, so his extension of Odyssean thematics to the "post-*Odyssey*" consequences of the *Mnesterophonia* brings dramatic closure at the end. Thus Zeus' omission of the consequences of Orestes' revenge in his Oresteia is itself polemical, since the omission raises in advance the question of how the paradigm can be made consistent with any limit on a man's sufferings at the hands of others in a world where the institution of the vendetta is pervasive and judicial remedies inadequate. The *Odyssey*'s answer to this contradiction is to identify the supernatural justice of Zeus with the dramatic conclusion of Odysseus' story. And this strategy, as I shall discuss in the next chapter, helps to obviate complicated engagements with epichoric traditions that narrated the consequences of the *Mnesterophonia*.

4

AFTER THE *ODYSSEY*

Z EUS' SETTLEMENT at the end of the *Odyssey* is meant to be permanent: Odysseus will "be ruler forever" (βασιλευέτω αἰεί, 24.483). Of course, this cannot come to pass literally; even the divinely favored Menelaos must cede Sparta and retire to Elysion (*Odyssey* 4.561-564). The clear implication is that Odysseus will rule Ithake until his death, at which point his heir will assume power.[1] Zeus' further stipulation that Ithake is to be peaceful and prosperous (24.486) also implies that Odysseus' line will proceed through orderly succession from father to son, without the disruptions that result from struggles for power among legitimate brothers, bastards and pretenders.

Indeed the *Odyssey* elsewhere represents Odysseus' family as so predisposed. Asked by the disguised Odysseus why no brothers help him to oppose the suitors (16.97-98), Telemachos asserts:

> ὧδε γὰρ ἡμετέρην γενεὴν μούνωσε Κρονίων·
> μοῦνον Λαέρτην Ἀρκείσιος υἱὸν ἔτικτε,
> μοῦνον δ᾽ αὖτ᾽ Ὀδυσῆα πατὴρ τέκεν· αὐτὰρ Ὀδυσσεὺς
> μοῦνον ἔμ᾽ ἐν μεγάροισι τεκὼν λίπεν.

> For thus our line the son of Kronos made single:
> Laertes was the only son Arkeisios bore,
> and again Odysseus was the only son his own father bore;
>   and again Odysseus
> bore me only in his halls before he left.

> *Odyssey* 16.117-120

---

[1] As is for instance the case with Aeneas: νῦν δὲ δὴ Αἰνείαο βίη Τρώεσσι ἀνάξει/καὶ παίδων παῖδες, τοί κεν μετόπισθε γένωνται, *Iliad* 20.307-308; similarly *Homeric Hymn to Aphrodite* 196-197.

Apart from the simple fact that Telemachos is an only son, this information is superfluous in the immediate context of Book 16, and seems motivated in part by the irony of having the son tell family lore to his own disguised father. But the ornate rhetoric, in particular the jingly anaphora built around *moun-*'only, single' suggests a more significant function. That function, I shall argue, is to be found in the implications of Telemachos' statement for the *Odyssey*'s relationship to non-Homeric traditions.

For, unlike the Homeric Odysseus, the non-Homeric Odysseus leaves a legacy comparable to that of Herakles, namely a host of *epigonoi*, sons born of various women and goddesses in various locations apart from the hero's home and sanctioned marriage. The offspring that the *Odyssey* denies its hero appear in contexts as diverse as Cyclic epic, mythography, Athenian drama, and Aristotelian political theory. The *Odyssey*'s choice to construct Odysseus' family as one characterized by unilineal descent can, I suggest, be explained in part by the fact that branching of the family tree would on the one hand compli-cate Zeus', or any, vision of a peaceful Ithake ruled by the house of Odysseus, and on the other hand would establish unwanted connections to epichoric versions of Odysseus' story.[2] There may, then, be further irony in the fact that the recipient of Telemachos' genealogical account is not only his father, but his father in the guise of a disseminator of false tales about Odysseus.

I suggested in the last chapter that the *Odyssey*'s aim to have the last word on Odysseus extends beyond its own narrative bounds, to the point of mapping out its hero's "post-*Odyssey*" life, that is, events in his mythical biography that fall after the main narrative of the Homeric epic. The task is a formidable one, for Odysseus' heroic identity resists closure, as for instance Dante and Kazantzakis perceived. As discussed in the Introduction, the Homeric project of forging a definitive, Panhellenic account of Odysseus faced a challenge in a "fact" of his larger mythological identity that militates against his story ending with the *Mnesterophonia*. For in every known version of Odysseus' story, the *Odyssey* included, the hero always leaves Ithake again after he kills the suitors.[3]

In this chapter I explore the manner in which non-Homeric Odysseus-traditions realize the hero's post-*Odyssey* adventures. Particular attention is

---

[2] Again, cf. Aineias, whose family is similarly characterized (at least until Romulus and Remus); *Iliad* 20.215-240. "Unilineal descent" here refers to the male line, along which family inheri-tance normally descended in ancient Greek literature and society; Odysseus does have a sister (*Odyssey* 15.363).

[3] Thus Lord 1960:182-183 observes that "everything in oral tradition points to the conclusion that . . . there should be departure from Penelope and another visit to that strange world from which the hero had been rescued or released."

paid to three themes that recur in these stories: Odysseus' exile, his siring of children other than Telemachos, and his death by violence or away from home. The *Odyssey* rejects these themes explicitly, but nevertheless preserves them in "false" tales and in allusions to discarded narrative possibilities. I then conclude by proposing that that the association of these non-Homeric accounts with major religious centers in west Greece may explain the *Odyssey*'s need to engage with them.

Odysseus after the *Odyssey*

The *Odyssey*'s conception of the journey Odysseus must take after his return is revealed, not at the end of the narrative, but near the middle, in the prophecy the hero receives from Teiresias. Once you have killed the suitors, Teiresias tells Odysseus,

> ἔρχεσθαι δὴ ἔπειτα, λαβὼν εὐῆρες ἐρετμόν,
> εἰς ὅ κε τοὺς ἀφίκηαι, οἳ οὐκ ἴσασι θάλασσαν ...
> καὶ τότε δὴ γαίηι πήξας εὐῆρες ἐρετμόν,
> ῥέξας ἱερὰ καλὰ Ποσειδάωνι ἄνακτι ...
> οἴκαδ' ἀποστείχειν ἔρδειν θ' ἱερὰς ἑκατόμβας
> ἀθανάτοισι θεοῖσι.

> Go then, taking a well-made oar,
> until you reach those who do not know the sea ...
> and then in the earth fix the well-made oar.
> When you have made pleasing sacrifices to lord Poseidon ...
> return home and dedicate sacred hekatombs
> to the deathless gods.
>
> > *Odyssey* 11.121-122, 129-130, 132-133 (cf. 23.269-281)

Through the appointed rituals, the hero will bring to an end his protracted conflict with his divine antagonist by entering the god's service, in which respect Odysseus resembles such figures as Erechtheus.[4] The transformation of Odysseus' relationship with Poseidon seems also a necessary precondition of Zeus' settlement for Ithake in Book 24, since a community of islanders depends naturally on a good relationship with the sea god (as the Phaiakes

---

[4] Odysseus' propitiation of Poseidon is in part a dramatization of the spread of the god's cults; thus Malkin 1998:120-126; Nagy 1990a:231-232; Heubeck *CHO* 2:84-85 ad 11.121-37; Hartmann 1917:73-75, 91. On Erechtheus, Poseidon, and Odysseus, see Cook 1995:128-170.

illustrate in Book 13). And while the predicted journey far inland seems likely to be arduous, no hazards or intrigues are noted, and Odysseus' safe return is guaranteed.

An important function of this part of Teiresias' prophecy, I suggest, is to explain the "fact" of the obligatory journey as a mere tidying up of the *Odyssey*'s own loose ends and to render it otherwise consistent with the themes that are identified with Zeus in the main narrative. In other words, since the larger tradition demands a post-*Mnesterophonia* voyage, the *Odyssey* realizes that voyage in terms that help to bring closure without pointing the way to a new series of adventures. The voyage likewise has no connection with the killing of the suitors, in which respect Odysseus is again assimilated to Zeus' Orestes, whose revenge is uncomplicated by guilt, retribution from mortals, or opposition from gods. As Odysseus describes it, the projected journey hints at the exotic locales that the proem associates with the *Apologoi* (compare 23.267 with 1.3); but Zeus' settlement circumscribes these adventures by reducing them to the victory lap of a blessed and pious man, leaving no purchase for sequels that would compromise Zeus' theodicy.

Similarly poor in dramatic possibilities is the death scenario that Teiresias reveals to Odysseus. Again, this scenario, or rather range of scenarios, is linked thematically to Zeus' settlement (the brackets are meant to preserve significant ambiguities in translation):

> θάνατος δέ τοι ἐξ ἁλὸς αὐτῶι
> ἀβληχρὸς μάλα τοῖος ἐλεύσεται, ὅς κέ σε πέφνηι
> γήραι ὕπο λιπαρῶι ἀρημένον· ἀμφὶ δὲ λαοὶ
> ὄλβιοι ἔσσονται.

> Your own death will be [far from/away from/out of] the sea,
> a very [gentle/feeble] sort it will be when it comes, which
>   kills you
> when you are worn out by sleek old age; and around you the
>   people
> will be prosperous.

> *Odyssey* 11.134b-137a (cf. 23.281-284)

The sympathy between Teiresias' prophecy and Zeus' settlement is evident in the stipulation that "the people will be prosperous" when Odysseus dies (cf 24.486). Further, Teiresias' scenario of a peaceful death, in old age, and during a time of prosperity, implies the seamless transfer of power from ruler to son Odysseus to Telemachos, that Zeus' settlement implies.

An altogether different death-scenario features in a number of the non-Homeric traditions to which I have alluded already. In these accounts, further significant adventures await Odysseus after the *Mnesterophonia*, including exile, marriage into another royal house, fathering of *epigonoi*, generalship in another war, and death either violent or abroad. One of the better known of these traditions in antiquity is represented by the Cyclic *Telegony*:

οἱ μνήστορες ὑπὸ τῶν προσηκόντων θάπτονται. καὶ Ὀδυσσεὺς θύσας Νύμφαις εἰς Ἦλιν ἀποπλεῖ ἐπισκεψόμενος τὰ βουκόλια καὶ ξενίζεται παρὰ Πολυξένωι δῶρόν τε λαμβάνει κρατῆρα, καὶ ἐπὶ τούτωι τὰ περὶ Τροφώνιον [5] καὶ Ἀγαμήδην καὶ Αὐγέαν.

ἔπειτα εἰς Ἰθάκην καταπλεύσας τὰς ὑπὸ Τειρεσίου ῥηθείσας τελεῖ θυσίας. καὶ μετὰ ταῦτα εἰς Θεσπρωτοὺς ἀφικνεῖται καὶ γαμεῖ Καλλιδίκην βασιλίδα τῶν Θεσπρωτῶν.

ἔπειτα πόλεμος συνίσταται τοῖς Θεσπρωτοῖς πρὸς Βρύγους, Ὀδυσσέως [10] ἡγουμένου· ἐνταῦθα Ἄρης τοὺς περὶ τὸν Ὀδυσσέα τρέπεται, καὶ αὐτῶι εἰς μάχην Ἀθηνᾶ καθίσταται· τούτους μὲν Ἀπόλλων διαλύει. μετὰ δὲ τὴν Καλλιδίκης τελευτὴν τὴν μὲν βασιλείαν διαδέχεται Πολυποίτης Ὀδυσσέως υἱός, αὐτὸς δ' εἰς Ἰθάκην ἀφικνεῖται. κἂν τούτωι Τηλέγονος ἐπὶ ζήτησιν τοῦ πατρὸς πλέων ἀποβὰς εἰς τὴν Ἰθάκην τέμνει τὴν νῆσον· [15] ἐκβοηθήσας δ' Ὀδυσσεὺς ὑπὸ τοῦ παιδὸς ἀναιρεῖται κατ' ἄγνοιαν. Τηλέγονος δ' ἐπιγνοὺς τὴν ἁμαρτίαν τό τε τοῦ πατρὸς σῶμα καὶ τὸν Τηλέμαχον καὶ τὴν Πηνελόπην πρὸς τὴν μητέρα μεθίστησιν· ἡ δὲ αὐτοὺς ἀθανάτους ποιεῖ, καὶ συνοικεῖ τῆι μὲν Πηνελόπηι Τηλέγονος, Κίρκηι δὲ Τηλέμαχος.

The suitors are buried by their relations. And Odysseus, having sacrificed to the Nymphs, sails to Elis, intending to look over his herds; and he is entertained by Polyxenos, and receives as a gift a mixing bowl, upon which are the stories of Trophonios [5] and Agamede and Augeas.

Then Odysseus sails to Ithake and performs the sacrifices spoken of by Teiresias. And after this he makes his way to the Thesprotians and marries Kallidike queen of the Thesprotians.

Then war breaks out with the Thesprotians against the Brygoi, and Odysseus [10] serves as commander; then Ares puts to flight those around Odysseus, and Athene engages him [Ares] in battle;

but Apollo parts them. Afterward Kallidike dies, and Polypoites, Odysseus' son [by her], receives the kingdom, and Odysseus himself makes his way to Ithake. At this point Telegonos, on a voyage in search of his father, reaches Ithake and attacks the island; [15] and when Odysseus comes to the defense, he is killed by his own son, who acts in ignorance. And Telegonos realizes his mistake and brings his father's body, along with Telemachos and Penelope, to his mother [Kirke]; and she makes them immortal, and Telegonos marries Penelope, and Telemachos marries Kirke.

Proklos 101.1-103.20 Bernabé, 109.5-27 Allen

A similar tradition is preserved in "Apollodoros": Odysseus, after killing the suitors,

θύσας δὲ Ἅιδηι καὶ Περσεφόνηι καὶ Τειρεσίαι, πεζῆι διὰ τῆς Ἠπείρου βαδίζων εἰς Θεσπρωτοὺς παραγίνεται καὶ κατὰ τὰς Τειρεσίου μαντείας θυσιάσας ἐξιλάσκεται Ποσειδῶνα. ἡ δὲ βασιλεύουσα τότε Θεσπρωτῶν Καλλιδίκη καταμένειν αὐτὸν ἠξίου τὴν βασιλείαν αὐτῶι δοῦσα. [35] καὶ συνελθοῦσα αὐτῶι γεννᾶι Πολυποίτην. γήμας δὲ Καλλιδίκην Θεσπρωτῶν ἐβασίλευσε καὶ μάχηι τῶν περιοίκων νικᾶι τοὺς ἐπιστρατεύσαντας. Καλλιδίκης δὲ ἀποθανούσης, τῶι παιδὶ τὴν βασιλείαν ἀποδιδοὺς εἰς Ἰθάκην παραγίνεται, καὶ εὑρίσκει ἐκ Πηνελόπης Πολιπόρθην αὐτῶι γεγεννημένον. [36] Τηλέγονος δὲ παρὰ Κίρκης μαθὼν ὅτι παῖς Ὀδυσσέως ἐστίν, ἐπὶ τὴν τούτου ζήτησιν ἐκπλεῖ. παραγενόμενος δὲ εἰς Ἰθάκην τὴν νῆσον ἀπελαύνει τινὰ τῶν βοσκημάτων, καὶ Ὀδυσσέα βοηθοῦντα τῶι μετὰ χεῖρας δόρατι Τηλέγονος <τρυγόνος> κέντρον τὴν αἰχμὴν ἔχοντι τιτρώσκει, καὶ Ὀδυσσεὺς θνήσκει. [37] ἀναγνωρισάμενος δὲ αὐτὸν καὶ πολλὰ κατοδυράμενος, τὸν νεκρὸν <καὶ> τὴν Πηνελόπην πρὸς Κίρκην ἄγει, κἀκεῖ τὴν Πενηελόπην γαμεῖ. Κίρκη δὲ ἑκατέρους αὐτοὺς εἰς Μακάρων νήσους ἀποστέλλει.

Sacrifices to Hades and Persephone and Teiresias, and going on foot through Epeiros arrives among the Thesprotians, and, in accordance with the prophecies of Teiresias, propitiates Poseidon with sacrifices. And the queen of the Thesprotians at the time, Kallidike, thought it right that he remain and gave to him the kingdom. [35] And joining with him she begets Polypoites. And having wed Kallidike he became king of the Thesprotians and in battle conquered those of the neighboring peoples who made war. And

Kallidike dies, so Odysseus hands the kingdom over to his son and proceeds to Ithake, and finds his son by Penelope, Poliporthes. [36] And Telegonos learns from Kirke that he is the child of Odysseus, and sails off in search of him. And having arrived at the island of Ithake he drives off some of the herds, and Odysseus goes to defend them, and Telegonos wounds him with a spear tipped with a point of <a stingray>[5]and Odysseus dies. [37] And recognizing him [Telegonos] laments much, and brings the body <and> Penelope to Kirke, and there marries Penelope. And Kirke sends them both to the islands of the Blessed.

"Apollodoros" *Epitome* 7.34-37

Though it has no part in Homeric tradition, Telegonos' story did evolve sufficiently to take a variety of forms, including references in Hesiodic epic and Attic tragedy.[6] Again, even if these specific accounts post-date the *Odyssey*, the latter at least evinces awareness of similar themes.[7] On the one hand, this awareness is betrayed through wholesale de-authorization, as in the case of Telemachos' assertion and Zeus' settlement. But the *Odyssey* also appears to target themes specific to antithetical versions of its hero's story.

Particularly suggestive in this latter respect is the connection between Odysseus and Thesprotia, the land of his non-Homeric exile, in the *Odyssey*. No Thesprotian characters or settings occur in the main narrative, but they do feature in a group of inset narratives, most of which the *Odyssey* constructs as false. To begin with, Thesprotia is one of the settings in the "Cretan tales," the lies that Odysseus tells after he has returned to Ithake disguised as a beggar.[8]

---

[5] The conjecture is based on such evidence as scholia to *Odyssey* 11.134. The *Odyssey* may allude to this tradition when Odysseus, after being wrecked by Poseidon, fears a god will send a sea monster against him (κῆτος, 5.421); note also the potential pun in the name of one of Odysseus' adversaries in the *Apologoi*, the Laistrygones (Λαιστρυγόνες).

[6] *Theogony* 1011-1014; see Frazer 1921 v. 2:303-305n2 for further references. Telemachos' absence from some of these accounts is consistent with traditions in which he leaves home to marry Nausikaa and live with the Phaiakes, on which see further below.

[7] Thus Kullmann 1980:76-79 suggests that the *Telegony* and *Odyssey* draw on conflicting *alte Motive*. A relatively early date for the former is supported by, e.g. Malkin 1998:126-133; Danek 1997:286; Schwartz 1924:134-156.

[8] My argument here parallels that of Malkin 1998:125-134 (quote from 125), who, drawing on the work of Merkelbach, proposes that the Cretan tales "may 'argue against' other versions of the *Odyssey* or may simply reflect them as (ironic and intertextual?) alternatives." Reece 1994 offers an analysis of the Cretan tales in terms that, while similar, rely on neither Merkelbach's multiple-poet theory nor Malkin's early dating of the *Odyssey* ("the *Odyssey*, as we know it, existed in the ninth century," 45).

A connection between Ithake and Thesprotia is natural, given their geographic proximity. The *Odyssey* seems to have exploited Thesprotia not simply as a geographically convenient setting, however, but as a kind of geographical symbol for a rich body of epichoric Odysseus-traditions that were current across the adjacent west Greek mainland.

In the Cretan tales, the disguised Odysseus tells Eumaios, and later Penelope, that he has recently visited Thesprotia and there received information about "Odysseus" (the disguised Odysseus' third-person representation of himself):

ἔνθα με Θεσπρωτῶν βασιλεὺς ἐκομίσσατο Φείδων . . .
ἔνθ' Ὀδυσῆος ἐγὼ πυθόμην· κεῖνος γὰρ ἔφασκε
ξεινίσαι ἠδὲ φιλῆσαι ἰόντ' ἐς πατρίδα γαῖαν·
καί μοι κτήματ' ἔδειξεν, ὅσα ξυναγείρατ' Ὀδυσσεύς . . .
τὸν δ' ἐς Δωδώνην φάτο βήμεναι, ὄφρα θεοῖο
ἐκ δρυὸς ὑψικόμοιο Διὸς βουλὴν ἐπακούσηι,
ὅππως νοστήσηι Ἰθάκης ἐς πίονα δῆμον,
ἤδη δὴν ἀπεών, ἢ ἀμφαδὸν ἦε κρυφηδόν.   330
ὤμοσε δὲ πρὸς ἔμ' αὐτόν, ἀποσπένδων ἐνὶ οἴκωι,
νῆα κατειρύσθαι καὶ ἐπαρτέας ἔμμεν ἑταίρους,
οἳ δή μιν πέμψουσι φίλην ἐς πατρίδα γαῖαν.

There the king of the Thesprotians, Pheidon, entertained
    me . . .
there I myself heard about Odysseus; for he kept saying
that he had hosted Odysseus and treated him kindly as
    he was going to his paternal land;
and he showed me possessions that Odysseus had
    gathered . . .
and he said that he had gone to Dodona, so that from
    the god's
lofty-leafed oak he might learn the plan of Zeus
    (*Dios boulē*),
how he would return home to the rich people
    of Ithake,
having already been away for a long time, either
    openly or in secret.   [330]
And he [Pheidon] swore to me myself as he was
    pouring libations in his house,
that a ship had been drawn down [to the sea] and

comrades were ready,
who will send him to his own paternal land.

Odyssey 14.316, 321-323, 327-333
(cf. 19.195-202; 14.325-330~19.294-299)

Such a mission would be plausible to Homeric audiences since historical Dodona was the site of a well-known oracle of Zeus. The question that "Odysseus" is to ask Zeus' tree-oracle at Dodona, regarding how he should arrive on Ithake, is reproduced in Teiresias' prophecy, which also admits the possibility of Odysseus' "open" return (again, ἠὲ δόλωι ἢ ἀμφαδὸν ὀξέι χαλκῶι, 11.120; cf. 14.330=19.299). Likewise, Nestor suggests to Telemachos that his father may return and exact *tisis* from the suitors "either alone or all the Achaians as well" (ἢ ὅ γε μοῦνος ἐὼν ἢ καὶ σύμπαντες Ἀχαιοί, 3.217).[9] What "Odysseus" is apparently pondering in these lying tales is the possibility of returning at the head of an army, for Pheidon has offered ships and men to aid in his repatriation. He is however leaving it to Zeus to decide the terms of his return, which is to say that control over the course of this ersatz Odyssey rests, as over that of the main narrative, with Zeus.

That "Odysseus" would return as a military commander seems in any case the natural consequence of an "open" arrival on Ithake. If the hero sails into the harbor with a company of soldiers, the situation will resemble that in Mykene at Agamemnon's return from Troy: those who have taken over the hero's *oikos* in his absence will be compelled either to relinquish it to him or, more likely, to face him and his escort in battle. The military return scenario also figures in another false tale told by another wandering liar, an Aitolian who, according to Eumaios, has earlier claimed that Odysseus would soon return "with godly comrades" (σὺν ἀντιθέοις ἑτάροισι, 14.385).[10]

In this light, it may be significant that Odysseus is represented elsewhere in the *Odyssey* as hostile to the Thesprotians, or at least aligned with their enemies, a people known as the Taphians. In a story mentioned in Chapter 3, Odysseus takes the side of Eupeithes when the latter incites the anger of the Ithakan *dēmos* by aiding the Taphians in their attacks on Thesprotia (16.424-430). Similarly, Athene, in disguise as Mentes, the leader of the Taphians (1.105; cf. 419), claims a guest-friendship relationship with Odysseus

---

[9] The *Odyssey*'s "false" story of Odysseus' Thesprotian visit prior to killing the suitors may also help to explicate the fragmentary *Telegony*, since it suggests a previously-established relationship with the Thesprotians as the reason why the hero takes up residence there, rather than in Elis, his first stop after leaving Ithake.

[10] On the Aitolian liar's tale as a "false" *Odyssey*, see Marks 2003:214-217.

(1.187; cf. 180-181, 259-264); and Odysseus' slave Eumaios purchases a slave of his own from Taphian merchant-pirates (14.449-452, though he does so without consulting those in charge of Odysseus' *oikos*). The "real" Odysseus, then, seems to favor the Taphian enemies of the Thesprotians, while the "false" Odysseus is a Thesprotian ally, potentially to the point of relying on Thesprotian forces to defeat the suitors. Even in the "false" story, Pheidon's subjects turn on Odysseus after they set sail for Ithake (14.337-347).[11] The message seems to be that Thesprotians are untrustworthy as are, by extension, narratives in which they appear.

A distinguishing characteristic of these "false" and non-Homeric accounts is a messy, "real-world" staging and outcome of Odysseus' return, which again stands in contrast with Zeus' *eklēsis*. This "false" scenario corresponds to a recurrent theme in ancient Greek myth and history: an ousted king or tyrant has himself reinstalled by the military forces of a neighboring ruler. Such a return is a recipe for a fleeting victory and a protracted struggle, on analogy of for instance the Theban saga or the career of the Peisistratids in historical Athens.

These messy, real-world themes include Odysseus' exile. According to another passage from "Apollodoros":

εἰσὶ δὲ οἱ λέγοντες ἐγκαλούμενον Ὀδυσσέα ὑπὸ τῶν οἰκείων ὑπὲρ τῶν ἀπολωλότων δικαστὴν Νεοπτόλεμον λαβεῖν τὸν βασιλεύοντα τῶν κατὰ τὴν Ἤπειρον νήσων, τοῦτον δέ, νομίσαντα ἐκποδὼν Ὀδυσσέως γενομένου Κεφαλληνίαν καθέξειν, κατακρῖναι φυγὴν αὐτοῦ, Ὀδυσσέα δὲ εἰς Αἰτωλίαν πρὸς Θόαντα τὸν Ἀνδραίμονος παραγενόμενον τὴν τούτου θυγατέρα γῆμαι, καὶ καταλιπόντα παῖδα Λεοντοφόνον ἐκ ταύτης γηραιὸν τελευτῆσαι.

But some say that Odysseus was prosecuted by the [suitors'] kin because of the dead, and that he took Neoptolemos, king of the islands around Epeiros, as judge, and that the latter, thinking that, with Odysseus out of the way, he would lay hold of Kephallenia,

---

[11] Note the undercurrent of class distinction here: the split between Odysseus and the rest of the Ithakans in attitudes toward Thesprotians is reproduced in the contrast between the positive valorization of king Pheidon in stark contrast with his subjects.

pronounced a judgment of exile, on account of which Odysseus came to Aitolia to Thoas, son of Andraimon, married his daughter, and, having left behind a child begotten of her, Leontophonos, died of old age.

"Apollodoros" Epitome 7.40

A fragment from the Aristotelian *Constitution of the Ithakans* preserves a related account:

τῶι Ὀδυσσεῖ μετὰ τὴν μνηστηροφονίαν οἱ ἐπιτήδειοι τῶν τεθνηκότων ἐπανέστησαν, [20] μεταπεμφθεὶς δ' ὑπ' ἀμφοτέρων διαιτητὴς Νεοπτόλεμος ἐδικαίωσε τὸν μὲν Ὀδυσσέα μεταναστῆναι καὶ φεύγειν ἐκ τῆς Κεφαλληνίας καὶ Ζακύνθου καὶ Ἰθάκης ἐφ' αἵματι, τοὺς δὲ τῶν μνηστήρων ἑταίρους καὶ οἰκείους ἀποφέρειν ποινὴν Ὀδυσσεῖ τῶν εἰς τὸν οἶκον ἀδικημάτων καθ' ἕκαστον ἐνιαυτόν. [25] αὐτὸς μὲν οὖν εἰς Ἰταλίαν μετέστη, τὴν δὲ ποινὴν τῶι υἱῶι καθιερώσας ἀποφέρειν ἐκέλευσε τοὺς Ἰθακησίους· ἦν δ' ἄλφιτα, οἶνος, κηρία, ἔλαιον, ἅλες, ἱερεῖα πρεσβύτερα φαγίλων. . . . τοὺς δὲ περὶ Εὔμαιον ἐλευθερώσας ὁ Τηλέμαχος κατέμιξεν [30] εἰς τοὺς πολίτας καὶ τὸ γένος ἐστὶ Κολιαδῶν ἀπ' Εὐμαίου καὶ Βουκολιδῶν ἀπὸ Φιλοιτίου.

After the killing of the suitors the relations of the dead rose up against Odysseus, [20] and Neoptolemos was sent for as an arbitrator by both sides and he gave a judgment that Odysseus was to depart and go into exile from Kephallenia and Zakynthos and Ithake for the killing, and that the companions and relations of the suitors were to pay yearly damages to Odysseus for the injustices done to his house. [25] He himself therefore moved to Italy, and transferred the payments to his son, ordering the Ithakans to bring them to him. These were grain, wine, honeycombs, olive oil, salt, and sacrificial animals. . . . And Telemachos freed those associated with Eumaios and mingled [30] them with the citizens; and the Koliad clan is descended from Eumaios, the Boukolid clan from Philoitios.

Aristotle *Constitution of the Ithakans* fr. 507 Rose
(= Plutarch *Moralia* 294D)

As in the *Telegony*, Odysseus departs, marries into the royal family, and fathers *epigonoi*; here, however, he does not return.[12] Most importantly, the present passages make explicit that Odysseus departs Ithake as a direct consequence of the *Mnesterophonia*.

As discussed in Chapter 3, the possibility of Odysseus' exile is raised in the main narrative (23.118-122; 24.430-431), but only as something that cannot or must not happen. The theme of exile also recurs in the lying tales, when the disguised Odysseus claims to have been driven from Crete (cf. 13.266-286; 14.207-210). Inclusion of the Aitolian ruler Thoas in the "Apollodoros" account is suggestive in this context. Thoas is Odysseus' ally in the *Iliad*, but the feckless victim of a ruse by "Odysseus" in another of the lying tales (14.457-522).[13] As mentioned above, the one other Aitolian character in the *Odyssey* spreads "lies" about Odysseus' return. In these cases, I again suggest, the *Odyssey* deauthorizes themes that allude to its own alternatives by placing them in the mouths of negatively-valorized characters. Thus the lying Aitolian and foolish Thoas are meant to convey the idea that Aitolian themes are unreliable on the subject of Odysseus' post-*Odyssey* life.

Awareness of such possible outcomes to Odysseus' story highlights the significance of Zeus' *eklēsis*, and of the *Odyssey*'s preference for relatively more fantastic over more real-world or political themes generally. Human institutions cannot, from the *Odyssey*'s perspective, obtain for Odysseus the outcome that he deserves; and on this point at least the non-Homeric accounts agree, for the human Neoptolemos proves an interested and corruptible party to the negotiations, the exact opposite of Zeus.[14] In this respect the effectiveness of

---

[12] Eustathios 1796.50-51 cites an account in which Leontophonos (also known as Doryklos) is Odysseus' son by a Thesprotian named Euippe, and attributes to Sophokles a play in which the son is called Euryalos; cf. Parthenios *Romances* 3; Pausanias 8.12.5-7 (quoted in Chapter 1); see Hartmann 1917:206 for a tabulation, and 140-143 on Odysseus' exile. Other sons of Odysseus include Agrios and Latinos (by Kirke) and Nausithoos and Nausinoos (by Kalypso), Hesiod *Theogony* 1011-1018. The aforementioned version that includes the marriage of Nausikaa and Telemachos (e.g. Hesiod fr. 221 MW) can explain why Odysseus finds Poliporthes, not Telemachos, on his second return to Ithake, since the Phaiakian custom seems to be for the husband to relocate to the wife's *oikos* (cf. *Odyssey* 6.244-245). The statement by "Apollodoros" that Odysseus "left behind" a son (καταλιπόντα, *Epitome* 7.40), could imply physical departure (LSJ s.v. 1), but there is no indication that the hero leaves Aitolia in this strand of the myth.

[13] Odysseus and Thoas appear alternatively as allies and antagonists in Cyclic and Hesiodic epic; their relationship is the subject of Marks 2003.

[14] Neoptolemos' hostility here recreates that between his father Achilleus and Odysseus (e.g. *Odyssey* 8.75-82, *Iliad* 19.155-237); cf. Malkin 1998:101-102, 127-128; Nagy 1979:15-25. The *Odyssey* may be specifically undermining the possibility of a role for Neoptolemos in Odysseus' post-*Odyssey* life when it has him preparing to rule his father's kingdom in east Greece (4.5-9).

the Odyssean Zeus can be seen to reside in part in the relative impartiality that distinguishes him from Neoptolemos, as it does from Athene and Poseidon. Zeus stands above faction, his allegiance being to abstract principles: his plan, his theodicy, and, if my larger argument be accepted, the *Odyssey*'s Panhellenic program.

We are now in a position to appreciate a further dimension of Odysseus' death scenario as outlined by Teiresias in Book 11. As discussed, the seer generally reinforces the terms of Zeus' settlement, but his account of Odysseus' death retains ambiguities that suggest awareness of non-Homeric themes. Thus Teiresias does not make clear whether Odysseus dies on Ithake (though οἴκαδε at 11.132 could imply this) or elsewhere, thereby leaving open such possibilities as exile to Aitolia or Italy. Similar possibilities inhere in the prediction that the hero's death will be ἀβληχρός (135). This adjective is usually translated as "gentle" here, but elsewhere seems to mean "feeble" or "easily penetrated,"[15] and thus could equally describe the old Odysseus dying at Telegonos' hands on an Ithakan beach. Lastly, Teiresias predicts that Odysseus' demise will come ἐξ ἁλός (134), a prepositional phrase that can mean either "far from the sea" or "out of the sea." Teiresias' prophecy therefore can be reconciled either (1) with "Apollodoros'" Aitolian account, since Thoas' court could be conceived of as "far from the sea" at the inland Aitolian royal city of Kalydon, or (2) with the *Telegony*, in that Telegonos' attack comes from "out of the sea," or even (3) with the scenario in which a spine from a creature "from out of the sea," the stingray, is responsible for Odysseus' demise.[16] What Teiresias perceives, according to the model I am advancing, are realizations of the "facts" that remain possible in the notional moment before Zeus has translated them into narrative reality.

To sum up my conclusions thus far, then, a number of themes distance the *Odyssey* from non-Homeric accounts of Odysseus' life after the *Mnesterophonia*. The divine aid given the hero in killing the suitors contrasts with the aid of

---

[15] Homeric ἀβληχρός: Aphrodite's hand pierced by Diomedes, *Iliad*; 5.337, Hektor's assessment of the Greek fortifications, *Iliad* 8.178. Peradotto 1990:66 and 74 discusses the consequences of various translations of the adjective at *Odyssey* 11.135.

[16] Ancient interpretations of ἐξ ἁλός at *Odyssey* 11.134 are surveyed by Bernabé 1987:104-105 ad *Telegonia* fr. 4; cf. Frazer 1921 v. 2:304n2. Malkin's 1998:120-125 conclusions about this verse and the development of Thesprotian and Arkadian traditions in relation to a fixed *Odyssey* seem not to take into account the ambiguity of the phrase, which is nevertheless preserved in his translation (121). See Burgess 2001:153-154 for the *Odyssey*'s acknowledgement of the parallel traditions embraced by this ambiguity. Representative further discussion in Heubeck *CHO* 2:86 ad 11.134b-7; Nagy 1990b:214; Stanford 1965 v. 1:387 ad 11.134-5; Schwartz 1924:140-141; Hartmann 1917:73-75.

a foreign political power, divine adjudication with that of a mortal, *eklēsis* with exile,[17] the hero's peaceful death at home with one violent or abroad. From this perspective, Aitolia and Thesprotia are representative of locales that Odysseus might visit within the parameters of the "facts" of Odysseus-tradition, but that are however associated with stories about the hero that are incompatible with the Homeric version. There is in this respect a light touch to the *Odyssey*'s strategy of engagement with non-Homeric themes; for although Zeus' settlement in *Odyssey* 24 de-authorizes them en masse, their existence is nevertheless acknowledged obliquely. The *Odyssey* does not in other words condemn to oblivion the versions of its hero's story with which it conflicts, but rather frames them in Panhellenic terms: the stories are false, but serve a strategic function in the hero's success. In this manner the *Odyssey* affords to members of its audiences who may have attached cultic and genealogical significance to such stories the consolation that their traditions are not so much untrue as based on misperception of the stratagems of the "real" Odysseus.

The *Odyssey* and west Greek epichoric tradition

It is then my argument that the geographical references to west Greece in these non-Homeric Odysseus stories, and in the *Odyssey*'s "false" stories, suggest that the region may have been a locus of particularly vigorous epichoric Odysseus-traditions. While the relationship between poetical and "real" geography need not be so transparent, it is nevertheless unsurprising to find Odysseus-tradition flourishing in the area of the hero's reputed homeland. The considerable body of non-Homeric literary evidence, as well as material evidence, allows for a fairly detailed examination of the relationship between the west Greek references in the *Odyssey* and the kinds of epichoric and proto-Panhellenic traditions with which the Homeric narrative may have engaged.

My purpose here is not to assess the accuracy of the Homeric view of west Greece. Rather, I survey the region with an eye to contexts in which stories about Odysseus may have been performed and disseminated. Admittedly, the evidence discussed here allows for a number of plausible reconstructions, but it is nevertheless possible to recover at least the broad outlines of the shadowy traditions that, by my interpretation, exerted a significant influence

---

[17] Malkin 1998:123-125 contrasts Zeus' erasure of memory in *Odyssey* 24 with "realistic options of exile."

on the Homeric conception of Odysseus. Ithake not surprisingly offers abundant connections with the hero. I further propose that Thesprotia and Aitolia appear as important settings in accounts of Odysseus' non-Homeric exile, and in de-authorized accounts of Odysseus in the *Odyssey*, because of the associations of these regions with the two major religious centers in ancient west Greece, the oracle of Zeus at Dodona and the cult of Zeus at Olympia, sites that could have served as the foci of regional Odysseus-traditions.

Ithake

The archaeological record makes clear that Odysseus received cult honors at a cave on Polis Bay on the northwest coast of Ithake. It is true that the earliest unmistakable material evidence for this cult is Hellenistic, and that dedications to Here and Athene at the site preceded or coexisted with this evidence.[18] Nevertheless, Odysseus is probably among the figures to be identified with a marked increase in activity at the Polis Bay site in the late ninth or the eighth century, at which time – before, by most accounts, the Homeric narratives had stabilized – tripods began to be deposited in the cave. These tripods have from their first discovery been compared with a reference in the *Odyssey* to a cave dedicated to local nymphs where Odysseus stores his gifts from the Phaiakes, which include tripods (cf. *Odyssey* 13.217-218, 345-350, 362-364).[19]

Given the relatively small size and population of ancient Ithake, Polis Cave was probably connected to other local cults.[20] Thus the site may have formed part of a system that included a precinct of (probably) Apollo at Aetos some 10 miles to the south, which reveals a similar pattern of activity and could in turn be linked to Odysseus through a tradition that the suitors are killed during a festival of Apollo (cf. *Odyssey* 21.267-268).[21] Likewise, reference to yearly contributions of "grain, wine, honeycombs, olive oil, salt, and sacrificial animals" to the house of Odysseus in the Aristotelian *Constitution of*

---

[18] A point emphasized by Antonaccio 1995:153-155.

[19] Activity seems to have ceased by the Roman period; Strabo (1.3.18) states that the Odyssean cave of the nymphs had by his day been lost owing to changes in the landscape. Antonaccio's (1995:152-155) argument that Odysseus-cult on Ithake is Hellenistic is effectively refuted by Malkin 1998:99-107. The latter's conviction that the dedications were made by people familiar with Homeric poetry is in turn refuted by Cook 2000; cf. Mazarakis Ainian 1997:310; Coldstream 1977:182-184, and 347 for the conclusion that "Odysseus could have been venerated . . . in [his] own land . . . quite independently of epic influence."

[20] As suggested by Morgan 1988:309.

[21] Mazarakis Ainian 1997:114, 241 and 309 discusses the case for identifying *Odyssey* 21.267-268 with cult activity at Aetos.

the Ithakans could relate to rites at Aetos and/or Polis Bay.[22] The Panhellenic nature of these sites is indicated by the broad provenience of the offerings in the Aarchaic period, and is explained by Ithake's strategic location on the sea-lane that ancient Greeks, preferring to sail in sight of land, followed northwest toward the Adriatic and across to Italy.[23]

It therefore appears that both Aetos and Polis Bay served the needs of the Ithakans, while also appealing to a broader constituency during the time the Homeric epics were taking shape.[24] Again, evidence for performance traditions associated with these or any pre-Classical Greek sites is of necessity inferential owing to the paucity of contemporary sources. I argued in Chapter 1, in the context of Penelope's tomb, that it is a priori likely that most or all cult sites gave rise to and were at the same time inspired by associated narratives. Here I propose another, related principle: the more a cult site develops and broadens its constituency, the more complex its attendant narrative traditions become, and the more formalized their performance.[25]

Approached this way, Ithakan Odysseus-tradition can usefully be envisioned as a spectrum, extending from informal and local to institutionalized and Panhellenic performance contexts. Toward one end of this spectrum, family traditions were presumably the source of such stories as the report in the Aristotelian *Constitution* that leading Ithakan families claimed descent from Eumaios and Philoitios. And although the most likely paths for the transmission of such traditions are informal, through storytelling within the *oikos*, such rituals as funerals and weddings offer the prospect of more institutionalized performances of narratives that related family history to heroes, gods, and cult sites (cf. *Odyssey* 13.405-408, which could suggest such cult sites asso-

---

[22] A link between the Aetos and Polis Bay sites is suggested by Malkin 1998:112-113, citing Morgan 1988:315 and Waterhouse 1996:309; Malkin also cites the Aristotelian passage apropos of the tripod dedications at Polis Bay (101-102).

[23] Malkin 1998:62-93.

[24] Thus for example Coldstream 1977:184 describes dedications brought "from all points on the compass" to Aetos, and Malkin 1998:114 describes Polis Bay as "a local Ithacan shrine that acquired an 'international' dimension," and (116) Aetos as a "major sanctuary." Morgan 1988:315, on the other hand, while concluding that Polis Bay was "an established cult place through the earlier Iron Age, and probably continued as such into the eighth century," is skeptical about the extent of cult activity at Aetos.

[25] A parallel phenomenon can be observed in modern Indic epic; see Blackburn 1989, in particular his argument (21-30) that Indic oral epics tend to de-emphasize death and deification of heroes as their range extends from local to "pan-Indian," which parallels the Panhellenic *Odyssey*'s blurring the issue of its hero's death.

ciated with the supposed descendants of Eumaios), and to which the community at large may have had a measure of access.[26]

Family traditions will almost certainly have been informed by, and taken into account, traditions that can be located more toward the other end of the spectrum, that is, those associated with the cults of the Ithakan *polis* or *poleis*. On analogy with better-known *polis*-cults, it is plausible that community processions, sacrifices, initiations, and similar rituals incorporated narratives about the exploits of gods and heroes performed by, if not professional singers, at least individuals versed in native composition-in-performance traditions.[27]

Moving further across the spectrum, these epichoric *polis*-traditions would feed into those associated with the Panhellenic sites at Aetos and Polis Bay. In accordance with the general principle adduced above, contact with other Greeks, and the logistics of orchestrating large-scale festivals, would favor the standardization of Ithakan Odysseus-traditions by helping to shape narratives by determining the length of performances and by favoring the presentation of epichoric stories in a way that would appeal to a broad constituency.[28] Neighboring communities would naturally be the source of the earliest and most frequent outsiders to take part in Ithakan ceremonies; thus Ithakan Odysseus-tradition, as it began to achieve broader diffusion, would likely have reacted to and influenced traditions associated with the west Greek mainland. As discussed, the Ithakan, Thesprotian, and Aitolian references in Odysseus' post-*Odyssey* adventures share similar themes.

Lastly, Greek travelers from further afield, a truly Panhellenic constituency, may have had the opportunity to experience Ithakan performance traditions. Narratives developing at nominally Panhellenic sites like Polis Bay and Aetos would however correspond to what I defined in the Introduction as a "proto-Panhellenic" register of the ancient Greek epic tradition. This is because the cults on Ithake itself never achieved the kind of prominence that would allow them to develop and disseminate a narrative tradition comparable in authority to the Homeric *Odyssey*. Nevertheless, Ithakan traditions

---

[26] Thomas 1989:100-108, apropos of the transmission of genealogical tradition in Classical Athens, argues that such institutions as funereal sumptuary laws imply that an important aspect of family rituals was display for the community.

[27] Thus Malkin 1998:151 argues for "an independent Ithacan version" of Odysseus' story.

[28] Benton:1934-1935 proposes, in part on the evidence of Hellenistic inscriptions, that Ithakans held games in Odysseus' honor; such games would, on analogy with other festivals (see below on the Olympics), offer a likely context for the performance of poetry. The shortcomings of some of Benton's arguments, for which see Malkin 1998:99-100; Antonaccio 1995:153-154; Morgan 1988:316, do not in my opinion undermine the main thesis.

could have been sufficiently well-known to have exerted an influence on the Homeric *Odyssey*, even as they were themselves influenced by it.

   To summarize my model of arenas for the performance of Odysseus-tradition, I distinguish six registers extending from highly particularized and narrowly diffused traditions to those aimed at a wider constituency:[29]

   1) family tradition: Ithakan clan names in the Aristotelian *Constitution*

   2) polis cult sites: Aetos, Polis Bay

   3) polis cult system: Aetos and Polis Bay

   4) regional: Aetos and Polis Bay in the context of nearby mainland cults

   5) proto-Panhellenic: visitors to Aetos and Polis Bay from outside west Greece

   6) Panhellenic: Odysseus and west Greece in the Homeric epics

Thesprotia

In historical Thesprotia,[30] two sites are of particular interest for the development of Odysseus-tradition, the oracles of Zeus at Dodona and of the dead (*nekyomanteion*) at Ephyre. Zeus' oracle, 30 or so miles inland from the coast opposite Corcyra and about 60 miles due north of Ithake, has been mentioned already in the context of the Odyssean Cretan tales. In these "false" accounts, "Odysseus" goes to Dodona to learn the "plan of Zeus from the god's lofty-leafed oak" (θεοῖο ἐκ δρυὸς ὑψικόμοιο Διὸς βουλὴν ἐπακούσηι, 14.327-328=19.296-297). The *Iliad* also refers to the site, when Achilleus prays to

> Ζεῦ ἄνα Δωδωναῖε Πελασγικέ, τηλόθι ναίων,
> Δωδώνης μεδέων δυσχειμέρου, ἀμφὶ δὲ Σελλοί
> σοὶ ναίουσ' ὑποφῆται ἀνιπτόποδες χαμαιεῦναι

> Zeus lord, Dodonan, Pelasgian, dwelling far off,
> ruling Dodona where the winters are harsh; and around
>   the Selloi

---

[29] My model is based in part on Nagy's (1996:50-56) scheme illustrating relative degrees of Panhellenism.

[30] In non-epic contexts, e.g. the "Apollodoros" passages quoted above, roughly the same region is also called Epeiros (cf. Strabo 7.7.5; Parke 1967:11-12), and in the Classical period Molossia, whose kings claimed descent from Neoptolemos; cf. *Nostoi* 95.13-16 Bernabé, 108.28-109.1 Allen; Pindar *Nemea* 7.40.

> dwell, your intepreters, their feet unwashed, sleeping on
> the ground
>
> *Iliad* 16.233-235

The reference to "interpreters" (ὑποφῆται) alludes to the status of Zeus' Dodonan cult as an oracle. That the oracle is assumed to be known to audiences of the *Iliad* is implicit in the fact that Achilleus, though his homeland is on the opposite side of the mainland, invokes Zeus by a west-Greek cult title, and is aware of peculiar practices of the priests of this cult.[31] The distinctive priesthood in the *Iliad* complements, rather than conflicts with, the prophetic trees referred to in the *Odyssey*, since both seem to have been aspects of the "real" cult of Zeus at Dodona.[32]

It is in fact unusual that the *Odyssey* represents the cult of Zeus at Dodona as already being in operation in the time of the Trojan War. More commonly, "epic distancing" seems to motivate Homeric suppression of cult sites assumed by Greeks to have developed after the Trojan War, such as Delphi and Olympia. Relevant perhaps is the fact that Dodona was among the places believed in antiquity to have been the original Greek homeland.[33] It is in any case striking that Dodona is one of only two major historical Greek religious sites referred to as such in the Homeric epics.[34] The belief in the reputed antiquity of the oracle at Dodona does not, however, seem to reflect the actual history of the site. The archaeological record is somewhat confused, but it appears that Dodona was little frequented until the eighth century. From this point the site became increasingly popular, and by the latter part of the seventh century there are signs of regional, even Panhellenic, activity, in the form of bronze dedications from Corinth and perhaps Crete.[35] By the end of the Archaic period, Dodona's

---

[31] The relationship between the *Iliad* 16 passage and historical Dodona is discussed in Malkin 1998:149-150; Hammond 1967:371-372; and Parke 1967:1-10.

[32] For the oracular trees and priests at Dodona see e.g. Hesiod frr. 240, 319 MW; Pindar frr. 57-60 SM; *Prometheus Bound* 831-835. Parke 1967:20-33 analyzes the complementary relationship between the two aspects of the cult.

[33] Thus for example Aristotle *Meterologika* 352a33-34 speaks of Dodona as ἡ Ἑλλὰς ἡ ἀρχαία, and Strabo 7.7.5 calls the Dodonan oracle παλαιόν τε καὶ ὀνομαστόν.

[34] The other is Delos, referred to as the site of an altar of Apollo at *Odyssey* 6.162. Some minor cult sites are mentioned, for instance in the Iliadic Catalog of Ships (2.506, 696, etc.).

[35] Surveys of the material evidence in Morris 1998:42; Mazarakis Ainian 1997:309; Morgan 1990:148-150; Coldstream 1977:185. Cretan bronzes of course need not have been dedicated by Cretans. That the Dodonans are not part of Odysseus' northwest Greek kingdom in the *Iliad*, but rather number among the Epirote contingent (2.748-755, with reference, not to the oracle, but to the area's hard winters, Δωδώνην δυσχείμερον, 750), is perhaps attributable to the generally confused nature of Odysseus' kingdom in the *Iliad*; cf. Kirk *IC* 1:182-183.

renown as an oracular site was comparable with that of Delphi, along with which it seems to have formed part of an early festival circuit.[36]

The Thesprotian oracle of the dead at Ephyre was less prominent in ancient Greek life than was Zeus' oracle at Dodona, but it did come to attract a Panhellenic constituency. This oracle, probably to be identified with a site some 30 miles southeast of Dodona, near where the river Acheron empties into the sea (cf. Thucydides 1.46.4), is not referred to as such in the Homeric epics, but is rather described as a community whose leaders have guest-friendships with local Greek heroes. It is at Ephyre that Odysseus is said to obtain arrow-poison (*Odyssey* 1.259-262); and it is from Ephyre, "by the river Selleis" (cf. the "Selloi" in Achilleus' prayer) that the Elean hero Phyleus obtains armor for his son Meges, who in the Trojan War leads the contingent from nearby Doulichion (*Iliad* 15.528-531).[37]

It is not clear whether Homeric silence on the *nekyomanteion* is due to epic distancing or to the relative lateness of the oracle's establishment at Ephyre. The earliest material evidence for the cult is Archaic, though the record is disturbed owing to later construction.[38] Herodotos' story (5.92η2) of the attempt by Periander, the late seventh- or early sixth-century tyrant of Corinth, to employ the "Thesprotians by the Acheron river . . . at the *nekyomanteion*" in order to communicate with his dead wife indicates that the historian's intended audience of Classical-period, cosmopolitan Greeks had at least heard of the site, and did or could believe it to have been long in operation.[39]

In the *Odyssey*'s Cretan tales, as discussed, "Odysseus" seeks from Zeus' oracle at Dodona information analogous to that he receives from Teiresias: in both cases alternative views of Odysseus' return are entertained, either "open" or "in secret" (again, ἢ ἀμφαδὸν ἦε κρυφηδόν, 11.120~14.330=19.299). Given

---

[36] Morgan 1990:209, 212-223 traces the festival circuit from beginnings in the eighth century to a "great age of state activity" from the "very end" of the seventh. If as well-known as Delphi, Dodona was not as well-funded; the earliest temple remains date to around 400.

[37] There is more than one Homeric Ephyre: the Ephyre referred to as the home of Sisyphos at *Iliad* 5.152 appears to be another name for Corinth; and scholia record a tradition that distinguishes Thesprotian Ephyre from the Ephyre where Odysseus obtains his poison; see S. West *CHO* 1:108 ad 1.257ff, Kirk *IC* 2:177 ad 6.152-3. No Thesprotian contingent appears in the *Iliad* (see Kirk *IC* 1 185), though see below on Tlepolemos at *Iliad* 2.659.

[38] Neither Mazarakis Ainian 1997 nor Antonaccio 1995 include Ephyre in their surveys of Early Iron Age religious sites; Janko *IC* 4:287 ad 15.531 states that "there is no need to assume that Homer knew of the Thesprotian Ephura." On the other hand, Burkert 1985:114 argues that the oracle "must be of ancient repute," and that "the association of Odysseus' journey to Hades with this spot is probably older than our *Odyssey*." The material evidence is surveyed by Hammond 1967:65.

[39] Strabo (9.2.4 with 13.1.3) relates a story about the oracle set near the time of the Trojan War.

this thematic link, the plausible suggestion has been made that Odysseus' visit to the underworld in *Odyssey* 11 corresponds to the visit by "Odysseus" to Dodona in the Cretan tales.[40] Odysseus' katabasis appears to have been one of the "facts" of his story; and here again a familiar dichotomy emerges. In the main narrative of the *Odyssey*, the remote world of the *Apologoi* serves as the point of departure for this adventure; in the "false" tale, the *nekyomanteion* at Ephyre seems to serve in this capacity.

This interpretation derives support from the fact that Homeric geography confuses Dodona and Ephyre, or rather perhaps conceives of them as connected. In the Iliadic Catalog of Ships, one branch of the underworld river Styx is said to surface in Dodona (*Iliad* 2.750-755); and the mother of Tlepolemos, leader of the Rhodian contingent, is said to have been seized by his father Herakles from "Ephyre by the river Selleis" (ἐξ Ἐφύρης ποταμοῦ ἄπο Σελλήεντος, 2.659–15.531), the name of the river again echoing that of the priests mentioned in Achilleus' prayer. To be sure, Homeric geography is often confused, or at least confusing; there were moreover a number of ancient places called Ephyre, and at least one other Homeric river Selleis.[41] Nevertheless, I suggest that these overlapping geographic details may allude *pars pro toto* to a system of west Greek cult sites that together preserved a set of traditions in which the themes of Odysseus' adventures were intertwined with the region's oracles of Zeus and the dead, and perhaps even one of the hero himself.[42]

For another Thesprotian cult that may have played a role in the dissemination of Odysseus-tradition is an oracle of Odysseus at Trampya, approximately 30 miles northeast of Dodona and near Bouneima, a settlement supposedly founded by the hero.[43] There is then the possibility that worship

[40] Thus Danek 1998:286; Malkin 1998:129. Huxley 1958 relates *Odyssey* 11 to the Thesprotian oracle, but does not raise the issue of Dodona; cf. also Lord 1960:182. Zeus' oracle at Dodona also played a role in Sophokles' *Odysseus Akanthoplex* (frr. 455, 456, 460, 461 Lloyd-Jones); and Pausanias (9.30.6) reports a local tradition locating Orpheus' *katabasis* there.

[41] Pausanias (1.17.5) argues that the Homeric account of underworld rivers draws on Thesprotian geography. Apollodoros of Athens (*FGrH* 244 F 181, 198; cf. Strabo 7.7.10, 8.3.5; Eustathios 315.44) connects the river Selleis and the Selloi priesthood; cf. Hammond 1967:372-374, 379-380; Parke 1967:7-8. The other Homeric Selleis flows into the Hellespont (*Iliad* 12.97) and is described with the same formula as the Thesprotian river, as Hainsworth *IC* 3:328 ad 12.96-7 observes.

[42] Also suggestive in this context is the tradition, preserved in the late antique compendium of Lucius Ampelius (*Liber Memoralis* 8, cited by Huxley 1958:246), that visitors to the *nekyomanteion* on occasion saw Zeus. A link between Zeus and the underworld is also prominent in the myth and cult of Persephone and Demeter; see Mylonas 1961:172, 282-289

[43] The site has not however been located definitively; Hammond 1967:708, cf. 382, 393-395, for instance, identifies Trampya with late Archaic remains at Voutonosi.

of Odysseus at Trampya developed independent of Homeric influence, in an epichoric context comparable to that in which I earlier located the Mantineian Penelope. Such a tradition could have fed into more broadly regional stories associated with the nearby oracles of Zeus and of the dead.

Rites and *aitia* relating to the oracles of Zeus, the dead, and Odysseus in Thesprotia, then, offer plausible contexts for the development of epichoric and proto-Panhellenic narrative traditions. This is not to say that Thesprotia was an unrecognized cultural dynamo of the Archaic period, but rather that certain Thesprotian religious centers may have sponsored a vigorous Odysseus-tradition. As observed in Chapter 1, Pausanias speaks of a *Thesprotis* that could represent one of the better-known of the west Greek traditions with which the *Odyssey* engages.[44] In the case of Dodona, Herodotos (2.55-57) heard local narrative traditions about the founding of Zeus' oracle; the historian claims to have gathered his information directly from religious officials, but, to recast earlier argumentation, a more efficient medium for the transmission and dissemination of such stories would be epichoric poetry. At least one poet is known to have visited the area: an inscription on a fifth-century tripod unearthed at Dodona reads Τερψικλῆς· τῶι Δὶ· Ναίωι· ῥαψωιδὸς· ἀνέθηκε ("Terpsikles the rhapsode dedicated [this tripod] to Zeus Naios").[45]

Aitolia and Elis

A third west Greek region that features in non-Homeric Odysseus-tradition and the *Odyssey*'s false tales is Aitolia, the mainland south of Thesprotia and east of Ithake (Akarnania is not distinguished in pre-Classical sources). As discussed, some accounts of Odysseus' post-*Odyssey* life find him at the court of the Aitolian king Thoas, who is portrayed negatively, as is the only other Aitolian character in the *Odyssey*. The Aristotelian *Constitution of the Ithakans* (fr. 508 Rose) appears to refer to another oracle of Odysseus and the dead in Aitolia, which is in turn linked to the name of an Ithakan clan.[46]

---

[44] Pausanias 8.12.5. Some argue that *Thesprotis* is simply another name for the *Telegony*; see Malkin 1998:126-127 and Davies 1988:156; at any rate, most editors of the Epic Cycle fragments do not include a *Thesprotis*. My arguments here, however, could be adduced in support of a distinction between a relatively more epichoric *Thesprotis* and a relatively more Panhellenic *Telegony*; and I note that the Cyclic *Kypria*, which takes its name from the island of Cyprus (Burkert 1992:103 and 207n10), offers a precedent for the formation of an epic's title from its place of origin.

[45] *GDI* 5786, quoted and discussed by Graziosi 2002:25-27.

[46] Sch. Vet. to Lykophron 799=Aristotle fr. 508 Rose: μάντιν δὲ νεκρὸν Εὐρυτὰν στέψει λεώς· Ἀριστοτέλης φησὶν ἐν Ἰθακησίων πολιτείαι Εὐρυτάνας ἔθνος εἶναι τῆς Αἰτωλίας ὀνομασθὲν ἀπὸ Εὐρύτονος, παρ' οἷς εἶναι μαντεῖον Ὀδυσσέως. Discussion of the passage in Malkin 1998:125-128; Hammond 1967:385; Hartmann 1917:139-140.

Yet Odysseus-tradition in historical Aitolia, whatever forms it may have taken, is unlikely to have made much of an impression on the Greek world at large, since the region remained something of a backwater until the Hellenistic period and could boast no attraction like the oracle of Zeus at Dodona or even Polis Cave.[47] It might therefore seem odd that Aitolians feature as prominently as they do in Panhellenic epic – in addition to Thoas, there are Meleagros, Diomedes, and Thersites in the *Iliad* – as well as being the focus of a widely-known saga, the Kalydonian boar hunt. An explanation for the broad circulation of these characters and settings may be found in connections between Aitolia and the influential west Greek region of Elis. Specifically, epichoric tradition identified the settlement of Elis, and the foundation of the Olympian festival there, with Aitolian heroes and settings. These "pseudo-Aitolian," Elean traditions seem to have overshadowed whatever stories may have been native to the historical inhabitants of ancient Aitolia.[48] Thus, by way of a preliminary example, Herodotos (8.73.2) refers to the city of Elis, which in the fifth century replaced Olympia as the administrative center of the region of Elis, as a *polis* "of the Aitolians."

In a sense, then, Eleans could lay claim to two sets of heroes, Aitolians and a less impressive group of native sons. In the *Iliad*, the Eleans, who are regularly called "Epeioi" (see 2.615-624), play a minor role at Troy, where at least two of the ἄρχοντες Ἐπείων fall in battle (Diores at 4.517, Amphimachos at 13.185). The Homeric Elean-Epeians remain tied closely to west Greece. Thus an Elean exile, the aforementioned Meges, leads the contingent from the nearby island of Doulichion (2.625-630); and Nestor recalls Elean games in which his father participated (11.686~698), and others in which he himself and other Pylians, Epeians, and Aitolians took part (at the funeral of the Epeian leader Amarynkeus, 23.630-42), as well as an epic struggle between Pylians and Eleans (11.670-761).

The *Odyssey* appears to engage with Elean themes in a manner similar to its engagement with Thesprotian ones: Elis surfaces mainly in "false" tales

---

[47] For this conclusion about Archaic and Classical Aitolia see Coldstream 1977:184-187. Thucydides at one point (3.94.4-5) characterizes Aitolians of his day as primitive and poorly-organized, though perhaps with malice since he does so apropos of their sound defeat of an invading Athenian army.

[48] "Aitolian" themes are not, however, limited to Elean epichoric tradition: Aitolians figured in the Athenian "Choes" festival (see Burkert 1983:222-223); the Phokians claimed that the cult statue in their temple of Athene was brought from Troy by the Aitolian hero Thoas (Pausanias 10.38.5); and the tomb of the Aitolian hero Endymion was claimed by Heraklea in Karia (Pausanias 5.1.4). Nevertheless, the number of connections in the available evidence suggests that Elean tradition drew significantly more on mythic Aitolia than did other Greek regions.

and paths not taken.[49] There are no Elean characters in the *Odyssey*, but in the Cretan tales the disguised Odysseus at one point names Elis as his intended destination (13.275), and the disguised Athene claims a debt is owed her there (in a variant reading for 3.367). As for paths not taken, Eupeithes worries, needlessly, that Odysseus will flee to Elis (24.430-431, quoted in Chapter 3); and, again, Elis is Odysseus' first stop on his post-*Odyssey* journey in the *Telegony* (102.4-6 Bernabé, 109.7-10 Allen). It is not however clear to where in Elis these passages refer.[50] Olympia is not named in Homeric (or Hesiodic or Cyclic) epic, though this may again be attributable to "epic distancing." If so, the distancing seems incomplete. Nestor's aforementioned references to games "in godly Elis" (ἐν Ἤλιδι δίῃ, *Iliad* 11.686, 698; cf. 2.615) suggest aware-ness of some version of the Olympic festival.[51] Also of potential significance is the Ithakan Noemon's statement in the *Odyssey* that he keeps horses in Elis (4.635-636), since Ithake is unsuitable for the animals (4.601-608), whereas Elis is "horse-nurturing" (ἱπποβότοιο, 21.347), Noemon's stable may allude to equestrian events at the Olympics.[52] Lastly, since all the characters connected with these events hail from west Greece, the Homeric epics could reflect a time when Olympia attracted a mainly regional constituency.

In any case, it is in the context of the Olympian festival that the Elean-Aitolian connection tends to be discussed in non-Homeric sources. A repre-sentative narrative can be reconstructed from Strabo, who cites as his main authority the fourth-century historian Ephoros (whose evidence is said to include Elean inscriptions, 10.3.2). In this account, the Eleans and Aitolians are linked not only by blood, but also, paradoxically, as founders of each other's communities (οὐ τὴν συγγένειαν μόνον ἀλλὰ καὶ τὸ ἀρχηγέτας ἀλλήλων εἶναι, 10.3.3): long before the Trojan War an Elean named Aitolos was driven from his homeland, and he established an eponymous kingdom north across the Corinthian gulf; one of his descendants, Oxylos, returned with the Herakleidai to Elis and reclaimed his ancestral (προγονικήν) land. At this time Elis was

---

[49] Similarly Malkin 1998:131, citing Ballabriga 1989, connects Thesprotia and Elis in the *Odyssey* with Odyssean "sequels and alternatives."

[50] The Elean Catalog of Ships entry is similarly vague, listing not cities but regions; cf. Kirk *IC* 1:218-219 ad 2.615-617.

[51] A connection between the games Nestor describes at *Iliad* 11.698-702 and the Olympics was made in antiquity (e.g. Strabo 8.3.30; cf. Pherekydes 3 *FGrH* 118); cf. Raaflaub 1997:2-3; Bölte 1934:319-347.

[52] The epithet ἱπποβότοιο 'horse-nurturing' is used only of Elis, Argos, and Trike in Homeric epic. Interestingly, Noemon's claim that he keeps mules as well seems to conflict with a belief that mules could not be conceived there (Herodotos 4.30); see Nagy 1990a:336 on the significance of mules for the ideology of the Olympics.

dedicated to Zeus (ἱερὰν εἶναι τοῦ Διός); and Oxylos' descendant Iphitos later established the Olympian games (8.3.33).[53]

The significant point about west Greek narrative traditions here is that the authority and prestige of the festival at Olympia was articulated in part through mythological links to the ostensibly more ancient Aitolian heroic lineage, which leads from the eponymous founder-figure Aitolos to such celebrated figures as Oineus, Meleagros and Thoas (cf. Pindar *Isthmia* 5.31-32). Suggestive of the polemical force of this link between "Aitolian" and Elean tradition is Pindar's reference to one of the Hellanodikai, judges at the historical Olympic games, as an "exacting Aitolian man" (ἀτρεκὴς Ἑλλανοδίκας ... Αἰτωλὸς ἀνήρ, *Olympia* 3.12). Here allusion to the festival's supposed Aitolian origins seems intended to stress the authority and legitimacy of the games in order to magnify the laundandus' victory.[54] It therefore appears that the festival at Olympia, given its significance in ancient Greek life (at least that of the elite class), is a more likely place than Aitolia itself where people across Greece would come into contact with "Aitolian" characters and stories.

Of course, such narratives could have influenced the *Odyssey* only if it remained fluid into the period of Panhellenic activity at Olympia. The material record of the site itself parallels roughly that of the sites discussed above, with the exception that Olympia did not in its early phase develop in the shadow of a nearby community. Thus Iron Age cult activity becomes detectable in the late tenth century, and use of the site remains largely or wholly local until around 800. By the end of the seventh century a permanent settlement had grown up around the precinct of Zeus, and votives from outside west Greece begin to appear.[55]

---

[53] Among the many other versions: Aitolos' father Endymion founds Elis (Pausanias 5.1.4, 5.8.1-9.5; "Apollodoros" *Bibliotheke* 1.7.5); Diomedes is linked with the return of the Herakleidai to Aitolia (Strabo 7.7.7), and Aitolos is killed by the Aitolians (9.3.12); his great-grandson Oxylos takes over Elis (BCDEQ scholia to Pindar *Olympian* 3.12; "Apollodoros" *Bibliotheke* 1.7.7). Ostensible founders of the Olympian festival include, in roughly (mythical) chronological order: Kronos and Zeus (Pausanias 8.2.2), Endymion (Pausanias 5.1.4; cf. 6.20.9), Aitolos (Strabo 8.3.33), Iphitos (Strabo 8.3.33), Oxylos (Pausanias 1.4.5, 5.4.5, 5.8.5), Pelops (Pindar *Olympian* 1.18-24), Peisos (Phlegon *FGrH* 257 F 1), Herakles (Pindar *Olympian* 2.3-4, on which see Nagy 1990a:119-120; Lysias 23.1; Pausanias 5.7.6, 8.1, 13.8; 14.7. 2; "Apollodoros" *Bibliotheke* 2.7.2). Another genealogy makes Thoas son of Andraimon the grandfather of Oxylos and brother-in-law of Herakles' son Hyllos (Pausanias 5.3.6-7).

[54] The A scholion to Pindar's ode cites Hellanikos and Asklepiades as the authority for the explanation that the Hellanodikai traced their offices to Oxylos; the BCDEQ scholia begin simply "Aitolian for Elean" (Αἰτωλὸς ἀντὶ τοῦ Ἡλεῖος) and proceed to summarize the story of Oxylos' takeover of Elis.

[55] On the development of Olympia as a Panhellenic site, see Mazarakis Ainian 1997:323; Morgan 1990:9, 49-56, 1993:20-27; Mallwitz 1988; Coldstream 1977:338-339.

These considerations suggest that performances of narrative poems about local heroes could have arisen at Olympia in a manner similar to that described above for Ithake and Thesprotia. Since Olympia was at first and for long a regional meeting place rather than a permanent settlement, the development of a synthetic, regional perspective on local west Greek myths there may have been precocious. The development of the festival at Olympia into a premier Panhellenic event, then, could have created opportunities for the emergence of narratives distinguished by an "Aitolo-centric" perspective on west Greek heroes, including accounts of Odysseus that, owing to close association with Olympia, presented a challenge for the Homeric attempt to divorce Odysseus' adventures from "real" Greek cult sites.[56]

West Greek epichoric tradition

It is now possible to hazard some conclusions about the relationship between the *Odyssey* and west Greek traditions. From roughly the mid-eighth to mid-sixth centuries, Panhellenic institutions were emerging at Dodona and Olympia, as well as at Delphi, Delos, Isthmia, Athens, and Mykale in Ionia.[57] During this same period, the *Odyssey* was emerging as a Panhellenic narrative, and I follow many modern scholars in connecting these two developments.[58] Panhellenic gatherings in west Greece thus offered opportunities for the promulgation of narratives about Odysseus that had broad appeal to Greeks familiar with differing but related traditions.

Further, if, as seems likely, many of the same west Greek performers and audiences visited Ithake, Dodona, Ephyre, and Olympia, there would be a tendency for west Greek Odysseus-traditions in these contexts to develop

---

[56] Evidence for poetic performances at the Olympics (and other Panhellenic festivals) is scanty and late, such as Diodoros' (14.109) account of rhapsodic performances in the Classical period, on which see Weeber 1991:52-55. Nevertheless, many scholars conclude that such performances were integrated into the festival earlier, for example Raschke 2002:5-6; Swaddling 1980:37. The lying Aitolian in *Odyssey* 14 may hint at an Odysseus-Olympia connection when he predicts the hero's return at the summer harvest (14.384): this seasonal setting conflicts with the main narrative of the *Odyssey*, which is informed by themes associated with year-end rituals (on which see Chapter 3), but is consistent with the timing of the Olympic festival (see Lee 2001:7 with bibliography).

[57] Morgan 1990:191-194 argues that Delphi and Olympia developed in competition; she also notes (208) that "Athens was the earliest state to follow Olympia so closely in the formation of its main civic festival," a point of significance for the development of the *Odyssey* in an Attic performance context; see further below.

[58] Representative arguments in Nagy 2002; Ford 1997:86-89.

a regional character.[59] There may thus have been a kind of west Greek *koinē* when it came to Odysseus-tradition. As observed above, a similar plot underlies many of the post-*Odyssey* stories set in west Greece. Perhaps owing to the precocious development of a strong west Greek perspective, this body of tradition may have been slow to disentangle itself from regional themes when the impetus toward a Panhellenic perspective began to be felt. In other words, the political and religious geography of west Greece may have become impressed too deeply on performance traditions in the area for any west Greek *Odyssey*, even one associated with the quintessentially Panhellenic site of Olympia, to compete with the Homeric epic, which for the most part keeps its hero clear of such entanglements.

Chapter conclusions

The *Odyssey*'s strategy of denying the authority of, and of severing links to, traditions that locate Odysseus in the "real world" and entangle him in its problems is, I conclude, one of its defining characteristics and crowning achievements. As discussed in previous chapters, the Homeric Penelope and Phaiakes are also treated in a manner that limits engagement with epichoric traditions. Similarly, the Homeric *Apologoi* are located in the fantastic world of monsters and witches rather than in the context of ancient Greek geography. Thus, for instance, though Sicily was considered by many to be the home of the Kyklopes, the *Odyssey* avoids any such identification and the attendant links to Sicilian epichoric tradition, though it demonstrates awareness of Greek activity there.[60]

Wherever possible, the fully Panhellenic narratives exploit strategies of inclusion, or obfuscation, in order to gloss over potential conflicts with epichoric traditions. Thus Teiresias' ambiguous account of Odysseus' death

---

[59] There is some material evidence for what could be termed a "west Greek consciousness" in this period. Coldstream 1977:187, for instance, identifies a "collective West Greek character" in Geometric pottery from Elis to Epiros; Morgan 1990:89-90 suggests that Dodona and Elis were visited by the same kinds of people; in 1993:20 and 38n11 she also observes that offerings at Olympia and Dodona are similar in the eighth century and that, since the material at Dodona is still largely unpublished, this may be true for the Archaic period as well. Hammond 1967:429 and 433 argues that Elean colonists enjoyed a close relationship with Dodona. Historians are not unanimous on the subject; Morris 1998:42 and 55, for example, separates Dodona from Olympia in his four "broad zones of material culture that seem to be very old" (11; note however that the overlap between the Elean and Thesprotian zones in his Figure 1 extends almost to Dodona).

[60] Thus the suitors mention Sicilian slave traders (*Odyssey* 20.383), and the lying Odysseus claims at one point to be "Sikanian" (24.307).

and the uncertain fate of the Phaiakes appear to leave open narrative possibilities inconsistent with Odyssean thematics. In the case of west Greek traditions about Odysseus' return from Troy, I propose, the inconsistencies were too fundamental, and the conflicting traditions too influential, to allow for inclusion or obfuscation, for which reason the *Odyssey* exploits another strategy, de-authorization through recontextualization. By framing as lies accounts of Odysseus' return in which he wanders "real" ancient Greece, takes control of Ithake through outright assault, and suffers exile, the Homeric account undermines traditions in which the hero's wander- and bloodlust deny him the opportunity to live happily ever after in accordance with the poem's larger themes.

What the Cretan tales and the paths suggested but not taken in the *Odyssey* seem to construct, then, is a non-Homeric Odysseus, one whose journey takes him from Troy to places like Crete, Egypt, and Phoenicia (perhaps receiving the aid of the metrically equivalent Phoinikes instead of the Phaiakes), as well as Thesprotia, Dodona, and at last Ithake, where his undisguised return issues in exile and an ignominious death. Not surprisingly, one of the themes lacking from these accounts is a *Dios boulē*.

Zeus' absence from the non-Homeric material may seem to problematize my association of these putative west Greek traditions with cult sites dedicated to him. However, not every narrative performed at a festival made conspicuous homage to the festival's patron deity. Thus, for example, though Athene is considerably less prominent in the *Iliad* than she is in the *Odyssey*, there remain strong arguments for associating both poems with the Panathenaia festival at Athens.[61] Further, from the perspective developed in this and the preceding chapter, Zeus' absence is consistent with the real-world, political orientation of the themes of exile and *epigonoi*, mundane concerns with which the epic Zeus normally plays no part, except when dealing with his own offspring.

A further consideration is that, if the equation of divine plan and narrative plan is as I propose specific to the Panhellenic register of ancient Greek epic, a *Dios boulē* theme would be out of place in narratives that were not compelled make the kind of narrative decisions I ascribe to the Panhellenic, and Panhellenizing, Zeus. It is in this respect noteworthy that the subordinate Olympians Athene, Ares, and Apollo seem to conduct themselves in the non-Homeric *Telegony* much as they do in the *Iliad* (cf. Proklos 102.11-12 Bernabé, quoted above), only without the direction or arbitration of Zeus. Conversely,

---

[61] On the relationship between Homeric poetry and the Panathenaia see Nagy 2002:7-35 and Ritoók 1993 with bibliography.

Zeus' only appearance in the Homeric passages discussed in this chapter is as the offstage oracular voice of Dodona in the Cretan tales, where he is invoked in order to define the parameters of the "false" plot, that is, to determine whether Odysseus will return openly or in secret. This function, I propose, is a specifically Panhellenic one. I shall be arguing in the next chapter that another account of the aftermath of the Trojan War in the *Odyssey*, one told by Nestor to Telemachos, also presents Zeus in a role analogous to that which he plays in the main narrative, as the guiding force behind the narrative decisions that reduce the mass of epichoric stories about returning Greek heroes to a Panhellenic synthesis that reinforces Homeric themes.

5

NESTOR'S NOSTOI

L IKE ODYSSEUS, THE MORTAL CHARACTER NESTOR focalizes a significant portion of the *Odyssey*. His narrative helps to establish further the poem's relationship to the Nostos-tradition, which, as discussed in previous chapters, forms the part of the *Odyssey*'s backstory that extends from the fall of Troy to the death of Agamemnon. In a speech that extends over more than a quarter of *Odyssey* 3 (130-200, 262-312), which I shall refer to as "Nestor's Nostoi," the old hero expands on themes introduced in Zeus' Oresteia – the *Odyssey*'s first step toward orienting itself with respect to Nostoi-tradition – and extends these themes to other Trojan War heroes, including Neoptolemos, Diomedes, Idomeneus and Odysseus himself. Menelaos' extended narratives in *Odyssey* 4 also draw on Nostoi-tradition, but the focus there remains on the internal narrator, as is the case with Odysseus' *Apologoi*. Nestor's perspective in *Odyssey* 3, by contrast, extends well beyond himself, so that his narratives provide a valuable supplement to the understanding of Homeric narrative offered by the other storytellers in the poem.

In fact, Nestor's perspective, along with his narrative techniques, reveal him to be a special kind of storyteller, one more like the Homeric narrator or an ἀοιδός 'singer of epics', such as Phemios or Demodokos.[1] Like these figures, Nestor tells a tale that embraces multiple perspectives on a sizeable portion of the epic tradition. Most significantly for my overall argument, one of the features that distinguishes Nestor's Nostoi from narratives such as Odysseus' and Menelaos' first-person accounts is the conspicuous and pervasive role Nestor gives to Zeus.

I argued in the previous chapter that the *Odyssey* attempts to suppress "post-*Odyssey*" traditions, or, more precisely, that it attempts to create a relatively uneventful vision of the latter phase of Odysseus' life, in order to

---

[1] Thus for instance Dickson 1995:37 observes that "to a significant extent Nestor's characterization draws on traits that identify him as an *aoidos* in his own right."

deny Homeric authority to stories that complicate the justice and plan of the Homeric Zeus. "Pre-*Odyssey*" events pose analogous problems, in that they frequently recur in conflicting versions with ties to various epichoric traditions. Naturally, since these stories prefigure the tale itself, they cannot be attenuated in so sweeping a manner as events that fall after the main narrative. Indeed, as discussed in Chapter 1, the *Odyssey*, far from attempting to divert attention from such events, references them from the beginning. Here I shall be arguing that it is in part in order to create a uniformly Odyssean vision of "pre-*Odyssey*" Nostoi-tradition that the *Odyssey* in effect stages a performance of an idealized *nostoi*-narrative, with Nestor serving as an idealized narrator who recreates in miniature a plan of Zeus.

Indeed, Nestor's status as the voice of return transcends the *Odyssey*. An illustrative example occurs in *Iliad* 15, when, as the Trojans threaten to annihilate the Greek forces, Nestor raises his hands to the sky and prays:

> Ζεῦ πάτερ, εἴ ποτέ τίς τοι ἐν Ἄργεί περ πολυπύρωι
> ἢ βοὸς ἢ ὄιος κατὰ πίονα μηρία καίων
> ηὔχετο νοστῆσαι, σὺ δ᾽ ὑπέσχεο καὶ κατένευσας,
> τῶν μνῆσαι καὶ ἄμυνον, Ὀλύμπιε, νηλεὲς ἦμαρ.

> Father Zeus, if ever for you someone in much-grained Argos
> used to burn rich thigh-pieces of ox or sheep
> and prayed to return home (*nostēsai*), and you yourself
>   promised and nodded,
> these things remember, and ward off, Olympian, the
>   pitiless day.

> *Iliad* 15.372-375

As in most Homeric prayers, a god is invoked, a past act of piety recalled, and a request made; but the rhetoric here is more complex than the usual *do ut des*. If Zeus allows the Greeks to perish, Nestor says, the god will be breaking his own promise that at least some of them achieve a return from the Trojan War. Zeus hears the prayer and thunders in response (377-378); and, since such omens in Homeric epic indicate that a prayer will be fulfilled, Zeus apparently accepts Nestor's premise.[2]

In the larger context of the Trojan War, Zeus' guarantee of return here is not simply Nestor's supposition or wishful thinking, but is rather an established part of the Iliadic perspective, along with other "post-Iliadic"

---

[2] The relationship between such omens and plot in Homeric epic is well explicated by de Jong 2001:51-53 ad 2.143-207 and Nagy 2003:55-59.

events such as the sack of Troy (e.g. *Iliad* 15.71). In this respect the *Iliad* acknowledges a "fact" of ancient Greek myth: some of the Greeks, in particular Nestor, return home from Troy in every known version of the story. Thus, while Nestor's prayer is motivated by its immediate context – reference to Zeus' promise dramatizes the peril to the Greek camp, and reassures Hellenophilic audiences that the tide of battle will turn[3] – it is particularly effective in these respects because it engages with the larger mythological and poetical tradition to which the *Iliad* belongs.

Nestor is a fitting character to make this intertextual gesture. His very name, which means something like "he who returns [his people] home" (**nes* + agent suffix *-tor*),[4] identifies him with the final stage of the Trojan War story. Because the linguistic connection between "Nestor" and "*nostos*" is transparent, the "speaking name," in any context, alludes to the stretch of the Trojan War story that falls between the main narratives of the two Homeric epics. So natural is the Nestor-*nostos* connection, so firmly embedded in the larger tradition, that it surfaces even proleptically in *Iliad* 15.

The *Odyssey*, on the other hand, defines itself at the outset as the ultimate *nostos*-narrative: "then all the others [except Odysseus] who escaped sheer death [at Troy] were at home" (ἔνθ' ἄλλοι μὲν πάντες, ὅσοι φύγον αἰπὺν ὄλεθρον/οἴκοι ἔσαν, 1.11-12). These themes have the potential to invoke Nestor's nominal identity, since they allude to the backstory, which it will be his main Odyssean function to supply. Significantly, Nestor receives responsibility for the *Odyssey*'s account of the Greeks' departure from Troy, in which Odysseus features prominently, in preference to Odysseus himself, whose account of his own story condenses this part of it into a single word, Ἰλιόθεν 'from Troy [we went]' (9.39).

I shall first be arguing that Nestor locates his Nostoi within the broader context of an at least loosely-defined system of mutually referential Trojan War stories that bear a more than passing resemblance to the narrative territories of the Homeric and Cyclic epics as we know them. Second, I make the case that roles played by Zeus and Athene in Nestor's Nostoi illustrate the centrality of the *Dios boulē* theme to Homeric composition in general.

---

[3] As observed by e.g. Janko *IC* 4:268-269 ad 15.377-80.

[4] The etymology is discussed in detail by Frame 1978:82-86, 96-99, 112; cf. Dickson 1995:202.

Nestor's perspective on the Trojan War

The immediate motivation for Nestor's Nostoi in *Odyssey* 3 is Telemachos' request for news of Odysseus. However, the young man already knows that his father survived most of the events Nestor goes on to describe (cf. 1.237-241), and has told him as much (3.86-89). Thus Telemachos' request is revealed as a dramatic device: Odysseus has been out of contact with the "real world," and therefore beyond Nestor's ken, for years, and even this fact is communicated to Telemachos not by Nestor but by Menelaos (4.556-560). Nestor's Nostoi in this respect responds to poetical problems – or, to anticipate my argument, opportunities – created by the *in medias res* narrative structure that characterizes the *Odyssey*, and for that matter any Trojan War narrative that does not begin at the beginning of the conflict. So for example the *Iliad*, which commences nine years into the war, fills in the background with scenes such as the *Teichoskopia*, positioned similarly in the third Book, in which Agamemnon, Odysseus, Telamonian Aias, and Idomeneus are introduced, and events preceding the main narrative discussed (*Iliad* 3.155-244).

In performance, these scenes would not be motivated by the need to supply information to Homeric audiences, who again were presumably acquainted with the Trojan War story through a variety of contexts. Indeed, a simple expository function is ruled out by the fact that Nestor's Nostoi and the *Teichoskopia* alike, though positioned near the beginnings of their respective narratives, nevertheless occur well after the characters they introduce have entered the action. In diachronic terms, it may be that formal structures – such as a traditional "observers on the walls" theme, or "old man tells young man about his father" theme – that developed in the performance tradition as a means to provide essential background have come to serve other functions in Homeric epic.[5]

The significance of this background for Homeric audiences, then, resides not in its value as information, but rather in the capacity of events previous to the narrative to explicate and reify its major themes.[6] Thus Nestor's Nostoi can from one perspective be seen as a particularly developed example of a series of speeches, like Athene's reference to Orestes in Book 1 (298-302), that draw on the *Odyssey*'s backstory in order to motivate Telemachos. Similarly, in the case of the *Teichoskopia*, the belated introduction of Odysseus with reference

---

[5] Cf. Kirk *IC* 1:286-287 ad 3.161-246.
[6] See for instance S. Richardson's (1990:38-39, 143-144) arguments that background generally is provided to deepen the understanding of the immediate context, and Atchity's (1978:260-264) discussion of the hortatory function of Nestor's speeches in the *Iliad*.

to his skillfully conducted but unsuccessful mission to negotiate a settlement with the Trojans in the early years of the conflict (*Iliad* 3.206-207) foreshadows the failure of the truce brokered between the Greeks and Trojans later in Book 3 and Odysseus' own failure in the embassy to Achilleus in Book 9.

Nestor's Nostoi, being longer and more elaborate than the *Teichoskopia*, engages in a correspondingly more complex manner with events that fall before the main narrative in which it appears. To begin with, Nestor, unlike Helen and the Trojan elders at the walls of Troy, prefaces his tale with an overview of the Trojan war. This survey takes up the story before the Greeks besiege Troy and carries it to the city's fall:

ὦ φίλ', ἐπεί μ' ἔμνησας ὀιζύος, ἣν ἐν ἐκείνωι
δήμωι ἀνέτλημεν μένος ἄσχετοι υἷες Ἀχαιῶν,
ἠμὲν ὅσα ξὺν νηυσὶν ἐπ' ἠεροειδέα πόντον   105
πλαζόμενοι κατὰ ληίδ' ὅπηι ἄρξειεν Ἀχιλλεύς,
ἠδ' ὅσα καὶ περὶ ἄστυ μέγα Πριάμοιο ἄνακτος
μαρνάμεθ' - ἔνθα δ' ἔπειτα κατέκταθεν ὅσσοι ἄριστοι·
ἔνθα μὲν Αἴας κεῖται ἀρήιος, ἔνθα δ' Ἀχιλλεύς,
ἔνθα δὲ Πάτροκλος, θεόφιν μήστωρ ἀτάλαντος,   110
ἔνθα δ' ἐμὸς φίλος υἱός, ἅμα κρατερὸς καὶ ἀταρβής,
Ἀντίλοχος, περὶ μὲν θείειν ταχὺς ἠδὲ μαχητής· -
ἄλλα τε πόλλ' ἐπὶ τοῖς πάθομεν κακά· τίς κεν ἐκεῖνα
πάντα γε μυθήσαιτο καταθνητῶν ἀνθρώπων;
οὐδ' εἰ πεντάετές γε καὶ ἑξάετες παραμίμνων   115
ἐξερέοις, ὅσα κεῖθι πάθον κακὰ δῖοι Ἀχαιοί·
πρίν κεν ἀνιηθεὶς σὴν πατρίδα γαῖαν ἵκοιο.
εἰνάετες γάρ σφιν κακὰ ῥάπτομεν ἀμφιέποντες
παντοίοισι δόλοισι, μόγις δ' ἐτέλεσσε Κρονίων.
ἔνθ' οὔ τίς ποτε μῆτιν ὁμοιωθήμεναι ἄντην   120
ἤθελ', ἐπεὶ μάλα πολλὸν ἐνίκα δῖος Ὀδυσσεὺς
παντοῖσι δόλοισι.

Ah, friend, since you have reminded me of pain, which in that
country [Troy] we endured, unbowed in might, we sons of Achaians,
as many wanderings with ships on misty sea   105
as we wandered for the sake of plunder, wherever Achilleus would lead,
and as many struggles as around the great city of

> lord Priam
> we struggled – there then did they perish, such as
>   were best:
> there lies warlike Aias, and there Achilleus,
> and there Patroklos, like the gods in counsel,   110
> and there my own son, both powerful and fearless,
> Antilochos, excelling in speed and battle –
> and many other evils we suffered in addition to these.
>   Who could
> tell all those things, who of mortal men?
> Not if five or even six years you remained   115
> would you enquire about such evils as godly Achaians
>   suffered there;
> sooner would you leave and reach your homeland.
> For nine years we stitched together for them [the Trojans]
>   evils, working
> all sorts of tricks; but at last Kronos' son brought it to
>   an end.
> There no-one was willing to contend in mental power,   120
> since by far godly Odysseus triumphed
> in all sorts of tricks.

Odyssey 3.103-122

As noted above, Nestor's speech here is unresponsive to Telemachos' question, a fact that has often been explained in terms of Nestor's proverbial garrulousness. Among its other shortcomings,[7] this interpretation fails to appreciate that Nestor's path toward the story Telemachos wants to hear is carefully structured, and that he takes care to explain how the information sought by Telemachos is embedded the larger story of the Trojan War.

In surveying this material, Nestor identifies the Trojan War story as a whole by an overarching theme, "pain" (ὀιζύς, 103), for which Zeus is ultimately responsible (μόγις δ᾽ ἐτέλεσσε Κρονίων, 119; cf. *Iliad* 1.5 and discussion of *Odyssey* 14.235-236 below). This pain-narrative Nestor then resolves into smaller units, specifically two ὅσα-clauses ("as many as").[8] The first covers

---

[7] An interpretation refuted effectively by Falkner 1989:31 (quoted in Dickson 1995:36).

[8] Compare for instance *Iliad* 12.10-17, where the Homeric narrator uses a series of temporal clauses in order to divide the Trojan War into four thematic groupings: events before the death of Hektor, the deaths of major Trojan and Greek heroes, the sack of Troy, and the return of the Greeks.

a series of plundering raids, "as many as" the Greeks make under the leadership of Achilleus (105-106). Second, after the raids, come conflicts, "as many as" the Greeks endure once they besiege Troy (106-107). No single figure dominates the latter events as Achilleus does the raids; rather, Nestor further resolves the siege into a series of deaths of major heroes, Aias, Achilleus, Patroklos, and Antilochos, each named in an ἔνθα-clause ("there [lies]").

The sequences of events covered in the ὅσα-clauses, the raids and the deaths, follow in chronological order. Nestor's sequence of deaths in the second clause, Aias-Achilleus-Patroklos-Antilochos, on the other hand, does not: the "facts" are that Achilleus' vengeance on the killers of Patroklos and Antilochos precipitates his own demise, and that Aias then dies as a result of a dispute over the dead Achilleus' armor. The non-chronological presentation of the series is not, however, attributable to Nestor, since other narrators use the same core sequence, Achilleus-Patroklos-Antilochos, with Aias last, elsewhere in the *Odyssey* (11.467-469, 24.15-17). It therefore appears that metrical and/ or formulaic factors are responsible for the order in which Nestor lists the deaths. Significant as well could be themes relating to the burial of Achilleus, whose remains were interred in the same amphora as those of Patroklos, with Antilochos' nearby in the second place of honor (*Odyssey* 24.76-79). In any case, the two ὅσα-clauses together cover the war to the point at which Troy falls (118). Then, at last, Nestor locates the hero whose fate he has been asked to tell (121-122).

At least three criteria can be discerned in this schematization of the Trojan War. On the broadest level, Nestor proceeds in part in chronological order, from Greek raids on the Troad to the siege of Troy and its fall. Second, he associates each sequence of events with a main theme, pain, which he then resolves into raids and conflicts, with the conflicts in turn resolving into a series of heroes' deaths, and with the fall of Troy capping the pain-theme. Third, each sequence is associated with a main hero or heroes: Achilleus with the raids; Telamonian Aias, Patroklos, and Antilochos with the deaths; and Odysseus, by association, with the Greeks' final triumph.

In this respect, Nestor can be seen to handle his narrative in the manner of a poet.[9] As discussed in the Introduction, the association of main hero, main theme, and chronology is a conventional way to identify or define an ancient Greek epic. So for example the *Odyssey*'s proem brings together "the man" (Odysseus), "return," and a call to the Muse to begin from some point

[9] Thus Dickson 1995:79-80 describes *Odyssey* 3.130-200 and 253-316 as a distinct narrative, "The Akhaian Nostoi," and observes therein "authorial structures, tropes and techniques familiar from the enframing tale" as well as from the *Iliad*.

(ἄνδρα . . . νόστον . . . τῶν ἀμόθεν, 1.1-10), that of the *Iliad* 'wrath', Achilleus, and a specific temporal reference (μῆνιν . . . Ἀχιλῆος . . . ἐξ οὗ δὴ τὰ πρῶτα, 1.1-6). Thus, keeping in mind that titles emerged only in the process of textualization, Nestor seems to use this bundle of themes to refer to discrete sections of the Trojan War story; that is, he conceptualizes his material as if he were a composer of epics.[10]

Nestor's explanation for dividing up the pain-narrative points to a similar conclusion. He asserts that this material, in its undigested form, threatens to overwhelm both himself, the mortal storyteller, and any audience unprepared to spend years listening to it (115-117).[11] Nestor in other words approaches the story of the Trojan War in terms of its performability, and his reflection on the limits of both storyteller and audience may have had a meta-theatrical effect during performances of the *Odyssey*. Roughly an eighth of the way through a long narrative, with the main hero nowhere in sight, a famously prolix character reflects on the difficulty of handling the enormous mass of Trojan War material. I suggest that the allusive thematic bundles consisting of hero or heroes, main theme, and temporal frame that occur in the opening section of Nestor's speech in effect refer the audience to an at least loosely-defined set of epic narratives.

The relationship between Nestor's thematic bundles and the Trojan War epics that have come down to us strengthens this impression. Specifically, Nestor's categorization scheme appears to reproduce the divisions among the *Iliad* and the poems of the Epic Cycle. To begin with, the raids under Achilleus' leadership in the first ὅσα-clause can be mapped onto the *Kypria*, which covers the opening phase of the Trojan War story up to around the point at which the *Iliad* begins (Proklos 43.66-68, 67.1-2 Bernabé, 105.16-20 Allen). In the *Kypria*, raiding is a recurrent theme, and Achilleus is as prominent as he is in the *Iliad*.[12]

---

[10] Dickson 1995:76-77 refers to what I have termed the chronological theme as the "point of departure," and defines the main theme as a "noun, generally specified by a short qualifier" that "identifies the theme and so functions as a title," which as he notes is akin to Ford's 1992:20 notion of "titling syntax." On the absence of titles in oral traditions generally, see Finnegan 1977:107.

[11] Declarations of aporia are conventional in Greek epic; cf. the beginning of the Catalog of Ships (*Iliad* 2.488-492). As Dickson 1995:77-78 observes, such declarations are "central to oral poetry," in that performance demands careful selection. For the pain-theme cf. Demodokos' use of πήματος in reference to an inflection point in the Trojan War (*Odyssey* 8.81).

[12] Raids in the *Kypria*: (40.36, 42.58-62 Bernabé, 104.4-8, 105.6-15 Allen). Achilleus in the *Kypria*: parents wed (Proklos 38.5-39.8 Bernabé, 102.14-18 Allen); he himself weds (41.39-40, 104.8-9); quarrels with Agamemnon (41.49-50, 104.23-24); kills the first Trojan (42.1-2, 105.2-3); prevents the Greek army from dissolving (42.61, 105.9-10); the object of Zeus' planning (43.66-67, 105.16-17). For the temporal scope of the *Kypria* and its junction with the *Iliad*, see Marks 2002; for an alternative reconstruction, Burgess 2001:136-140.

Turning now to the heroes' deaths introduced by Nestor's second ὅσα-clause, that of Patroklos is a peak dramatic moment in the *Iliad* and a natural way for Nestor to refer to the Iliadic portion of the war, since Achilleus has already been identified with the raiding sequence. The other deaths Nestor mentions, those of Antilochos, Achilleus and Aias, are narrated in the *Aithiopis*; the latter is in addition the first event in the *Ilias Parva* (Proklos. 74.3-5 Bernabé, 106.20-23 Allen). The absence of a single dominating presence in Nestor's second ὅσα-clause, observed above, is consistent with our evidence for these epics, which appear to have been built episodically around the sequential losses of Greek and Trojan heroes.[13] Nestor also includes a catch-all category, the "many other evils we suffered in addition to these" (113), that can account for any ancillary story, which is perhaps to say any epichoric myth.

The death of Aias brings Nestor's narrative to a point in the overall story of Troy that corresponds to the junction between the *Aithiopis* and the *Ilias Parva*. This death also raises the specter of the hero toward whom Nestor has been working, since it is after losing to Odysseus in the contest for the dead Achilleus' armor that Aias perishes by his own hand (74.3-5 Bernabé, 106.21-23 Allen; cf. *Odyssey* 11.543-548; "Apollodoros" *Epitome* 5.6). After his remark on the magnitude of the pain-narrative, Nestor resumes his survey at the end of the war, a sequence covered in the *Ilias Parva* and another Cyclic epic, the *Iliou Persis*. By way of transition, Nestor reflects for a moment on the theme of trickery and cleverness (δόλοι, μῆτις, 119-122; cf. 163). This theme is of course central to Odysseus' heroic identity; in the *Odyssey*, for example, he introduces himself to the Phaiakes as "Odysseus son of Laertes, a concern to men for all sorts of tricks," or, more grandly, "to all men for my tricks" (Ὀδυσεὺς Λαερτιάδης, ὃς πᾶσι δόλοισιν/ἀνθρώποισι μέλω, 9.19-20).

After the ὅσα-clauses, then, Nestor has arrived at a major inflection point in the overall story of the Trojan War, and in the story of Odysseus. For it is after the deaths of Patroklos, Antilochos, Achilleus, and Telamonian Aias that the gods are prepared to let Troy fall and that the tricks and stratagems at which Odysseus excels become decisive in the struggle between the Greeks and Trojans. Odysseus is to be sure a significant, and occasionally tricky, character in earlier events. Other figures, however, in particular Achilleus, dominate the first nine years of the Trojan War story. Moreover, it is at this point that Nestor asserts a special affinity between himself and Odysseus (*Odyssey* 3.126-129), which claim both appeals to the internal audience, Telemachos, and reinforces the significance of Odysseus in *nostos*-traditions. Nestor's nominal identity can

---

[13] See Burgess 2001:144-145.

explain the fact that the old hero too only at this point becomes an actor in his own narrative: with the fall of Troy, themes associated with "Mr. Nostos" naturally come to the fore.

Nestor's characterization of this final stage of the Trojan War agrees with what is known of the two Cyclic epics that covered these events. For in the *Ilias Parva* and the *Iliou Persis*, Odysseus is responsible for nearly every step the Greeks make toward taking the city. He gathers intelligence by capturing Helenos and entering Troy in disguise, brings Philoktetes and Neoptolemos to Troy, helps to steal the Trojan Palladion, and plays a role in the construction of the wooden horse (74-75, 88-89 Bernabé, 106.23-107.8 Allen; cf. *Odyssey* 8.500-520). Considering the entire Trojan War story, then, the fall of Troy is Odysseus' main moment in the spotlight apart from the *Odyssey* itself.

To sum up the argument thus far, I am proposing that Nestor's conception of the Trojan War corresponds to the Trojan War epics that have come down to us as follows. The pain-theme embraces the entire Trojan War story; Nestor's first ὅσα-clause covers the narrative territory of one epic, the *Kypria*; the second ὅσα-clause is distributed into ἔνθα-clauses that cover the narrative territories of the *Iliad*, *Aithiopis*, *Ilias Parva*, and *Iliou Persis*. The final stage of this overall narrative, the returns of the surviving heroes, is covered in the Cyclic *Nostoi* and *Telegony* and the Homeric *Odyssey*. Thus, in tabular form:

portion of Trojan War	narrative tradition
Trojan War as a whole	"pain-narrative" (unperformable)
raiding expeditions	*Kypria*
death of Patroklos	*Iliad*
deaths of Antilochos and Achilleus	*Aithiopis*
death of Aias	*Aithiopis*, *Ilias Parva*
sack of Troy	*Ilias Parva*, *Iliou Persis*
returns of surviving Greeks	*Nostoi*, *Odyssey*, *Telegony*

My proposal that Nestor references a kind of epic cycle is made in full awareness of the uncertainties about the narrative bounds of various Trojan War traditions and of the probability that the episodes associated with each narrative tradition varied over time. The model advanced in the Introduction accounts for such variation, for in its terms the *Odyssey* documents a time in the evolution of the epic tradition when standardization was occurring but was not complete. Again, I am not arguing, as have Analyst and Neo-Analyst critics, that the *Odyssey* derives material from an already fixed set of Cyclic poems, but rather that Homeric and Cyclic traditions were mutually referential throughout their development.

Thus Nestor can be seen to acknowledge, and in a sense to take part in, this process of engagement. His schematization could even be interpreted as a diachronic recapitulation of the larger tradition. Viewed this way, the two ὅσα-clauses document a time when narratives corresponding to the *Kypria* and *Aithiopis* covered the war up to the *nostoi*-narratives, while the division of the second ὅσα-clause into smaller units documents the subsequent encroachment, on the one hand, of Iliadic tradition on the narrative territory of the *Kypria*, and, on the other, of the *Ilias Parva* and *Iliou Persis* on the territory of the *Aithiopis*.[14]

This evolutionary scheme is of course speculative; nor is it possible to know with any certainty how distinct an idea Homeric audiences had of the narratives that came to be associated with the Cyclic and other epics. I do hope to have demonstrated at least that Nestor conceives of the Trojan War in terms of performable sections. The same can be said, I shall now argue, of Nestor's Nostoi proper, which is again neither random nor ad hoc, but rather embeds the perspective and conventions of established narrative traditions.

The gods of return

In contrast with the elliptical references that make up the opening section of Nestor's narrative, his Nostoi proper provides a considerable amount of detail, including chronological and geographical settings and a measure of character development. Most importantly for my larger argument, Nestor traces causation back to the gods, among whom Zeus is the decisive figure.

Nestor's claim to describe the actions of the gods raises a key interpretive issue. For, as discussed in Chapter 2 in the context of Odysseus' narration of his *Apologoi*, mortal characters remain only vaguely aware of divine activity unless they witness an undisguised god in action or receive information from a divine source. This phenomenon, commonly referred as "Jørgensen's law," admits of two general exceptions: seers, such as Halitherses in *Odyssey* 2 and 24, and divinely-inspired singers of epic, such as Demodokos in *Odyssey* 8, have steady and reliable information about the gods. Nestor's knowledge of divine activity assimilates him to these latter characters, singers such as the Homeric

---

[14] For arguments that the *Kypria* and *Aithiopis* were more comprehensive than the extant evidence implies, see Burgess 2001:26-27, 141-143; Kullmann 1960:224, 358.

narrator and the professionals to whom the Muse (*Odyssey* 1.1, 8.62-64, 479-481, 22.347; *Iliad* 1.1, 2.484-487) provides access to the gods' involvement in events on earth and those that take place on Olympos (*Odyssey* 8.266-366).

The *Iliad* also attributes exceptional knowledge of divine activity to Nestor. In another extended account of things past, the so-called "Pylian Epic" in *Iliad* 11 (670-761), he tells how, in the final phase of a conflict in which he himself took part, Zeus (753) and Athene (758) combine forces to orchestrate a Pylian victory. The gods' actions, which, coordinated as they are, suggest a divine council scene analogous to the one at the beginning of the *Odyssey*, should be beyond Nestor's ken.[15] And since Nestor alone of mortal characters that are neither seers nor singers fails to conform to Jørgensen's law, it is difficult to dismiss the divine apparatus in both his Pylian Epic and his Nostoi as lapses.[16] Nestor's compositional tendencies are however consistent with the interpretation advanced here, that he is in both Homeric epics assimilated to the character of a "singer of tales." Thus I note that the Pylian Epic identifies at the outset a main hero (Nestor himself), a temporal frame, and main theme, "when there was a conflict between the Epeioi and us"(ὁπότ' Ἠλείοισι καὶ ἡμῖν νεῖκος, 671).

While Nestor's initial mention of Zeus as responsible for the Trojan War (*Odyssey* 3.119) might thus be explicable in terms of Jørgensen's law, his Nostoi proper marks the debut of what can fairly be called a divine apparatus:[17]

---

[15] Cf. *Iliad* 11.721, 750-752. Thus Hainsworth *IC* 3:298 ad 11.670-762 observes that Nestor "tells his tale generally in the same manner as the narrator of the *Iliad* . . . like the poet he knows what the gods did." Nestor even seems to evince knowledge of divine activity in the main narrative, for he implicates Thetis and Zeus in Achilleus' refusal to fight (*Iliad* 11.795). Similarly, Atchity 1978:261 observes that "Nestor resembles the poet inasmuch as he shares the poet's transcendence of time."

[16] de Jong 2001:76-77 ad 3.130-85 observes that "Nestor partly has an exact understanding of the gods . . . [and] partly expresses himself . . . according to Jørgensen's law," and explains away the former ability as "*ex eventu* commentary;" left unexplained, however, is how Nestor comes by this information even after the fact, and the novelty of his exceptional status. Attempts like Calhoun's (1940:269-275) to explain such exceptions to the law in terms of ad hoc decision-making by the poet demand the acceptance of his overall conclusion, opposite the one advanced here, that the Homeric gods are "purely ornamental" (276).

[17] Thus Dickson 1995:80-81 argues that the gods Nestor names in *Odyssey* 3 serve "as the deep mechanism that steers the homebound Akhaians and *a fortiori* the tale itself . . . [along] nodes from which different trajectories for the tale can veer off towards different destinations, and upon whose 'grid' the singer maps his story out. Nestor demonstrates precisely the same 'navigational' control over these paths as does the narrator of the larger tale in which his is embedded."

αὐτὰρ ἐπεὶ Πριάμοιο πόλιν διεπέρσαμεν αἰπήν,
βῆμεν δ' ἐν νήεσσι, θεὸς δ' ἐκέδασσεν Ἀχαιούς,
καὶ τότε δὴ Ζεὺς λυγρὸν ἐνὶ φρεσὶ μήδετο νόστον
Ἀργείοις, ἐπεὶ οὔ τι νοήμονες οὐδὲ δίκαιοι
πάντες ἔσαν· τῶ σφεων πολέες κακὸν οἶτον ἐπέσπον
μήνιος ἐξ ὀλοῆς γλαυκώπιδος ὀβριμοπάτρης,   135
ἥ τ' ἔριν Ἀτρείδῃσι μετ' ἀμφοτέροισιν ἔθηκε.

But after we sacked Priam's high city,
we boarded the ships, but a god scattered the Achaians,
and right then Zeus was devising in his thoughts a lamen-
    table homecoming
for the Argives, since in no way right-thinking nor just
were they all; therefore many of them fell upon an evil fate
on account of the destructive wrath of the grey-eyed
    daughter of a powerful father [i.e. Athene]
who made strife between the sons of Atreus.

Odyssey 3.130-136

After a summary statement that "a god" scattered the Greek ships (θεός, 131), Nestor explains that it was Zeus who devised the *nostos* generally (132), and Athene who, on account of her wrath, brought the power of Olympos to bear on the returning heroes (135; cf. 145-147). More specifically, Zeus intended a "lamentable" return for the Greeks (λυγρός, 132), and Athene made it so by inciting strife between their leaders (135-136).

The coordinate action of Zeus and Athene mirrors that which, I have been arguing, motivates the main narrative. In both cases, the lesser Olympian plays an active, and partisan, role in human affairs, while Zeus deliberates. Nestor's reference here to the wrath of Athene has parallels in songs performed by the *Odyssey*'s professional singers. Thus Demodokos conceives of the Trojan War as an overall pain narrative that is motivated by Zeus (πήματος ἀρχὴ/Τρωσί τε καὶ Δαναοῖσι Διὸς μεγάλου διὰ βουλάς, 8.81-82), while he assigns specific responsibility for the wooden horse episode to Athene (διὰ μεγάθυμον Ἀθήνην, 8.520); Phemios also associates his own Nostoi with Athene (Ἀχαιῶν νόστον ἄειδε/λυγρόν, ὃν ἐκ Τροίης ἐπετείλατο Παλλὰς Ἀθήνη, 1.326-327).[18]

---

[18] Nestor's reference to the wrath of Athene alludes to acts of sacrilege committed by the Greeks during the sack of Troy, in particular desecration of the goddess's sacred image by Oileian Aias (*Iliou Persis* 89.15-20 Bernabé, 108.2-6, 11-13 Allen; cf. *Odyssey* 4.502). So also in "Apollodoros" *Epitome* 6.5 Athene asks Zeus to send a storm against the returning Greeks. Phemios' elision of Zeus' role and emphasis on Athene in his account of the *nostoi* is paralleled by Hermes (*Odyssey* 5.108-111).

Nestor explains Zeus' involvement with the Greeks' sufferings after Troy in terms of their unlawful behavior (ἐπεὶ οὔ τι νοήμονες οὐδὲ δίκαιοι πάντες ἔσαν, 133-134). Here again, Nestor's themes resonate with the main narrative, for divine justice and human culpability are central to Zeus' Oresteia, as well as to the sufferings that Odysseus' crew, the Phaiakes, and the suitors endure – in all of which Zeus is implicated.[19] In terms of my overall model for the *Odyssey*, Zeus here in Nestor's Nostoi can be seen to incorporate Athene's narrow concern for her own divine prerogatives into a plan that involves all of the returning Greeks. In other words Nestor, by defining Athene's motivation narrowly, subordinates the goddess to Zeus in the chain of causality that undergirds his Nostoi, thus recreating the relationship between the two gods that runs through the main narrative.

This interpretation is consistent with the fact that, as Nestor proceeds with his tale, Zeus continues to direct the overall progress of the Greeks' returns. Athene, by contrast, ceases to play a role once she has caused the strife between the Greek leaders (134-158), and even in this case Nestor comments that "Zeus was fashioning misery of evil" (ἐπὶ γὰρ Ζεὺς ἤρτυε πῆμα κακοῖο, 152).[20] Zeus then again harries the returning Greeks by causing a further round of strife among them (Ζεὺς δ' οὔ πω μήδετο νόστον/σχέτλιος ὅς ῥ' ἔριν ὦρσε κακὴν ἔπι δεύτερον αὖτις, 160-161), as a consequence of which Nestor's narrative passes a crucial inflection point. He himself parts company with Odysseus (162-163) and afterward has no more to say about him. Likewise, in the main narrative, Athene, after active participation in the opening phase of the story, plays a small role in Odysseus' *nostos* in Books 5-13.

Nestor's special qualities as a narrator become particularly clear when his Nostoi is compared with Odysseus' *Apologoi*. Odysseus offers neither a synoptic view of the Greeks' wanderings nor a coherent account of the gods' role in them (again, cf. 9.39). Further, Zeus is absent from Odysseus' *Apologoi*, except for the divine council in Book 12 cited above to illustrate Jørgensen's law, and for unmistakable *ex eventu* supposition that conforms to this law (e.g. 9.553-555). Likewise the absence of Athene, the other pillar of the *Odyssey*'s, and Nestor's, divine apparatus, during the return portion of Odysseus' story is so palpable that the goddess herself is called on to explain it away (13.341-343).

---

[19] Cf. de Jong 2001:77 ad 3.130-66; Clay 1983:47-49.
[20] Agamemnon's awareness of Athene's wrath in this passage (*Odyssey* 3.143-145) is explicable in the context of scenes, such as in *Iliad* 1, in which he and the assembled army are informed of the gods' displeasure by the seer Kalchas, who indeed survives the war and appears in the Cyclic *Nostoi*.

There is however one circumstance in which Odysseus does take on powers as a narrator comparable to Nestor's: when he tells his false tales. Thus, after returning to Ithake in disguise, Odysseus refers to Zeus or makes him responsible for a number of events in his false past. It has been argued that the knowledge of Zeus' actions that Odysseus' persona claims, because it is only of a general sort, conforms to Jørgensen's law, and this is true in most instances (e.g. 14.268, 17.424).[21] However, the role that the disguised Odysseus assigns to Zeus on occasion parallels closely that in the "real" story, as when he claims that Zeus and Helios destroyed his ship and crew (19.276; cf. 12.374-387); and his declaration that Zeus was responsible for the Trojan War (14.235-236), though perhaps a commonplace, nevertheless echoes similarly programmatic statements by Nestor and the Homeric narrator discussed above. Building on the perspective developed in the previous chapter, the lying Odysseus, through his claims about his own fate and Zeus' role in it, is constructed as a false singer performing a counterfeit tradition. His avowed knowledge of Zeus' activities represents one more preposterous claim, like that of being a peer of Menelaos during the Trojan War (14.470-471).

Nestor's divine apparatus, then, reproduces the conventions that inform the representation of the gods in the main narrative. His Nostoi overlays the sufficient dramatic motivation of a lesser god responding to immediate, localized circumstances – Athene's anger at the Greeks – with the more comprehensive and impersonal motivating force of the supreme god Zeus. Given the compressed nature of his account, it is remarkable that Nestor mentions the gods at all, let alone in such detail, and by means of powers normally unavailable to mortal characters.

Variations on the *nostos*-theme

Odysseus exits Nestor's Nostoi when the two part ways at Tenedos (*Odyssey* 3.159-164), but the story continues, like the Cyclic *Nostoi*, through to the Oresteia. Having seen Diomedes safely home, Nestor completes his own return without difficulty, thereby fulfilling his nominal destiny as "Mr. Nostos." Back in Pylos, he receives news about other distinguished Trojan War veterans, namely Neoptolemos ("the glorious son of great-hearted Achilleus"), Philoktetes and Idomeneus, who return home uneventfully and safely

---

[21] Thus de Jong 2001:355 ad 3.192-359. Contrast for instance *Odyssey* 11.558-560: in narrating a "real" event, Odysseus' surmise about Zeus' responsibility for the strife between himself and Telamonian Aias is expressed in terms consistent with Jørgensen's law; cf. the similar terms in which Agamemnon blames Zeus for his conflict with Achilleus (cf. *Iliad* 19.86-87).

(188-192), and Agamemnon, who does not (193-200). After a brief interlude, Nestor concludes his Nostoi with an expanded version of Agamemnon's story (262-312). Nestor's Pylos can thus be seen as a kind of Panhellenic clearing-house for the larger Trojan War tradition (cf. 94-95); so Nestor also mediates Telemachos' pursuit of further news from Menelaos (317-328). Stories arrive and are organized into a coherent narrative at a site from the heroic past, Pylos, whose location was a mystery to ancient Greeks (cf. Strabo 8.3.24), and therefore removed from epichoric tradition. Thus, while local epic singers such as Phemios on Ithake and Demodokos on Scherie receive and transmit Trojan War stories, the quality of their information is perceived to be inferior to that of Nestor, since Telemachos would not be motivated to travel to Pylos unless he could expect to learn more there than he could from Phemios.

Like those of other characters in the *Odyssey*, Nestor's account of the returning heroes proves to be polemical. It is for one thing selective: Nestor mentions neither the death of Oileian Aias at the hands of Athene and Poseidon (related by Menelaos at 4.499-511), for instance, nor Kalchas, who has a prominent role in other accounts (e.g. *Nostoi* p. 94.7-9 Bernabé, 108.22-24 Allen; "Apollodoros" *Epitome* 5.23-6.4). Most significant for the present discussion, Nestor's shaping of the stories he does tell mirrors the *Odyssey*'s shaping of Odysseus' story. For the safe returns of Diomedes, Neoptolemos, Philoktetes, and Idomeneus contrast starkly with non-Homeric accounts, in which these heroes are driven from home to find new adventures in the west.[22]

Such traditions grew up particularly thick around the returning Diomedes. While his return is uneventful in the Cyclic *Nostoi* as it is in the *Odyssey* (94.5 Bernabé, 108.19 Allen; cf. "Apollodoros" *Epitome* 6.1), other non-Homeric accounts give Diomedes a story like that of the non-Homeric Odysseus, including a dangerous, Klytaimnestre-like wife, post-Trojan War wanderings, and death in an adopted home, in this case, Apulia.[23] The non-Homeric Neoptolemos, as discussed in the previous chapter, leaves Troy either to rule the Molossians or the Epirotes. The non-Homeric Philoktetes is also driven to the west, where he was connected with a settlement and a cult of

---

[22] Strabo (6.1.15; cf. 5.2.5), associates only "those accompanying Nestor from Ilion" (τῶν ἐξ Ἰλίου πλευσάντων μετὰ Νέστορος) with the foundation of Metapontion, and Nestor's stay in Italy need not be permanent, since "Mr. Nostos" is unlikely to have had an unsuccessful return in any traditional version, though see Malkin 1998:213 for a contrary view.

[23] According to Mimnermos fr. 22 W, Aphrodite corrupts Diomedes' wife in revenge for his wounding of her (cf. *Iliad* 5.412-415); for possible Iliadic suppression of this faithless wife, see Chapter 1 n27. For Diomedes' wanderings, see Servius ad *Aeneid* 8.9; for his colonization of Apulia and death there, Strabo 6.3.9.

Apollo near Croton.[24] The non-Homeric Idomeneus likewise is cuckolded while at Troy; his wife's seducer then takes control of Crete and repels the hero when he returns, so that Idomeneus ends up settling in Calabria.[25]

Again, such foundation myths are the stuff of epichoric tradition. Nestor does not, however, take care to pare away potential connections to epichoric traditions until he comes to name these heroes as safely returned. Before this point in his narrative, he describes, for instance, stops on Tenedos (159-164), the historical inhabitants of which claimed descent from Trojan captives released by the Greek army (Pausanias 2.5.4), as well as at Geraistos in Euboia (173-179), where a temple to Poseidon was said to commemorate sacrifices by Nestor and Diomedes to thank the god for their safe return to Greece (Strabo 10.1.7). Perhaps because none of these events conflicts with its view of Odysseus, the *Odyssey* allows Nestor to set this part of his tale in the "real world" of ancient Greek geography.

The uneventful homecomings that Nestor describes for Diomedes, Neoptolemos, and Idomeneus may be motivated in addition by a desire to de-authorize stories in which Odysseus is indirectly responsible for the aforementioned seduction of their wives. According to these non-Homeric accounts, Odysseus, in some versions with the aid of Diomedes, falsely accuses the Greek hero Palamedes of theft and engineers his execution; in revenge, Palamedes' father Nauplios travels to the absent heroes' homes – though not to Ithake, where there is apparently sufficient temptation for Penelope already – and arranges matches between their wives and various usurpers (*Kypria* 43.66 Bernabé, 105.15-16 Allen; cf. "Apollodoros" *Epitome* 6.8-9). Nestor's Nostoi at least reinforces the exclusion of Palamedes from both Homeric epics, presumably on the grounds that his story is irreconcilable with the Homeric Odysseus. Similarly, the safe returns of Neoptolemos and Diomedes in effect place a seal of divine approval on questionable acts in which they assist the non-Homeric Odysseus: the theft of Athene's sacred image from Troy and the luring of Philoktetes to Troy, respectively.

Suggestive in any case is Odysseus' close relationship with each of these heroes in both Homeric and non-Homeric contexts. Odysseus and Diomedes

[24] For Philoktetes' Italian wanderings see "Apollodoros" *Epitome* 6.15b; [Aristotle] *De Mirabilis Auscultationibus* 107 (115), cited in Frazer 1921:261n3 *ad loc.*; Strabo 6.1.3; *Aeneid* 3.402. He is not mentioned in the extant evidence for the Cyclic *Nostoi*.

[25] For Idomeneus' return see "Apollodoros" *Epitome* 6.9-10 with Appendix XII in Frazer 1921 v. 2. His exile was known to Virgil (*Aeneid* 3.121-122; 11.264-265; cf. Servius ad *Aeneid* 3.121 and 11.264). Like Philoktetes, Idomeneus is not mentioned in the extant evidence for the Cyclic *Nostoi*.

work together in battle (e.g. *Iliad* 10) and during the taking of Troy (*Ilias Parva* 75.15-18 Bernabé, 107.7-8 Allen). Neoptolemos is alternatively Odysseus' ally (*Odyssey* 11.506-537; *Ilias Parva* 74.10-11 Bernabé, 106.29 Allen), and, as discussed in Chapter 4, his foe. Philoktetes is mistreated and tricked by Odysseus in non-Homeric tradition (e.g. "Apollodoros" *Epitome* 5.8; Sophokles *Philoktetes*); it is perhaps in part for this reason that the *Odyssey* has Odysseus voice regard for Philoktetes' skill as an archer (8.219). Lastly, Idomeneus is, like Diomedes, a frequent companion of Odysseus at Troy (the two are together in scenes in *Iliad* 4, 5, 7, 13, and 1), and he is associated with the Cretan persona and Odysseus in the Cretan tales (13.259, 14.237, 19.181, 190) and in the story that the lying Aitolian tells Eumaios (14.382).[26]

Lastly, Nestor shapes his account of Agamemnon (3.193-200, 262-312) in a manner that recalls Zeus' Oresteia. Thus Nestor omits Klytaimnestre from his initial account, and then casts her as a victim of Aigisthos, and perhaps of the gods, in an expanded version (264-269). This version, which Nestor produces at Telemachos' specific request (248-252), is also of interest for the reappearance of the gods, who have been absent from Nestor's narrative since Zeus contrived the strife among the Greeks at Tenedos (160). Nestor's statements that Aigisthos' initial success was due to the "fate of the gods" (μοῖρα θεῶν, 269), and that Menelaos' wanderings were the result of an attack by Apollo (279-283),[27] suggest a familiar constellation of themes. The "fate of the gods," an expression that is, as discussed in the Introduction, related to the *Dios boulē* theme, implies coordinated divine action, which is dramatized conventionally in a divine council scene over which Zeus presides. Apollo's attack again reveals Nestor's unique knowledge of divine activity and recalls the theme of the angry subordinate god who instigates the action among mortal characters, as Apollo does at the beginning of the *Iliad* (1.9).

Nestor's Nostoi, then, alternately emphasizes and suppresses themes in a manner that mirrors the handling of analogous themes in the main narrative. Space prevents a detailed consideration of the epichoric roots of the non-Homeric traditions discussed here. I have however tried to suggest places where an approach like that applied to west Greek Odysseus-traditions in the previous chapter could yield plausible contexts for the performance of epichoric and proto-Panhellenic narratives that were early and influential enough to invite the *Odyssey*'s engagement. By way of further

---

[26] Idomeneus also appears on Telemachos' itinerary in variant readings at *Odyssey* 1.93 and 285; see Reece 1994:166-169. On the lying Aitolian see Chapter 4.

[27] The site of Apollo's attack, Cape Sounion off Athens (*Odyssey* 3.278), also figured in epichoric tradition; see Burgess 2001:37-38.

illustration, stories about Palamedes appear to have been associated with the Argolid (Strabo 8.6.2); and citizens of Lokris, for whom Oileian Aias was a local hero, may have entertained very different accounts of Athene's anger at the returning Greeks than those in the *Odyssey* and Cyclic *Nostoi*, where he is a prime offender against the goddess.

Chapter conclusions

Nestor, I have argued, is a unique narrator in the *Odyssey*, in that his compositional strategies are assimilated to those of epic singers and the Homeric narrator. Thus "Mr. Nostos" has access to information about the gods that is normally unavailable to mortal characters, and he locates his Nostoi within the broader context of a loosely-defined system of mutually referential Trojan War stories that, by my interpretation, recall some the narratives we know as the *Iliad* and Cyclic epics. Also like a traditional singer, Nestor identifies the narratives that make up this system in terms their performability and by a characteristic bundle of themes.

Conspicuous among these themes is a divine apparatus that provides the overall motivation for Nestor's Nostoi. This divine apparatus, consisting of the main god Zeus acting in concert with one or more subordinate gods, parallels that of the *Odyssey* itself and of other epics. From this perspective, the Zeus of Nestor's Nostoi is thematically equivalent to the Zeus of the *Odyssey*'s main narrative and to the Zeus Nestor invokes in *Iliad* 15, where the fated, inevitable return of "Mr. Nostos" is represented as the dispensation of the supreme god.

More specific to the *Odyssey*'s perspective on the Trojan War is Nestor's shaping of *nostos*-stories that parallel Odysseus' return. The stories of heroes who are associated with Odysseus in other contexts, and whose return-stories parallel his, are subjected to the kind of selective treatment that Zeus gives the Oresteia and that Odysseus receives in the main narrative. Thus Nestor's Diomedes, Neoptolemos, and Idomeneus journey home uneventfully, without adventures to which epichoric traditions attach, and they return apparently to untroubled marriages and contented subjects. The return of Agamemnon, on the other hand, becomes for Nestor what it was for Zeus at the beginning of the narrative, a negative paradigm for Odysseus.

Nestor's uniqueness as a character, I suggest, arose as epic tradition became invested in constructing him as a voice of authority over the portion of the Trojan War story that is conjured up by his very name. In the *Odyssey*, this authority serves to complete the task, assigned initially to Zeus, of situating its hero's story within the context of the many and conflicting accounts of the Greeks' returns from Troy. As a consequence, Nestor's Nostoi recreates in miniature the *Odyssey*'s own compositional tendencies, in particular the fundamental equation of divine plan and narrative plan.

6

DIVINE PLAN AND NARRATIVE PLAN

THUS FAR I HAVE ARGUED that the *Dios boulē* theme serves two interconnected functions in the *Odyssey*: it lends shape and coherence to the narrative, and it mediates the *Odyssey*'s relationship to other Odysseus-traditions. The attraction of Zeus to the interface between the Homeric and non-Homeric accounts I have explained in terms of the Panhellenic orientation of the former: the *Odyssey* was crafted to appeal to heterogeneous audiences familiar with, and patriotically attached to, differing epichoric accounts of the Trojan War. To sum up my argument in a single, if unwieldy, sentence: the *Dios boulē* theme is a Panhellenic and proto-Panhellenic realization of a traditional way of conceptualizing ancient Greek epic narratives.

Such interpretations are naturally incapable of proof due to the dearth of ancient Greek testimony on the practical aspects of poetics. Yet in order for my, or any, model of the *Odyssey*'s narrative structure to be plausible, it is necessary to consider how concepts that have been deduced from textual evidence could have arisen and functioned in the oral tradition from which the texts derive. Some of these issues were raised in the Introduction, when I considered the potential for subtext in a medium without texts. As a kind of summary of my findings in general, I return in this chapter to the significance of the plan, and of Zeus, for composition-in-performance of epics like the *Odyssey*.

An at least partial reason why a composer, or a narrative tradition, might bother to elaborate so formalized a conception of a song can, I propose, be found in the mechanics of oral poetry. Specifically, comparison with living (or recently deceased) epic traditions, for which first-person accounts of the practical aspects of poetics are available, suggests that the overarching perspective that I have identified in the Homeric *Dios boulē* theme is a broader phenomenon, and is indeed essential to the composition-in-performance of extended oral narratives. Thus, even if my model overestimates the significance of Zeus in the *Odyssey*, I maintain that the operation of some other character or principle must be inferred that carries out the functions I assign to the *Dios boulē*.

The *Dios boulē* in performance

The deployment of an overarching theme is a core concept in Albert Lord's model of oral composition-in performance, for it is in this theme that he located the identity of a song. Employing the comparative methodology pioneered by his teacher Milman Parry, Lord deduced from then flourishing South Slavic epic traditions some general principles concerning this level of narrative structure that he then applied to the Homeric epics. A traditional singer's perspective on the subject is documented in one of Lord's earlier publications:

> A Yugoslav singer told me last year that when he learned a new song he made no attempt at word-for-word memorization but learned only the "plan" of the song, which he explained as "the arrange-ment of the events." This plan he then proceeded to fill in with the themes which he already knew.[1]

As this singer explained it, the identity and stability of an orally composed and transmitted narrative is founded, not on verbatim adherence to an archetypal composition, but on a different unit of content, the "plan." Here we may wonder whether Lord's translation of the Slavic singer's category with this particular English word is not in part conditioned by his own familiarity with Homeric epic, specifically the Διὸς δ' ἐτελείετο βουλή of the *Iliad* proem.[2]

In any case, further study led Lord to conclude that, regarding the overall shape of a traditional oral narrative,

> His [the singer's] idea of stability, to which he is deeply devoted, does not include the wording, which to him has never been fixed . . . He builds his performance, or the song in our sense, on the stable skeleton of narrative, which is the song in his sense.[3]

The emphasis has been added because without attention to this phrase Lord's model can be misunderstood. The plan of a traditional oral narrative is not simply a general template for improvisation. It is rather a specific way to organize characters and action patterns into a coherent narrative. For while the "stable skeleton" does not impose word-for-word fixity on a song, it does establish firm limits on the amount of variation that occurs when the song is performed. Thus Lord observed in general "a conservativeness in regard to

---

[1] Lord 1951:74.
[2] See for instance Lord 1960:188-189.
[3] Lord 1960:99.

story," concomitant with significant variation in the actual wording, across performances of what singers described as the "same" song.[4] The song remains "the same" from the singer's perspective when each performance preserves the essential themes, organized according to the most essential theme of all, the plan.

Subsequent research has corroborated Lord's findings and established a broader comparative perspective for his model of composition-in-performance. Relevant here is the work of David Rubin, a cognitive psychologist who has applied models and methods developed in his own field to the study of memory in oral traditions, including ballads and nursery rhymes as well as epics. His understanding of large-scale structure in orally composed and transmitted narratives is that

> The song is a system made up of systems ... such as the spatial and object systems of imagery or the rhyme and alliteration patterns. Similarly, the song is embedded in a system, the genre, which itself is embedded in the class of all oral traditions, and so forth. . . . Each of the systems at each level interacts. . . . The song has a boundary, which defines what is inside and what is outside the systems. Variants of one song are within the possible manifestations of the systems, but different songs are not. . . . The particular words making up the song change over time, though the basic organization does not. . . . The song maintains itself.[5]

By way of translation, Rubin's "systems" as I understand them are functionally equivalent to Lord's "themes," which are defined as "basic units of content" that manifest varying capacities to organize a song.[6] Likewise, what Lord described as a song's "plan" can be rendered in Rubin's terms an overarching system, which interacts with the song's sub-systems, its "spatial and object systems," and with the broader systems of communication in the context of which the song arises.

What Rubin offers is not simply a multiplication of terms, but a complementary perspective on large-scale narrative structure. Modern systems theory helps to balance a tendency in Homeric studies to concentrate on the units of composition rather than the interactions among them, and helps to solve problems inherent in the analysis of structures in which dependent

---

[4] Lord 1960:113, 123; cf. Finnegan 1977:134-169.

[5] Rubin 1995:96-97; for his debt to Lord see 4-9, 137-141.

[6] See Lord 1960:68-69 for this definition of "theme."

and independent variables interact.[7] Conceived of as a system that organizes other systems, the *Dios boulē* as I have described it extends in the *Odyssey*, as in the *Iliad*, through the system of divine councils that fall at the main inflection points in the narrative, where they provide the motivation for the plot as it unfolds. At the same time, this overarching theme or system serves as an interface between the *Odyssey* and the larger system of the ancient Greek epic tradition.

In this latter respect, Rubin's concept of the "boundary" is especially useful, for it describes one of the two functions that, according to my own model, Zeus performs in the *Odyssey*. The boundary in the first place separates the narrative from what precedes and follows it; as we have seen, the distinction of the *Odyssey* from previous and succeeding events is effected by Zeus in the divine council scenes in Books 1 and 24. And again, the boundary also distinguishes the *Odyssey* from parallel Odysseus-traditions; it is in this capacity that I have analyzed Zeus' role in the fate of the Phaiakes and in the cycle of reciprocal violence on Ithake. Lastly, the boundary can also be assimilated to the concept of the "facts" of the larger tradition, in that its operation implies the systematization of narrative possibilities at a level that transcends any one performer, performance, or narrative.

Plan and boundary, then, can be understood as different aspects of what is, from a functional perspective, the same theme. The special nature of this theme is apparent in its scope when compared with an epic's other themes or systems, that is, its formulas, type-scenes, and larger patterns such as withdrawal-and-return. The plan alone embraces the entire narrative and therefore has the unique potential to impinge on all other themes.

A further distinction is that a plan is acquired in a manner different from less comprehensive themes. These latter themes may recur in any number of narratives, for a traditional singer internalizes them during training, and devotes to them no more conscious thought than a traditional musician does to scales. By contrast, a singer consciously acquires plans that can organize basic themes into performable, transmissible, and distinct songs.[8] And while a plan allows for substitution of non-essential themes and for the expansion or contraction of the narrative in response to performance circumstances, it at the same time imposes strict limits on essential features, such as overall chronology, setting, and characters. From the perspective of poets who do not rely on written texts for their repertoire, the plan is the song.

---

[7] Rubin 1995:95-96.

[8] In cognitive-psychological terms, basic themes or systems, e.g. meter, reside in "implicit memory;" the plan, by contrast, resides in "explicit memory;" see Rubin 1995:191.

Turning now to Homeric narrative, I suggest that Zeus, as the character traditionally endowed with the greatest power to control other characters and the world they inhabit, is a natural figure with which to identify an over-arching plan. In the case of the *Odyssey*, the *Dios boulē* theme carries out the functions that Lord and Rubin assign to the plan or boundary in oral compo-sition-in-performance.[9] Zeus, identified with the top of the hierarchy of the *Odyssey*'s themes, provides the stable skeleton for the poem's overall thematic coherence and unity and establishes the boundary between pre- and post-Odyssean events as well as between Homeric and non-Homeric Odysseus-traditions. Zeus' essential role, though obscured by his own strategies and rhetoric, is nevertheless communicated through his dramatic appearances at the cardinal points of the narrative, and may well have commanded the atten-tion of Homeric audiences, which were accustomed by familiarity with the larger tradition to expect divine motivation at just such junctures.

Zeus Panhellenikos

Its centrality to the *Odyssey* aside, the *Dios boulē* was not, according to my model, the only, or even the most common, form that the essential plan theme assumed in the ancient Greek epic tradition. Rather, I have suggested that equation of Zeus' divine plan with the epic narrative plan was a specifically Panhellenic phenomenon. Panhellenism is often understood as a synthetic process, whereby epichoric traditions were blended into narratives and practices that emphasized similarities and downplayed differences. Many aspects of the Olympian system can indeed be explained in this way. Thus the gods who appear in the epics are those who were worshipped in one form or another in most or all Greek communities, to the exclusion of more localized deities, such as the Cretan-Aiginetan Britomartis or Boiotian-Thessalian Kabeiroi. Likewise, the Homeric (and Hesiodic) gods are departicularized: Poseidon, for instance, appears in his widely recognized role as sea-god, while his less common association with horse cult is largely unobserved. The Panhellenic synthesis can in these respects be understood as an abstraction from the prevailing beliefs about the gods in Greece at the time when the epics were taking shape.

---

[9] On the functional nature of a divine apparatus in an oral medium cf. M. Edwards 1987:131-134, Havelock 1961:169-171. Admittedly, Lord himself considered Zeus' speech at the beginning of the *Odyssey* to be "ornamental" (1951:76; see Chapter 3 n8), but I respectfully submit that, on this particular occasion, my interpretation of the *Odyssey* is closer to the spirit of Lord's model than is his own.

It might then be expected that Zeus' position of dominance in Panhellenic epic reflects a dominant role in ancient Greek religious life. However, it appears that Zeus did not attract the intensity of attention, measured in terms of resources devoted to him and symbolic status accorded to him, that Greek communities directed to other divinities portrayed in the epics. It is this very fact, I suggest, that made Zeus especially well suited to preside over Panhellenic narratives. For while Zeus was recognized in most or all ancient Greek communities, and seems to have maintained, perhaps as an outgrowth of his conception as a sky god, some vague claim to supremacy over other deities, actual cult activity devoted to him was largely restricted to contexts that were outside the domain of the *polis*, residing either entirely within the *oikos*, or at the level of Panhellenic cult, which transcends the *polis*. The relatively low profile of the supreme god of the epic pantheon in other contexts is particularly significant given that many if not most aspects of Greek religion centered on the *polis*.[10] As a consequence, Zeus was relatively less encumbered than any other deity by associations with particular communities or regions.[11]

It will be useful to approach this line of argumentation, which appears at first glance counterintuitive, in diachronic terms. To begin with, there can be no doubt that worship of Zeus was deeply ingrained in ancient Greek religion. The earliest documents in Greek, written in the so-called Linear B syllabary and dating mainly to the thirteenth and twelfth centuries, establish that Zeus was among the deities – along with Dionysos, Hephaistos, Here, Hermes, and Poseidon (certainly), and Athene and Ares (possibly), but not Apollo, Demeter, Aphrodite, or Artemis – whose worship persisted after the Bronze Age. Alphabetic Greek "Zeus" corresponds to Linear B *di-w-*, a name that appears in the palace archives in connection with a shrine at Pylos (dedicated to *di-wi-jo*), as the name of a month at Knossos (*di-wi-jo-jo*), and as a component of personal names at Thebes, Knossos, and possibly Mykene. Moreover, *di-w-* is associated with *e-ra*, later Greek "Here," at Pylos, and with a different goddess, *di-wi-ja* 'Dione', at Pylos and perhaps Knossos; there also may have been a common cult of Zeus and Dionysos at Chania. That the relationships among these deities were to some degree systematized is suggested by

[10] Thus for instance Sourvinou-Inwood 1988:259 argues that "the polis provided the fundamental, basic framework in which Greek religion operated, [and it] anchored and legitimated, and mediated, all religious activity."

[11] Thus Hall 1997:101 argues that "on the ritual level at which Greek religion ultimately operated, there is little evidence that the Homeric vision of the society of gods, headed by the patriarchal Zeus, found much of an early material realisation in the cultic geography of the various Greek *poleis*."

dedications "to all gods" (*pa-si te-o-i*) at Knossos, to an apparent triad of divinities at Thebes, and also by references to a "mother of the gods" (*ma-te-re te-i-ja*) and possibly to a "son of Zeus" (*di-wo i-je-we*) at Pylos.[12]

Bronze Age Greeks, then, recognized Zeus and associated him with other gods. The relationships among these deities can only be inferred, but it is at least worth noting that the scanty evidence gives no indication that Zeus was reckoned as the leader of the gods, or even as one of the more significant among them. In the archives at the best-documented site, Pylos, the relative frequencies of divine names, and the activities and functionaries with which these names are associated, imply greater emphasis on Poseidon and the goddess Potnia than on Zeus. Other deities appear to have been more important than Zeus at the other palace centers, and there is no clear reference at all to Zeus as a god at Thebes or Mykene.[13]

This trend in Zeus-worship persists in later Greek religion. To review briefly the well-known facts, the collapse of the Bronze Age palace communities, a process complete by around 1050 BCE, occasioned or was followed by a steep decline in population, so that Greek communities of the Early Iron Age (1050-800) were few, small, and isolated compared with those of earlier and later periods. Early Iron Age Greece also contrasts with preceding and succeeding periods in the complete absence of literacy and of monumental architecture, and the near-absence of representational art.[14] Greek religion after the Bronze Age, not surprisingly, displays both continuity and change. By the time written records begin to become available again in the eighth century (and with them the possibility of capturing epic poetry in performance), the aforementioned new pantheon has become established in Greece, while new religious systems have emerged in place of those sustained by the palaces.

Among the elements of continuity in religion from the Late Bronze Age to the Classical period, if we except the evidence of the epics themselves, is Zeus'

[12] Zeus' shrine at Pylos: Mb1366, An42; Tn316; month named for Zeus at Knossos: Fp5; personal names: Thebes, Ug11, Of26, Of33; Knossos, Vc293; Mykene Oe103; Zeus and Here: Tn316 (Here appears to have been worshipped in Thebes also, Of28, and perhaps Knossos, Da 1323, Fh 357); Zeus-derived goddess: Pylos, An607, Tn316, Cn1287; Knossos, Xd97 (this deity may resurface as Dione, the mother by Zeus of Aphrodite at *Iliad* 5.370-417 (cf. Hesiod *Theogony* 17), and as Zeus' consort at the oracle of Dodona); "son of Zeus": PY172 = Tn316 (Burkert 1985 43, 46; contrast Palmer 1963 264 with Ventris and Chadwick 1973 s.v. *i-je-<re>-we*); sacrifice to "all gods": e.g. Fp1+, Gg705; "mother of gods": Fr1202; divine triad at Thebes: Fq121. Discussion in Schachter 2000; Ventris and Chadwick 1973:125-126, 286-289; Mylonas 1966:158-161; Palmer 1963:235-268 *passim*.

[13] Cf. Palmer 1963:103; Schachter 2000:15.

[14] My understanding of the post-Bronze Age "collapse" has been informed in particular by Morris 2000:195-198; Shelmerdine 1997:580-584; Snodgrass 1980:20-23.

lack of prominence as suggested by the Linear B documents, which obtains throughout the Archaic and Classical periods. For again, deities that are represented as subordinate to Zeus in the epics played a more prominent role than him in Greek religious life. This conclusion emerges clearly from an analysis of the most complete tabulation of the post-Bronze Age religious archaeology of ancient Greece to date, Alexander Mazarakis Ainian's massive survey of 304 Early Iron Age to archaic sites in mainland Greece, Ionia, and Magna Graecia:

Survey Early Iron Age to Archaic period sanctuaries and cult sites[15]

divine dedicatee	number of sites associated with dedicatee
Apollo	44
Athene	33
Artemis	32
Demeter	18
Zeus	17
Here	12
Aphrodite	9
Poseidon	7
Dionysos	6
Hermes	3
Ares	1
Hephaistos	1
subtotal:	**186**
other deities or heroes	86
unidentified	87
total attributions:	**359**

[15] Mazarakis Ainian 1997:420-424; cf. Coldstream 1977:327-328. My tabulation includes every possible attribution to a deity at a given site; thus some sites are counted more than once, which is why the 359 total attributions exceed the 304 sites actually considered. My category "other deities and heroes" includes Mazarakis Ainian's attributions to hero, chthonic, household, and ancestor cults, as well as to (relatively rare) non-Olympians such as Pan; under "unidentified" I include cases where cult activity cannot be established with certainty. Omitted are sites for which Mazarakis Ainian cites only Homeric authority.

Zeus here ranks well behind Apollo, Athene, and Artemis in terms of the number of cult sites dedicated to him from the end of the Bronze Age to the dawn of the Classical period. To be sure, caveats are in order. The recipient of cult has not been identified for about half of the sites surveyed by Mazarakis Ainian; attributions to activity before around 600 are mostly conjectural if often uncontroversial; and multiple deities or different deities at different times may have been worshipped at the same site. Further, the figures in are influenced by the varying tendencies of communities to set up the inscriptions that offer the firmest evidence, and by the tendency among archaeologists to focus on certain regions of ancient Greece (particularly Attica). Historical circumstances may also distort the picture; thus for example Poseidon's relatively low ranking on the table could be linked to Persian encroachment on Ionia, where worship of the sea god is thought to have been especially popular.[16]

Nevertheless, the sample size is large enough, and the variation in the attention given to individual gods sufficiently marked, to support the general conclusion that Zeus was no more prominent in later Greek communities than he appears to have been in those of the Bronze Age. Moreover, Zeus' Iron Age cult sites tend to be located on mountain tops (e.g. his sanctuary on Mt. Hymettos in Attica) or similarly remote places and to lack substantial material remains, in contrast with the tendency for the more numerous sites dedicated to Apollo, Athene, and Here to be located within or near communities.[17]

The overall trend in cult activity is similarly consistent with Zeus' absence from the list of deities to which the earliest monumental stone temples were dedicated. In partial vindication of my analysis of Mazarakis Ainian's findings, three other gods ranked high in Table 00 seem to have been the only recipients of this expensive and labor-intensive honor before the seventh century: Here at Samos and Argos, Apollo at Corinth and Eretria, and Artemis at Ephesos.[18] A parallel trend can be found in a striking aspect of community-sanctioned Zeus-worship: although every Greek *polis* identified itself with a divine patron, or "poliad" deity, such as Athene at Athens or Here at Argos, not one community is known to have worshipped Zeus in this capacity before the Hellenistic period.[19]

---

[16] For Poseidon's association with Ionia see Herodotos 1.148; Burkert 1985:136.

[17] Morgan 1990:26-29, who suggests that Zeus may have been worshipped more as an agriculture deity in the period before the relatively late appearance of his cult in civic contexts.

[18] 8th-century stone temples: Snodgrass 1980:33-34, 58-62, 141-149; Mazarakis Ainian 1997:425.

[19] Zeus' lack of poliad status is observed by e.g. Burkert 1985:130; de Polignac 1995; Graf OCD^3 s.v. "Zeus." Note that Zeus' post-Classical role as poliad occurs at colonies, such as Baktria, whose settlers were drawn from many *poleis* – that is, the populations of these later colonies were Panhellenic.

Again, it is in contexts that were either more personal or more broadly based than those of the *polis* that the worship of Zeus is most evident in Archaic and later Greece. On the one hand, cult titles associated with the *oikos*, including Zeus Herkeios ("of the wall [around the *oikos*]"), Xenios ("of guest-friendship," i.e. formal relationships among *oikoi*), and Ktesios ("of [household] property") demonstrate that Zeus was a significant figure at what might be called the "sub-*polis*" level. Likewise, individuals could appeal to Zeus Soter ("of safety") and Hiketesios ("of suppliants") for personal protection. Recognition of Zeus by these titles was sanctioned in some circumstances by some *poleis*, but this phenomenon appears to be an extension of his association with *oikos*. Thus, for example, candidates for archonships at Athens were required to display a household or family shrine to Zeus Herkeios.[20] Not surprisingly, sub-*polis* aspects of Zeus-worship were represented in the most general terms in Panhellenic narratives; thus the *Odyssey* for instance acknowledges Zeus Herkeios, Hiketesios, and Xenios without naming any attendant rites or narrative traditions.

The other major locus of Zeus-worship was in "super-*polis*" contexts; and this brings us back to the subject of Panhellenism. For Zeus' most conspicuous role in Archaic Greek religious life is as the patron deity of Panhellenic festivals and cults, in particular at Dodona, Nemea, and most famously Olympia. The material evidence, as discussed in Chapter 4, implies that these sites were either undeveloped or entirely local in orientation during the Early Iron Age, and only in the Archaic period began to evince intense activity and a Panhellenic orientation.[21] This was clearly the case at Olympia, where not until the seventh century did a permanent settlement grow up around the sanctuary of Zeus and a significant number of votives from outside west Greece begin to appear, while at the same time the cult of Here at Olympia was at least as prominent in the early Archaic period. The same is true at Dodona, where evidence of a sustained Panhellenic constituency appears late in the Archaic period.[22] And at Nemea, where no material evidence predates the late

---

[20] Zeus Herkeios: *Odyssey* 22.334-335; *Athenaion Politeia* 55.3 (on qualification for archonship). Xenios: *Odyssey* 14.389; cf. Burkert 1985:248. Ktesios: Isaios 8.15-16. Soter: Xenophon *Anabasis* 3.2.9. Hiketesios: *Odyssey* 16.422-423. Polis-sanctioned worship of Zeus Olympios and Polios, at least in Athens, dates to the sixth-century; cf. Simon 1983:15-16 and Parke 1967:144-145 (contra: Robertson 1992:139-140). Cults of Zeus Agoraios ("of the market"), attested in Sparta, Elis, and Thebes (Pausanias 3.11.9, 5.15.4, and 11.24.1, respectively), presumably date to a similar period.

[21] Contra: Morris 1998:55, who suggests that Dodona was a regional center already in the tenth century, despite the lack of evidence he acknowledges earlier in his article (42).

[22] For Olympia and Dodona see Chapter 4; for the cult of Here at Olympia, see Mazarakis Ainian 1997:323 and Morgan 1990:42.

ninth century, Zeus' association with the site cannot be confirmed prior to the establishment of the Panhellenic festival there in 573.[23]

This comparative and material evidence, then, suggests that Zeus' supremacy in the canonical epics reflects circumstances that brought together Greeks from different communities and regions. Viewed this way, the emergence of Zeus-worship outside the *oikos*, and of the Olympian system described in the epics, are interrelated phenomena, to be associated with the rise of an interstate elite class as a community apart from epichoric, *polis*-based affiliations.[24] The social institution by which this elite class established and maintained interstate relationships was *xenia*, which can be seen as a bypassing of *polis*-tradition through the extension of Zeus' function in the *oikos* under the cult title Xenios. These elites developed interstate sanctuaries and associated festivals as places to define their status relative to one another in the Greek world at large. In this respect the *Iliad*, which dramatizes the assembly of an elite group drawn from many *poleis* to compete for *kleos*, can be seen as a metaphor for the formation of elite groups in the arenas of Panhellenic festivals.

In sum, Zeus' failure to number among pre-Hellenistic poliad deities, and among dedicatees of early stone temples, implies that he was less central to the rituals and myths of individual communities than were Athene, Apollo, Here, and Artemis. Conversely, because he was no city's poliad deity, Zeus was a natural choice to preside over a Panhellenic religious system that claimed authority, at least on special occasions, over the variegated mass of epichoric beliefs and practices.[25] In these Panhellenic contexts, the goddess worshipped on the Athenian acropolis, for instance, would not be subordinated to the sea god worshipped at the Panionion, or vice versa.

The transcendent perspective of a Panhellenic Zeus may have been reinforced in turn by his apparently age-old role as a weather god, whose power descends from the sky and is felt in the *polis* where Athene and Apollo reside, in the liminal spaces where Artemis resides, on the sea where Poseidon resides, and so on. The figure of an otiose, or at least disengaged, father or sky god is

---

[23] The emergence of Olympia, Dodona, and Nemea as fully Panhellenic only in the late Archaic period corresponds chronologically with the emergence of Panhellenic sites dedicated to other deities, such as Apollo at Delos (Morgan 1990:205-208) and Delphi (Fontenrose 1988:121, 125), Isthmia (Morgan 1994, esp. 121-125), and Poseidon at the Panionion.

[24] Morgan 1993:130 urges that "it would be wrong to assume that a pan-Hellenic system of values had early origins, or that pan-Hellenic sanctuaries were pre-state institutions."

[25] Cf. Burkert 1985:130: "Zeus is...uniquely qualified to be the god of all Greeks."

certainly precedented in ostensibly cognate mythological systems.[26] In any case, it is my reading of this evidence that the Olympian system represents a synthesis of epichoric religious perspectives under the authority of what was in the Archaic period a new principle, a Panhellenizing Zeus.[27]

In a synthetic, Panhellenic narrative, then, Zeus' plans either gratify or frustrate other gods' "local" aims, aligning the narrative with, or distancing it from, various epichoric traditions. More figuratively, as the plan of Zeus sanctions a series of negotiations among the local and competing aims of lesser divinities, the Homeric epics themselves represent by analogy Panhellenic syntheses of conflicting epichoric traditions. That is, conflicts among epichoric traditions are dramatized in the Panhellenic epics as conflicts among poliad deities and of these deities with Zeus. Zeus himself, on the other hand, being relatively free of epichoric attachments, subsumes competing aims and authorizes a coherent path through the tangle of parallel narrative possibilities. By presenting a song as a "plan of Zeus," then, an epic singer could draw attention away from the variety of beliefs and practices with which the members of individual Greek *poleis* identified, in order to create for the emerging Panhellenic elite a synthetic vision of Hellenicity.

My model can be refined here with a consideration of what I have termed the "proto-Panhellenic" register of the ancient Greek epic tradition. As discussed in the Introduction, the non-Homeric *Kypria* is an example of an epic that deploys a prominent *Dios boulē* theme, but that does not represent a canonical, or in other words fully Panhellenic, tradition. The strategy of this epic as I see it was however similar to that of the canonical epics: the *Kypria* tried to present the story of the early part of the Trojan War in a way that appealed to most or all Greeks, and it is in part for this reason that the *Dios boulē* theme is prominent in surviving summaries and fragments.[28] Though many scholars have followed Aristotle (*Poetics* 1459b) in attributing the failure of the *Kypria* to achieve canonicity to aesthetic factors,[29] the historical context

---

[26] Thus for example the cognate ancient Indic god *Dyaus* is a minor character in the Vedas, while in the Germanic pantheon the thunder god Thor is subordinate to the war god Odin, and the earliest account of the their pantheon ranks the Gauls' equivalent of Iuppiter below that of Mercury (Caesar *Gallic Wars* 6.16-17). On the obsolesence of sky gods, see Nagy 1990b:94-95n53.

[27] Not to be confused with the Roman-period cult of Zeus Panhellenios, on which see Price 1999:157.

[28] Marks 2002 explores Zeus' role in the *Kypria*.

[29] An argument made forcefully by Griffin 1977.

is equally worthy of consideration. For absorption of Greek Ionia into the Persian empire in the later Archaic period, at the moment when Panhellenic institutions were developing, led to the marginalization of Greek communities in the east, including those on Cyprus, a probable locus of *Kypria*-tradition, with the result that narrative traditions from this region were in a sense denied the opportunity to achieve, or at least to compete for, full Panhellenic authority.

Conclusions

I have tried in this chapter to frame my interpretation of Zeus' role in the *Odyssey* in terms of the epic's status as a traditional orally-derived text that was intended to appeal to a Panhellenic audience. I note that my approach here combines synchronic and diachronic perspectives. As a tool or strategy of performance, the *Dios boulē* theme in the *Odyssey* can be seen as one aspect of a synchronic "snapshot" of the Homeric performance tradition. On the other hand, as a specifically Panhellenic construct, the *Dios boulē* can be seen as a mechanism that evolved diachronically in response to historical developments in Greek religion and in performance contexts for epic narratives.

The overarching *Dios boulē* theme in the *Odyssey*, then, is both an essential feature of epic composition-in-performance and a manifestation of a specifically Panhellenic (and proto-Panhellenic) perspective on the defining event of ancient Greek mythical history, the Trojan War. Thus the main story is tied to Zeus, first with his programmatic Oresteia, from which an outline of the *Telemachia* and *Mnesterophonia* can be deduced, again in Book 5, where the god himself defines the terms of the hero's return, including an opening for the *Apologoi* sequence, which in turn reifies the themes that inform the main narrative, and lastly at the end of the story, where Zeus is deployed in order to achieve closure in a manner consistent with the themes that he has been identified with throughout the narrative. Thus the *Dios boulē* theme offers to performers and to audiences a unifying perspective on the action, and a convenient way to conceptualize, and to keep track of, themes that are essential to the Homeric version of Odysseus' story.

I have argued that a complementary function of the *Dios boulē* theme is to authorize a specific set of narrative choices among the various traditional accounts of Odysseus' story over which the Panhellenic *Odyssey* claims authority. Zeus' plan for the *Odyssey* relies on themes that distinguish the Homeric account from one or more epichoric accounts: the hero must have a single son, a faithful wife, a lack of allies outside his own *oikos*, and no defense against the social repercussions of the revenge that he is bound by the tradition to exact. Zeus' one appearance outside the main narrative, when he destroys Odysseus' crew in Book 12, dramatizes the significance of these themes, for it is this act that closes off the possibility that Odysseus may return like Agamemnon at the head of an army and fight, rather than scheme, for control of Ithake.[30] Zeus' plan for the closure of the narrative in turn truncates the consequences of the *Mnesterophonia* and in so doing de-authorizes traditions in which reaction to the suitors' deaths undermines Odysseus' political and social position. Zeus' power to negotiate the *Odyssey*'s engagement with non-Homeric traditions can also, I have proposed, be seen in the case of the Phaiakes, whose fate has far-reaching consequences for Odysseus' and Telemachos' later adventures and was therefore left to be articulated through the character of Zeus during each performance of the epic.

The manner in which Zeus exerts this control over the Odyssean narrative is notable for its subtlety. Rather than issuing decrees, as he regularly does in the *Iliad*, Zeus in the *Odyssey* relies on Athene to pick up on verbal cues, so that her interests are organically subsumed under his own. Zeus employs the same delicacy with which he handles the goddess of *mētis* when he deals with the other major divine character in the *Odyssey*, Poseidon, the bluff god of *biē*. Zeus' plan for Odysseus' return incorporates Poseidon's wishes, and even relies on him as an agent. The angry god Helios is treated with similar finesse in Book 12. In each of these cases, the subordinate deities' narrow perspectives and parochial interests can be compared to "epichoric viewpoints." That is, the *Dios boulē* theme in the *Odyssey* embraces and imposes order on Odysseus-tradition in a manner analogous to Zeus' coordination of Athene's, Poseidon's, and Helios' competing concerns.

I have suggested that the relationship between divine plan and narrative plan in the *Odyssey* is obscured for those outside the tradition by the economy and strategy of Zeus' interactions with other gods. For those within the tradition, however, ancient Greeks who were familiar with narratives like the *Iliad* and the *Kypria*, there may have been the expectation that a Panhellenic narrative would have as its "internal" architect the supreme god Zeus. By Panhellenic convention, in other words, gods that are in other contexts poliads come into conflict over the fate of a hero, while the relatively less partisan Zeus decides the issue.

---

[30] Cook 1995:121-127 draws attention to the importance for the *Odyssey*'s theodicy of the fact that Zeus (rather than Helios) destroys the last of Odysseus' crew.

To return to an earlier formulation, Zeus' harmonization of the conflicting aims of Athene and Poseidon in the *Odyssey* can be seen as a staged metaphor for the process of the *Odyssey*'s own composition and for the evolution of its Panhellenic perspective. As the epic Zeus manipulates and cajoles other deities into furthering his plan within the narrative, the *Odyssey* finesses, as far as possible, the competing claims of non-Homeric traditions, according to each as much recognition and authority as Homeric thematics allow.

BIBLIOGRAPHY

Texts

West, M., ed. 1998. *Homerus Ilias Volumen Prius Rhapsodias I-XII Continens.* Stuttgart and Leipzig.

West, M., ed. 2000. *Homerus Ilias Volumen Alterum Rhapsodias XIII-XXIV Continens.* Munich and Leipzig.

van Thiel, H., ed. 1991. *Homeri Odyssea.* Zurich and New York.

Allen, T., ed. 1912. *Homeri Opera V: Hymnos Cyclum Fragmenta Margiten Batrachomyomachiam Vitas Continens.* Oxford.

Bernabé, A. 1987. *Poetae Epici Graecae: Testimonia et Fragmenta Pars 1.* Leipzig.

Commentaries

IC 1=Kirk, G. 1985. *The Iliad: a commentary. Volume I: books 1-4.* Cambridge.

IC 2=Kirk, G. 1990. *The Iliad: a commentary. Volume II: books 5-8.* Cambridge.

IC 3=Hainsworth, B. 1993. *The Iliad: a commentary. Volume III: books 9-12.* Cambridge.

IC 4=Janko, R. 1992. *The Iliad: a commentary. Volume IV: books 13-16.* Cambridge.

IC 5=Edwards, M. 1991. *The Iliad: a commentary. Volume V: books 17-20.* Cambridge.

IC 6=Richardson, N. 1993. *The Iliad: a commentary. Volume VI: books 21-24.* Cambridge.

Ameis-Hentze-Cauer=Ameis, K., and Hentze, C. 1920-1940. *Homers "Odyssee".* Revised edition in 4 volumes by P. Cauer. Leipzig.

CHO 1=Heubeck, A., West, S., and Hainsworth, J. 1988. *A Commentary on Homer's Odyssey. Volume I: Introduction and Books I-VIII.* Oxford.

CHO 2=Heubeck, A., and Hoekstra, A. 1989. *A Commentary on Homer's Odyssey. Volume II: Introduction and Books IX-XVI.* Oxford.

CHO 3=Russo, J., M. Fernández-Galiano, and A. Heubeck. 1992. *A Commentary on Homer's Odyssey. Volume III: Introduction and Books XVII-XXIV.* Oxford.

Articles and books

Alcock, S. and Osborne, R., eds. 1994. *Placing the Gods: Sanctuaries and Sacred Space in Ancient Greece.* Oxford.
Antonaccio, C. 1995. *An Archaeology of Ancestors: Tomb Cult and Hero Cult in Early Greece.* Lanham, MD.
Arend, W. 1933. *Die typischen Szenen bei Homer.* Berlin.
Atchity, K. 1978. *Homer's Iliad: The Shield of Memory.* Carbondale and Edwardsville, IL.
Austin, N. 1975. *Archery at the Dark of the Moon: Poetic Problems in Homer's Odyssey.* Berkeley.
Bakker, E. 1997. *Poetry in Speech: Orality and Homeric Discourse.* Ithaca, NY.
—— 2002. "Remembering the God's Arrival." *Arethusa* 35:63-81.
Bakker, E. and Kahane, A., eds. 1997. *Written Voices, Spoken Signs: Tradition, Performance, and the Epic Text.* Cambridge, MA
Ballabriga, A. 1989. "La prophétie de Tirésias." *Métis* 4:291-304.
Benardete, S. 1997. *The Bow and the Lyre: A Platonic Reading of the Odyssey.* Lanham, MD.
Benton, S. 1934-5. "Excavations in Ithaca, III. The Cave at Polis, I." *Annual of the British School at Athens* 35:45-73.
Blackburn, S. 1989. "Patterns of Development for Indian Oral Epics." In Blackburn et al. 1989: 15-32.
Blackburn, S. et al., eds. 1989. *Oral Epics in India.* Berkeley.
Bölte, F. 1934. "Ein pylisches Epos." *Rheinische Museum* 83:319-347.
Bowra, M. 1962. "Composition." In Wace and Stubbings 1962:38-74.
Bremmer, J. 1983. "Scapegoat Rituals in Ancient Greece." *Harvard Studies in Classical Philology* 87:299-320.
Burgess, J. 1999. "Gilgamesh and Odysseus in the Otherworld." *Echos du Monde Classique/Classical Views* XLIII n.s. 18:171-210.
—— 2001. *The Tradition of the Trojan War in Homer and the Epic Cycle.* Baltimore, MD and London.
Burkert, W. 1960. "Das Lied von Ares und Aphrodite." *Rheinische Museum* 103:130-144.
—— 1979. *Structure and History in Greek Mythology and Ritual.* Berkeley.
—— 1983. *Homo necans* (trans. P. Bing). Berkeley.
—— 1985. *Greek Religion* (trans. J. Raffan). Cambridge MA.
—— 1992. *The Orientalizing Revolution: Near Eastern Influence on Greek Culture in the Early Archaic Age.* Cambridge, MA.
Calhoun, G. 1940. "The Divine Entourage in Homer." *American Journal of Philology* 61:257-277.
Carlier, P. 1999. *Homèr.* Lille.
Chantraine, P. 1968-1977. *Dictionnaire étymologique de la langue grecque.* Paris.

Clark, M. E. 1986. "Neoanalysis: A Bibliographic Review." *Classical World* 79:379-391.

Clark, M. 1997. *Out of Line: Homeric Composition Beyond the Hexameter.* Lanham, MD.

Clay, J. 1983. *The Wrath of Athena: Gods and Men in the Odyssey.* Princeton, NJ.

—— 1999. "The Whip and Will of Zeus." *Literary Imagination* 1:40-60.

Cohen, B., ed. 1995. *The Distaff Side: Representing the Female in Homer's Odyssey.* Oxford.

Coldstream, J. 1977. *Geometric Greece.* London.

Conte, G. 1986. *The Rhetoric of Imitation: Genre and Poetic Memory in Virgil and Other Latin Poets* (trans. C. Segal). Ithaca, NY and London.

Cook, E. 1995. *The Odyssey in Athens: Myths of Cultural Origins.* Ithaca, NY.

—— 2000. Review of I. Malkin, *The Returns of Odysseus: Colonization and Ethnicity.* Berkeley, 1998. *Bryn Mawr Classical Review* 00.03.22 (2000), http://ccat.sas.upenn.edu/bmrc/2000/2000-09-12.html.

Cunliffe, R. 1963. *A Lexicon of the Homeric Dialect.* Norman, OK.

Danek, G. 1998. *Epos und Zitat: Studien zu den Quellen der Odyssee.* Vienna.

Davies, M., ed. 1988. *Epicorum Graecorum Fragmenta.* Göttingen.

Dickson, K. 1995. *Nestor: Poetic Memory in Greek Epic. Albert Bates Lord Studies in Oral Tradition* 16. New York and London.

Dodds, E. 1951. *The Ancient Concept of Progress and other Essays on Greek Literature and Belief.* Oxford.

Doherty, L. 1995. *Siren Songs: Gender, Audiences, and Narrators in the Odyssey.* Ann Arbor, MI.

Dougherty, C. 2001. *The Raft of Odysseus: The Ethnographic Imagination of Homer's Odyssey.* Oxford.

Dowden, K. 1996. "Homer's Sense of Text." *Journal of Hellenic Studies* 116:47-61.

Edwards, A. 1985. *Odysseus against Achilles: The Role of Allusion in the Homeric Epic.* Königstein.

Edwards, M. 1980. "Convention and Individuality in Iliad 1." *Harvard Studies in Classical Philology* 84:1-28.

—— 1987. *Homer, Poet of the Iliad.* Baltimore, MD.

Ehnmark, E. 1935. *The Idea of God in Homer* Dissertation, University of Uppsala.

Erbse, H. 1972. *Beiträge zum Verständnis der Odyssee.* Berlin and New York.

—— 1986. *Untersuchungen zur Funktion der Götter im homerischen Epos.* Berlin.

Falkner, T. 1989. Ἐπὶ γήραος οὐδῷ: Homeric Heroism, Old Age and the End of the Odyssey." In Falkner and de Luce 1989:21-67.

Falkner, T., and de Luce, J., eds. 1989. *Old Age in Greek and Latin Literature.* Albany, NY.

Felson, N. 1994. *Regarding Penelope: From Character to Poetics.* Princeton, NJ.

Fenik, B. 1974. *Studies in the Odyssey.* Wiesbaden.

Finley, M. 1965. *The World of Odysseus*. New York.

Finnegan, R. 1977. *Oral Poetry: Its Nature, Significance and Social Context*. Cambridge.

Fisher, N. and van Wees, H., eds. 1998. *Archaic Greece: New Approaches and New Evidence*. London.

Flaig, E. 1994. "Das Konsensprinzip im Homerischen Olymp: Uberlegungen zum Gottlichen Entscheidungsprozess Ilias 4.1-72." *Hermes* 122:13-31.

—— 1995. "Tötliches Freien: Penelopes Ruhm, Telemachs Status und die sozialen Normen." In Lindner and Schindler 1995:364-388.

—— 1997. "Processus de Décision Collective et Guerre Civile: L'exemple de l'Odyssée Chant XXIV, vv. 419-470." *Annales* 1:3-29.

Flensted-Jensen, P., ed. 2000. *Further Studies in the Ancient Greek Polis*. Stuttgart.

Foley, J. 1998. "Individual Poet and Epic Tradition: Homer as Legendary Singer." *Arethusa* 3:149-178.

Fontenrose, J. 1988. "The Cult of Apollo and the Games at Delphi." In Raschke 1988:121-140.

Ford, A. 1992. *Homer: The Poetry of the Past*. Ithaca, NY.

—— 1997. "The Inland Ship: Problems in the Performance and Reception of Homeric Epic." In Bakker and Kahane 1997:83-109.

Frame, D. 1978. *The Myth of Return in Early Greek Epic*. New Haven, CT.

Fränkel, H. 1962. *Dichtung und Philosophie des frühen Griechentums: Eine Geschichte der griechischen Epik, Lyrik, und Prosa bis zur Mitte des fünften Jahrhunderts*. Munich.

Frazer, J., ed. 1921. *Apollodorus: The Library*. 2 vol. Cambridge, MA.

Friedrich, R. 1989. "Zeus and the Phaeacians: Odyssey 13.158." *American Journal of Philology* 110:395-399.

Gehrke, H., ed. 1994. *Rechtskodifizierung und soziale Normen im interkulturellen Vergleich*. Tübigen.

Gentili, B. 1988. *Poetry and Its Public in Ancient Greece: From Homer to the fifth century* (trans. T. Cole). Baltimore, MD.

Gordon, C. 1962. *Before the Bible: The Common Background of Greek and Hebrew Civilisations*. London.

Graziosi, B. 2002. *Inventing Homer: The Early Reception of the Epic*. Cambridge.

Griffin, J. 1977. "The Epic Cycle and the Uniqueness of Homer." *Journal of Hellenic Studies* 97:39-53.

Gunn, D. 1971. "Thematic Composition and Homeric Authorship." *Harvard Studies in Classical Philology* 75:1-31.

Hall, J. 1997. *Ethnic Identity in Greek Antiquity*. Cambridge.

Hammond, N. 1967. *Epirus: The geography, the Ancient Remains, the History and the Topography of Epirus and Adjacent Areas*. Oxford.

Hartmann, A. 1917. *Untersuchungen über die Sagen vom Tod des Odysseus.* Munich.

Haubold, J. 2000. *Homer's People: Epic Poetry and Social Formation.* Cambridge.

Havelock, E. 1963. *Preface to Plato.* Cambridge, MA.

Heubeck, A. 1954. *Der Odyssee-Dichter und die Ilias.* Erlängen.

Hölscher, U. 1988. *Die Odyssee: Epos zwischen Märchen und Roman.* Munich.

Hölkeskamp, K. 1994. "Tempel, Agora und Alphabet. Die Entstehungsbedingungen von Gesetzgebung in der archaischen Polis." In Gehrke 1994:135-164.

Huxley, G. 1958. "Odysseus and the Thesprotian Oracle of the Dead." *Parola del Passato* 13:245-248.

de Jong, I. 2001. *A Narratological Commentary on the Odyssey.* Cambridge.

Jørgensen, O. 1904. "Das Auftreten der Götter in den Büchen i-m der Odyssee." *Hermes* 39:357-382.

Katz, M. 1991. *Penelope's Renown: Meaning and Indeterminacy in the Odyssey.* Princeton, NJ.

Kirchoff, A. 1879. *Die homerische Odyssee und ihre Entstehung.* Berlin.

Kirk, G. 1962. *The Songs of Homer.* Cambridge.

Kullmann, W. 1960. *Die Quellen der Ilias.* Munich.

—— 1980. "Tragische Abwandlungen von Odysseethemen: Ein Beitrag zur Wirkungsgeschichte der Odyssee." *Archaiognosia [Athen]* 1:75-89.

—— 1985. "Gods and Men in the Iliad and the Odyssey." *Harvard Studies in Classical Philology* 89:1-23.

—— 1992. *Homerische Motive: Beiträge zur Entstehung, Eigenart und Wirkung von Ilias und Odyssee.* Stuttgart.

Lang, M. 1983. "Reverberation and Mythology in the Iliad." In Rubino and Shelmerdine 1983:140-164.

Latacz, J. 1996. *Homer, His Art and His World* (trans. J. Holoka). Ann Arbor, MI.

Lee, H. 2001. *The Program and Schedule of the Ancient Olympic Games. Nikephoros Beihefte: Beiträge zu Sport und Kultur im Altertum 6.* Hildesheim.

Lesky, A. 1967. *Homeros.* Stuttgart.

Lindner, R. and Schindler, N., eds. 1995. *Historische Anthropologie: Kultur, Gesellschaft, Alltag.* Heft 3. Köln.

Lloyd-Jones, H. 1971. *The Justice of Zeus.* Berkeley.

Lohmann, D. 1970. *Die Komposition der Reden in der Ilias.* Berlin.

Lord, A. 1951. "Composition by Theme in Homer and Southslavic Epos." *Transactions of the American Philological Society* 82:71-80.

—— 1960. *The Singer of Tales.* Cambridge, MA.

—— 1991. *Epic Singers and Oral Tradition.* Cornell, NY.

Lowe, N. 2000. *The Classical Plot and the Invention of Western Narrative.* Cambridge.

Lowenstam, S. 1993. *The Sceptre and the Spear.* Lanham, MD.

Louden, B. 1999. *The Odyssey: Structure, Narration and Meaning.* Baltimore, MD.

Mackay, E., ed. 1999. *Signs of Orality: The Oral Tradition And Its Influence In The Greek And Roman World. Mnemosyne Supplementum 188.* Leiden.

Maitland, J. 1999. "Poseidon, Walls, and Narrative Complexity in the Homeric Iliad." *Classical Quarterly* 49:1-13.

Malkin, I. 1998. *The Returns of Odysseus: Colonization and Ethnicity.* Berkeley.

Mallwitz, A. 1988. "Cult and Competition Locations at Olympia." In Raschke 2002:79-109.

Marinatos, N. and Hägg, R., eds. 1993. *Greek Sanctuaries: New Approaches.* London.

Marks, J. 2002. "The Junction between the Kypria and the Iliad." *Phoenix* 56:1-24.

—— 2003. "Alternative Odysseys: The Case of Thoas and Odysseus." *Transactions of the American Philological Society* 133:209-226.

—— 2005. "The Ongoing neikos: Thersites, Odysseus and Achilleus." *American Journal of Philology* 126:2-31.

Mazarakis Ainian, A. 1997. *From Rulers' Dwellings to Temples: Architecture, Religion and Society in Early Iron Age Greece.* Jonsered.

Meiggs, R. and D. Lewis, eds. 1988. *A Selection of Greek Historical Inscriptions to the End of the Fifth Century BC.* ed. 2. Oxford.

Merkelbach, R. 1951. *Untersuchungen zur Odyssee.* ed. 2 Munich.

Morgan, C. 1988. "Corinth, the Corinthian Gulf, and Western Greece during the Eight Century B.C." *Annual of the British School at Athens* 83:313-338.

—— 1990. *Athletes and Oracles: the Transformation of Olympia and Delphi in the Eighth Century BC.* Cambridge.

—— 1993. "The Origins of Pan-Hellenism." In Marinatos and Hägg 1993:18-44.

—— 1994. "The Evolution of a Sacral 'Landscape': Isthmia, Perachora, and the Early Corinthian State." In Alcock and Osborne 1994:105-142.

Morris, I. 1986. "The Use and Abuse of Homer." *Classical Antiquity* 5:81-138.

—— 1998. "Archaeology and Greek History." In Fisher and van Wees 1988:1-92.

—— 2000. *Archaeology as Cultural History: Words and Things in Ancient Greece.* Malden, MA.

Morris, I. and Powell, B., eds. 1997. *A New Companion to Homer.* Leiden, New York, and Cologne.

Moulton, C. 1974. "The End of the Odyssey." *Greek Roman and Byzantine Studies* 15:153-169.

Muellner, L. 1996. *The Anger of Achilles: Mênis in Greek Epic.* Ithaca, NY.

Murnaghan, S. 1987. *Disguise and Recognition in the Odyssey.* Princeton, NJ.

—— 1995. "The Plan of Athena." In Cohen 1995:61-80.

Murray, G. 1934. *The Rise of the Greek Epic.* ed. 4. Oxford.

Mylonas, G. 1961. *Eleusis and the Eleusinian Mysteries.* Princeton, NJ.

—— 1966. *Mycenae and the Mycenean Age.* Princeton, NJ.

Nagler, M. 1974. *Spontaneity and Tradition: A Study in the Oral Art of Homer.* Berkeley.

Nagy, G. 1979. *The Best of the Achaeans.* Baltimore, MD. *Revised paperback edition 1999.*

—— 1990a. *Pindar's Homer: The Lyric Possession of an Epic Past.* Baltimore, MD.

—— 1990b. *Greek Mythology and Poetics.* Ithaca, NY.

—— 1996. *Homeric Questions.* Austin, TX.

—— 2002. *Plato's Rhapsody and Homer's Music: The Poetics of the Panathenaic Festival in Classical Athens.* Washington, DC.

—— 2003. *Homeric Responses.* Austin, TX.

—— 2004. *Homer's Text and Language.* Urbana and Chicago.

Nichols, S. 1961. *Formulaic Diction and Thematic Composition in the Chanson de Roland. University of North Carolina Studies in the Romance Languages and Literatures* 36. Chapel Hill, NC.

Olson, S. 1995. *Blood and Iron: Stories and Storytelling in Homer's Odyssey.* Leiden.

Ong, W. 1982. *Orality and Literacy: The Technologizing of the Word.* London.

Page, D. 1955. *The Homeric Odyssey.* Oxford.

Palmer, L. 1963. *The Interpretation of Mycenaean Greek Texts.* Oxford.

Parke, H. 1967. *Oracles of Zeus: Dodona, Olympia, Ammon.* Oxford.

Parker, R. 1983. *Miasma.* Oxford.

Parry, M. 1971. *The Making of Homeric Verse: The Collected Papers of Milman Parry* (ed. and intro. A. Parry). Oxford.

Pedrick, V. 1992. "The Muse Corrects: The Opening of the Odyssey." *Yale Classical Studies* 29:39-62.

Peradotto, J. 1990. *Man in the Middle Voice: Name and Narration in the "Odyssey".* Princeton, NJ.

Pfeiffer, R. 1968. *History of Classical Scholarship: From the Beginning to the End of the Hellenistic Age.* Oxford.

de Polignac, F. 1995. *Cults, Territory and the Rise of the Greek City-State.* Chicago.

Prag, A. 1985. *The Oresteia: Iconographic and Narrative Tradition.* Chicago.

Price, S. 1999. *Religions of the Ancient Greeks.* Cambridge.

Pucci, P. 1987. *Odysseus Polutropos: Intertextual Readings in the "Odyssey" and the "Iliad".* Ithaca, NY. *Revised paperback edition 1995.*

Raaflaub, K. 1997. "Politics and Interstate Relations in the World of Early Greek Poleis: Homer and Beyond." Antichthon 31:1-27.

Race, W. 1993. "First Appearances in the Odyssey." *Transactions of the American Philological Society* 123:79-107.

Raschke, W., ed. 1988. *The Archaeology of the Olympics: the Olympics and Other Festivals in Antiquity.* Madison, WI. *Revised paperback edition 2002.*

Reece, S. 1994. "The Cretan Odyssey: A Lie Truer than Truth." *American Journal of Philology* 115:157-173.

Richardson, S. 1990. *The Homeric Narrator.* Nashville, TN.

Ritoók, Z. 1993. "The Pisistratus Tradition and the Canonization of Homer." *Acta Antiqua Academiae Scientiarum Hungaricae.* 34:39-53.

Robertson, Noel. 1992. *Festivals and Legends: The Formation of Greek Cities in the Light of Public Ritual.* Toronto.

Rose, G. 1967. "The Quest of Telemachos." *Transactions of the American Philological Society* 98:391-398.

Rose, P. 1992. *Sons of the Gods, Children of Earth: Ideology and Literary Form in Ancient Greece.* Cornell, NY.

Rousseau, P. 1996. Ἐπὶ γήραος οὐδῷ: *Destin des héros et dessein de Zeus dans l'intrigue de l'Iliade.* Doctorat d'Etat thesis, Université Charles de Gaulle-Lille III.

Rubin, D. 1995. *Memory in Oral Traditions: The Cognitive Psychology of Epic, Ballads, and Counting-out Rhymes.* New York and Oxford.

Rubino, C. and Shelmerdine, C., eds. 1983. *Approaches to Homer.* Austin, TX.

Rüter, K. 1969. *Odysseeinterpretationen: Untersuchungen zum ersten Buch und zur Phaiakis.* Göttingen.

Rutherford, R. 1985. "At Home and Abroad: Aspects of the Structure of the Odyssey." *Proceedings of the Cambridge Philological Society* 211:133-149.

Salmon, J. 1984. *Wealthy Corinth: A History of the City to 338 BC.* Oxford.

Scaife, R. 1995. "The Kypria and Its Early Reception." *Classical Antiquity* 14:164-197.

Schachter, A. 2000. "Greek Deities: Local and Panhellenic Identities." In Flensted-Jensen 2000:9-17.

Schadewaldt, W. 1958. "Der Prolog der Odyssey." *Harvard Studies in Classical Philology* 63:15-32.

—— 1966. *Iliasstudien.* Darmstadt.

—— 1970. "Neue Kriterien zur Odyssee-Analyse." *Hellas und Hesperien. Ges. Schr. zur Antike und zur Neuren Literatur in Zwei Bänden.* Zürich.

Schwartz, E. 1924. *Die Odyssee.* Munich.

Scodel, R. 1982. "The Achaean Wall and the Myth of Destruction." *Harvard Studies in Classical Philology* 86:33-50.

—— 1999a. *Credible Impossibilities: Conventions and Strategies of Verisimilitude in Homer and Greek Tragedy. Beiträge zur Altertumskunde* 122. Stuttgart and Leipzig.

—— 1999b. "Odysseus' Evasiveness and the Audience of the Odyssey." In Mackay 1999:79-93.

Seaford, R. 1994. *Reciprocity and Ritual: Homer and Tragedy in the Developing City-State.* Oxford.

Shelmerdine, C. 1997. "Review of Aegean Prehistory VI: The Palatial Bronze Age of the Southern and Central Greek Mainland." *American Journal of Archaeology* 101:537-585.

Silk, M. 1987. *The Iliad.* Cambridge.

Simon, E. 1983. *Festivals of Attica: An Archaeological Commentary.* Madison, WI.

Slatkin, L. 1991. *The Power of Thetis: Allusion and Interpretation in the Iliad.* Berkeley.

Snodgrass, A. 1980. *Archaic Greece: The Age of Experiment.* Berkeley.

Sourvinou-Inwood, C. 1988. "Further Aspects of Polis Religion." *Annali Istituto orientale de Napoli: Archaeologica e storica antica* 10:259-274.

Sowa, C. 1984. *Traditional Themes and the Homeric Hymns.* Chicago.

Stanford, W., ed. 1965. *The Odyssey of Homer, 2 vols.* ed. 2. London.

Stanley, K. 1993. *The Shield of Homer: Narrative Structure in the Iliad.* Princeton, NJ.

Stehle, E. 1997. *Performance and Gender in Ancient Greece.* Princeton, NJ.

Swaddling, J. 1980. *The Ancient Olympic Games.* Austin, TX.

Taplin, O. 1992. *Homeric Soundings.* Oxford.

Thalmann, W. 1984. *Conventions of Form and Thought in Early Greek Epic Poetry.* Baltimore, MD.

—— 1998. *The Swineherd and the Bow: Representations of Class in the Odyssey.* Ithaca, NY.

Thomas, R. 1989. *Oral Tradition and Written Record in Classical Athens.* Cambridge.

Tracy, S. 1997. "The Structures of the Odyssey." In Morris and Powell 1997:360-379.

Usener, K. 1990. *Beobachtungen zum Verhältnis der Odyssee zur Ilias.* Tübingen.

van Wees, H. 1992. *Status Warriors: War, Violence, and Society in Homer and History.* Leiden.

Ventris, M. and Chadwick, J., eds. 1973. *Documents in Mycenean Greek.* ed. 2. Cambridge.

Vidal-Naquet, P. 1986. *The Black Hunter: Forms of Thought and Forms of Society in the Greek World* (trans. A. Szegedy-Maszak). Baltimore and London.

Wace, A., and Stubbings, F., eds. 1962. *A Companion to Homer.* New York.

Waterhouse, H. 1996. "From Ithaca to the Odyssey." *Annual of the British School at Athens* 91:301-317.

Weeber, K.-W. 1991. *Die unheiligen Spiele: Das antike Olympia zwischen Legende und Wirklichkeit.* Zürich and Munich.

West, M. 1997. *The East Face of Helicon: West Asiatic Elements in Greek Poetry and Myth.* Oxford.

—— 1999. "The Invention of Homer." *Classical Quarterly* 49:364-382.

West, S. 1989. "Laertes Revisited." *Proceedings of the Cambridge Philological Society* 35:113-143.

Whitman, C. 1958. *Homer and the Heroic Tradition.* Cambridge, MA.

Wilson, D. 2002. *Ransom, Revenge and Heroic Identity in the Iliad.* Cambridge.

Wolf, H-H. and Wolf, A. 1968. *Der Weg des Odysseus: Tunis-Malta-Italien in den Augen Homers.* Tübingen.

Zeitlin, F. 1995. "Figuring Fidelity in Homer's Odyssey." in Cohen 1995:117-152.

Zielinski, T. 1899-1901. "Die Behandlung gleichzeitiger Ereignisse im antiken Epos." *Philologus* suppl. 8. 405-449.

APPENDIX 1

HOMERIC SCENES IN WHICH ZEUS APPEARS AND REFERENCES TO HIS ACTIONS

CITATIONS INCLUDE SCENES in the main narrative, as well as scenes that, while outside the main narrative, impinge on it (such as the encounter between Helios and Zeus in *Odyssey* 12) or proceed directly from it (such as the destruction of the Greek fortifications predicted in *Iliad* 7 and 12). Not included are scenes that are outside the main narrative and tangential to it (such as Demodokos' song of Ares and Aphrodite in *Odyssey* 8), nor references to Zeus that can be explained in the generalizing terms described by Jørgensen's Law (on which see Chapters 2 and 5).

Iliad

1.5 (proem); 1.493-533, 8.370-372 (promise to Thetis); 1.533-611 (Zeus and gods on Olympos); 2.3-15; 2.38-40 (Agamemnon's dream); 2.786-787 (message to the Trojans); 3.302; 4.1-72 (duel between Paris and Menelaos); 5.421-431 (consoles wounded Aphrodite); 5.753-766, 906 (conflict between Athene and Ares); 6.234 (Glaukos' trade of armor); 7.443-464, 12.25-26 (future destruction of Greek wall); 8.2-52, 397-408, 438-484, 20.4-31, 155 (ban on divine intervention in battle); 8.69-75, 132-135, 216, 12.37, 174, 13.1-9, 794, 15.567, 592-604, 16.103, 17.627 (favors the Trojans); 8.130-136 (curbs Diomedes); 11.3-4 (dispatches Eris to Greeks); 11.163-164, 182-194, 202-209, 300, 12.292-293, 437, 450, 15.241-242, 610-612, 636-638, 694-695, 17.198-210 (and Hektor); 11.336-337, 542-544, 12.436-437, 13.1-9, 345-355 (manages the battle); 5.662, 12. 290-293, 402-403, 16.431-457, 661-662, 666-675, 21.388-390 (and Sarpedon); 14.293-353, 15.4-79, 95-109, 146-148, 152-167, 174-217, 220-235, (*Dios apate* and aftermath); 16.249-252, 644-656, 799, 17.268-273, 321, 400-401, 441-456, 544-546 (and Patroklos); 18.356-368, 19.340-349 (concern for Achilleus); 20.300-308, 21.229-232, 290 (rescue of Aineias from Achilleus); 21.505-514 (laughs at wounded Artemis);

15.610-611, 16.799-800, 22.166-186, 209-212, 403-404, 24.65-77, 100-120, 133-137, 143-159, 173-176, 194-196, 331 (death of Hektor and return of his body); 2.303-330, 7.478-479, 8.76-77, 133-135, 170-171, 245-252, 9.236, 11.52-55, 12.200-209, 252-255, 15.377-378, 16.458-459, 17.547-548, 593-596, 648-650, 20.56-57, 24.314-320 (omens)

Odyssey

1.22-95, 5.3-43 (Zeus and Athene plan for Odysseus' return); 12.374-388 (and Helios); 12.415-417 (destruction of Odysseus' crew); 13.127-165 (and Poseidon); 24.472-487 (resolves civil war on Ithake); 2.146-54, 20.102-121, 21.413, 24.539-540 (omens)

APPENDIX 2

TYPOLOGY OF DIVINE COUNCILS
IN THE *ODYSSEY*

I HAVE THROUGHOUT THIS STUDY referred to the five scenes in which Zeus has a speaking role in the *Odyssey*, in Books 1, 5, 12, 13 and 24, as "divine councils." From the standpoint of the oral tradition in which the Homeric epics originated, these narrative settings can be described as "type-scenes." This level of organization in Homeric narrative was first described systematically in the 1930s by Walter Arend, working in ignorance of Milman Parry's pioneering and then relatively unknown work on orality in Homeric composition. Arend explained repeated narrative sequences in Homeric epic such as arrivals, messages, and dreams, which he defined as *typischen Scenen*, in terms of the workings of Homer's mind.[1] Reviewing the study, Parry was appreciative of Arend's achievement in identifying the phenomenon, but rejected his "philosophic and almost mystic" explanation for it. These "fixed action patterns," he theorized, were analogous to the noun-epithet formulas he had himself shown to be characteristic of oral composition-in-performance.[2] Parry's student Albert Lord went on to document type-scenes in South Slavic epic, and subsequent analysis has shown this structural feature to be ubiquitous in oral communication.[3]

Repetition among instantiations of a given type-scene in a narrative is not verbatim, but rather represents a pattern for connecting related ideas. In the *Iliad*, for example, arming scenes, stock descriptions of warriors preparing for battle, take the form of nine or ten similar hexameters that describe Agamemnon, Achilles, and others donning greaves, corselet, sword, shield,

---

[1] Arend 1933.

[2] Parry 1971:404-407.

[3] Lord 1960:88-94; cf. the informative overview by M. Edwards 1987:71-77; recent perspectives and bibliography in Rubin 1995:210-220. Fenik 1974 surveys and analyzes type-scenes in the *Odyssey*.

helmet, spear, and so on, generally in the same order, but with some omissions or additions.[4] In the case of a more complex action pattern such as an assembly, scenes share such themes as summoning by heralds, seating of the attendants, set speeches, and dismissal, while the purpose of the assembly, the speakers, and subjects discussed, vary according to context.

Homerists classify assemblies generally, whether of gods or men, as a kind of type-scene.[5] Here I explore the formal features shared by Odyssean divine councils in order to demonstrate that they can indeed be described as variations on a theme. In terms of my larger argument, the divine council represents a thematic reflex of the narrative plan as a *Dios boulē*. Formalization of Odyssean divine councils thus reflects the unity of divine action across the narrative; and Zeus is the only god present at all of them.[6] The setting is Olympos, with other gods in attendance. Each council can be described schematically as some combination of seven themes: *assembly, complaint, surprise, invitation, proposal, modification,* and *implementation.*[7] In what follows, I survey the occurrence of these themes in each Odyssean divine council scene and consider narrative instances that may have prompted Homeric audiences to infer a council where one is not expressly described.[8]

Zeus and Athene I (*Odyssey* 1.26-102)

Most of the constituent themes of Odyssean divine councils can be deduced from the opening scene in Book 1. As the action of the *Odyssey* begins, the gods are *assembled,* "massed together in the halls of Olympian Zeus" (Ζηνὸς ἐνὶ μεγάροισιν Ὀλυμπίου ἀθρόοι, 1.27), and Zeus addresses them; in the remaining

---

[4] On Homeric arming scenes see Rubin 1995: 201-220 with bibliography.

[5] Cf. M. Edwards 1980:26, who notes some general differences between assemblies of gods and those of men.

[6] Finnegan 1977:58, citing Nichols 1961, draws attention to a parallel phenomenon in the *Chanson de Roland*, where "the poet uses as a vehicle for his composition ... the many councils in *Roland* and the recurrent stages within the council episodes."

[7] In keeping with the reservations of Hainsworth *CHO* 1:250, I note that my aim is not to describe strict units of composition, but rather general concepts in Homeric composition.

[8] While Iliadic divine councils are beyond the scope of this book, I note in anticipation of further study that these themes occur there as well, though with the addition of some themes that do not occur in the *Odyssey*, such as hostility. Gunn 1971 demonstrates that Iliadic and Odyssean type-scenes are in general often indistinguishable. Likewise, mortal councils in both Homeric epics share some of the themes I discuss here, but differ significantly from divine councils in featuring more speakers, a less formalized leadership structure, and settings of various inclusivity, from the council of leaders who meet to discuss Agamemnon's dream in *Iliad* 2 to the assemblies of the Ithakans in *Odyssey* 2 and 24 analyzed in Chapters 1 and 3.

Odyssean councils, on the other hand, Zeus always responds to another god. The speech Athene delivers (45-62) in response to Zeus' Oresteia introduces the next theme, another god's *complaint* to Zeus concerning Odysseus.[9] Zeus reacts to her complaint with *surprise*, here the mildly admonitory formula, "what word has escaped the barrier of your teeth?" (64), and *invites* help from all the gods in contriving Odysseus' homecoming (76-77). Athene responds with the *proposal* for her own and Hermes' departure from Olympos (81-95), and proceeds to *implement* it (96-103).

These individual thematic elements can be described, following Lord, as "minor" or "basic," in that each by itself lacks comprehensiveness.[10] Woven together, however, these minor themes comprise the larger, "essential" divine council theme. The divine council theme also interweaves "ornamental" themes, such as Athene's arming scene (96-101) and the genealogy of the Kyklops given by Zeus (71-74), which neither convey necessary information nor have a fixed place in the typology. Nevertheless, minor themes can communicate significant information: thus for example the genealogy Zeus gives the Kyklops demonstrates awareness of Odysseus' situation and at the same time distinguishes the Odyssean Kyklops from the similarly-named sons of Gaia and Ouranos who forge thunderbolts for Zeus in the Hesiodic *Theogony* (139).

Zeus, Athene and Hermes (*Odyssey* 5.3-54)

The first meeting of the gods on Olympos, and the typology of the divine council theme, is not, however, complete. As discussed in Chapter 2, the divine councils at the beginnings of Books 1 and 5 seem to narrate a single event depicted sequentially, as described by "Zielinski's law" (discussed in Chapter 2). At the beginning of Book 5, the gods are *assembled* in council at their "seating place," "and among them Zeus" (οἱ δ' θεοὶ θῶκόνδε καθίζανον, ἐν δ' ἄρα τοῖσι/Ζεύς, 3-4). Athene again *complains* to Zeus about Odysseus, stuck on Kalypso's island, and about the ambush that awaits his son (11-20). Zeus evinces *surprise* at the complaint (22=1.64), and *invites* Athene to carry on with "her plan" and see Telemachos home (25-27). He then instructs Hermes to set in motion Odysseus' homecoming (29-42). Zeus' instructions go beyond Athene's original proposal, and as such can be described as a *modification* of

[9] Cf. the 'Klage eines Gottes' Motivbereich described by Usener 1990:71-72.
[10] Lord 1960:146-147; see Chapter 6 for further discussion of Lord's concept of "theme" in oral performance.

Athene's vague proposal in the form of a detailed narrative signpost. Hermes then departs to *implement* the plan (43-54).[11]

The divine council at the beginning of Book 5 adds a crucial theme to Homeric divine council typology, namely, *modification* of the complaining god's proposal. In each Odyssean divine council, the impression that Zeus merely responds to other divinities is undercut by the fact that the plan that emerges from their deliberation has undergone significant modification at the hands of Zeus.

The two "halves" of the council scene that unfolds in Books 1 and 5, when taken together, provide a complete picture of the themes that structure all Odyssean divine councils. All of these themes are not assembled again in the *Odyssey*. However, because the audience has now been provided with a complete paradigm for divine interactions in the *Odyssey*, fewer themes are needed to set the scene for these interactions.[12]

Zeus and Helios (*Odyssey* 12.374-388)

While telling his adventures to the Phaiakes, Odysseus claims to have learned about an exchange between Zeus and Helios from Kalypso, who in turn heard it from Hermes (12.398-390). Thus embedded in three narrative layers, this council unsurprisingly does not receive full treatment. Helios *complains* (378-381) to the *assembled* (Ζεῦ πάτερ ἠδ' ἄλλοι μάκαρες θεοί, 377) Olympians about the slaughter of his cattle by Odysseus' crew. If the crewmembers are not made to pay for their act, the sun god threatens to go down to Hades and shine among the dead (382-383). This threat resembles a *proposal*, since it induces Zeus to act. Zeus' conciliatory response, an offer to destroy the offenders himself with a thunderbolt (385-388), serves the *modification* function, in that Zeus responds to the other god's complaint in a manner consistent with his own larger goals. Odysseus presently describes the *implementation* of Zeus' plan from his own perspective (415-425).

---

[11] The non-Olympian goddess Ino/Leukothea, who helps Odysseus reach Scherie (*Odyssey* 5.333-353), knows the outcome of the "second" divine council, specifically, that the Phaiakes will aid Odysseus (cf. 344-345 with 34-37). Thus "pity" (ἥ ῥ' Ὀδυσῆ' ἐλέησεν, 336) does not seem to be the sole motivation for Ino's aid to Odysseus, a situation with which we may compare Hera's concern for the Greeks dying from Apollo's plague (*Iliad* 1.I 55-56): in both cases the possibility remains that unexpressed divine councils were understood by Homeric audiences to precede the divine intervention.

[12] S. Richardson 1990:99-100 applies Genette's term, "paralipsis," to the omission of individual themes from larger thematic complexes in Homeric narrative. Cf. discussion of "filling in" by Lord 1960:68-98.

Zeus and Poseidon (13.125-160)

Near the beginning of Book 13, Poseidon *complains* to Zeus that the Phaiakes' return of Odysseus will cause the gods to dishonor himself (13.128-138). Although Poseidon was last seen departing for his residence at Aigai (5.381), the setting seems to be Olympos, as there is no precedent in the *Odyssey* (or in the main narrative of the *Iliad*) for Zeus visiting another god. Zeus shows *surprise* with a mildly admonitory formula (ὢ πόποι ... οἷον ἔειπες, 140), and *invites* Poseidon to do as he wishes (ἔρξον ὅπως ἐθέλεις καί τοι φίλον ἔπλετο θυμῶι, 145); the latter in turn *proposes* striking the Phaiakes' ship as it returns from Ithake and covering their city with a mountain (149-152). Zeus responds that he should do what "seems best" to him (ὡς μὲν ἐμῶι θυμῶι δοκεῖ εἶναι ἄριστα, 154), but submits a *modified* proposal that the Phaiakes' ship be turned to stone (155-158). Poseidon then departs to *implement* the modified proposal (160). This council exhibits most of the major themes adduced above, with one exception. Presumably because the three preceding council scenes have established that Zeus is regularly seated among the gods, the *assembly* element does not recur in Odyssean divine councils.[13]

Zeus and Athene II (*Odyssey* 24.472-88)

Following Odysseus' slaughter of the suitors, Athene again *complains* about Odysseus' situation (24.473-474), being concerned whether Zeus will bring to pass war or peace among the Ithakans (475-476). Athene's two options amount to a *proposal*, to which Zeus responds with *surprise* (τέκνον ἐμόν, τί με ταῦτα διείρεαι ἠδὲ μεταλλᾶις, (478; 24.477-480=5.21-24), and *invites* her to "do as she wishes" (ἔρξον ὅπως ἐθέλεις, 24.481a=13.145a). Again, however, Zeus offers as a *modification* of her proposal what "seems best" to him (ἐρέω δέ τοι, ὡς ἐπέοικεν, 481; cf. 13.154), namely the program for quelling the incipient civil war on Ithake (481-486). Athene then departs to *implement* the proposal (487-488). As with the previous council, absence of the *assembly* theme is explained by the fact that the first three councils have established that the gods are usually seated together.

---

[13] Lord 1960:146 observes that the Homeric Olympian family "is usually always together except for individuals away on a mission."

Odyssean divine council typology summarized

I hope to have demonstrated that all Odyssean divine councils can be described as the kind of complex of themes that scholars define as a "type-scene." In such scenes, the gods are assembled; a lesser Olympian makes a complaint to Zeus concerning Odysseus; Zeus expresses surprise; Zeus issues an invitation to address the complaint; the other god makes a proposal; Zeus offers a modification; and a lesser god sees to the implementation of the modified proposal. Although not every theme is expressed in every council, the mechanics of composition by theme justifies the classification of all the scenes in which the gods meet in the *Odyssey* as multiforms of a "typical" narrative sequence. In the following tabulation of these findings, the columns represent the god who interacts with Zeus at each council, and each row represents one of the seven themes:

Zeus' interlocutor	Book 1: Athene	Book 5: Athene	Book 12: Helios	Book 13: Poseidon	Book 24: Athene
assembly	26-27	3-4	377		
complaint	45-62	11-20	378-381	128-138	473-474
surprise	64	22		140	478
invitation	76-77	25-27		145	481
proposal	81-95		382-383	149-152	475-476
modification		29-42	387-388	154-158	481-486
implementation	96-103	43-54	415-425	160	487-488

No other divine councils as I have defined them – on Olympos, with Zeus as one of the participants – are linked chronologically or causally with the main narrative of the *Odyssey*. There are however other analogous scenes that merit brief consideration.

Demodokos' song of Ares and Aphrodite
(*Odyssey* 8.266-366)

As accompaniment to a dance, the Phaiakian bard Demodokos sings a song
about how Hephaistos, having been cuckolded by Ares, calls from the porch
of his house on Olympos (303-304) to the *assembled* gods (πᾶσι θεοῖσι, 305).[14]
Like Athene and Helios, Hephaistos *complains* to "Zeus father and other
powerful gods who always are" (Ζεῦ πάτερ ἠδ' ἄλλοι μάκαρες θεοὶ αἰὲν ἐόντες,
306=5.7=12.377; the same line appears in prayers, e.g. 12.371). Zeus, however,
has no further role, speaking or otherwise, in Demodokos' song, and the rest
of the typology is truncated. Nevertheless, it appears that Demodokos, like the
Homeric composer-performers who created and recreated him, composes by
type-scene.

"crypto-councils"?

Divine actions in the *Odyssey* do occur without mention of previous discussion
on Olympos. With the exception of Poseidon's attack on Odysseus in Book 5,
which is carried out in express opposition to the god's perception of Olympian
policy, these actions explicitly further the Olympian agenda. Within the
main narrative, Athene for instance travels to Sparta to prompt Telemachos'
return to Ithake (15.1-43); outside the main narrative, Hermes visits Aiaia in
order to provide Odysseus with the drug that allows him to overcome Kirke
(10.277-307). In both cases, the god then departs for Olympos (15.43, 10.307),
which implies that their missions originated there.[15] By contrast, after his
"independent" attack on Odysseus in Book 5, Poseidon departs not to Olympos,
but to his home in Aigai (381).

---

[14] According to the *Iliad*, each Olympian has his or her own dwelling (δῶμα) on Olympos (*Iliad*
1.606-608; cf. *Odyssey* 8.324-325); that Hephaistos is able to address them all at once implies that
they are gathered together.

[15] Thus Cook 1995:122n28 on Hermes. S. West *CHO* 1:79 ad 1.37ff, by contrast, concludes that the
god acts on his own initiative; however, the only Homeric parallel for independent action by
Hermes is an Iliadic digression on his seduction of a mortal woman (16.179-186). The *Odyssey*
is not entirely consistent in this respect; Athene departs to Athens after facilitating Odysseus'
approach to Alkinoos' home on Scherie (7.80), which act furthers the plan specified in Zeus'
instructions to Hermes in Book 5 (34-37).

The Homeric audience may have been conditioned to assume that divine deliberation precedes divine action, so that action by a subordinate god presumes a divine council over which Zeus presides, unless conditions are expressly said to be otherwise (as in the case with Poseidon's attack).[16] In other words, the mere mention of what I have described as the "implementation" theme may have been sufficient to conjure up in the minds of the audience a divine council in which Zeus has approved a given course of action in discussion before the assembled gods on Olympos. Similar "crypto-councils" may perhaps also be inferred at *Odyssey* 5.382-387, 6.13-16 and 13.189-191; examples from the *Iliad* include 1.194-195 with 1.221, 3.121-138 and 17.544-546.

[16] Thus M. Edwards *IC* 5:115 ad 17.545-546 notes, apropos of Athene's mission to rally the Greeks protecting Patroklos' corpse, that "it can well be argued that 545-6 provide a condensed version of the conversation with Zeus which is the usual preliminary of Athene's missions to inspire a hero."

INDEX

omens, 28, 62, 113
Oresteia, 14, 44, 69, 125, 129, 144
Orestes, 17

N

Nagy, Gregory, 10
nemesis, 65

P

Palamedes, 128
Pan, 29
Panhellenism, 4, 60, 76, 98, 102,
    107, 108, 136, 141
Parry, Milman, 133, 149
Patroklos, 118
Peisistratos, 77
Penelope, 17, 88
performance, 3, 10, 19, 26, 56, 59,
    82, 98, 100, 122, 133, 136, 144
Phaiakes, 14, 20, 82, 125, 135, 145,
    152-153
Phemios, 124, 127
Philoktetes, 126
Phoenicia, 110
poinē, 69
Poseidon, 14, 15, 21, 36, 42, 44, 82,
    136, 140, 145, 153-156
Pucci, Pietro, 9
Pylos, 126, 137, 138

R

ring structure 52, 64
Rubin, David, 134

S

scapegoat, 80
Scherie, 44
Sicily, 109
Slatkin, Laura, 10
suitors, 8, 14, 20, 55, 62, 91, 125, 145

T

Taphians, 91
Teiresias, 70, 85
Telegonos, 88
Telemachos, 14, 17, 55, 83, 88, 93,
    115, 151, 155
Thesprotia, 89
Thoas, 93
timē, 65, 69
tisis, 62
Trampya, 103
Trojan War, 5, 113, 115
Troy, 77
type scene, 13, 149-150, 154-155

X

xenia, 71, 142

Z

Zielinski's law, 37, 151

INDEX LOCORUM